THE PRIVACY FIX

Online surveillance of our behavior by private companies is on the increase, particularly through the Internet of Things and the increasing use of algorithmic decision-making. This troubling trend undermines privacy and increasingly threatens our ability to control how information about us is shared and used. Written by a computer scientist and a legal scholar, The Privacy Fix proposes a set of evidence-based, practical solutions that will help solve this problem. Requiring no technical or legal expertise, the book explains complicated concepts in clear, straightforward language. Bridging the gap between computer scientists, economists, lawyers, and public policy makers, this book provides theoretically and practically sound public policy guidance about how to preserve privacy in the onslaught of surveillance. It emphasizes the need to make tradeoffs among the complex concerns that arise, and it outlines a practical norm-creation process to do so.

Robert H. Sloan is Professor and Department Head of Computer Science at University of Illinois Chicago.

Richard Warner is Professor and Faculty Director of the Center for Law and Computers at Chicago-Kent College of Law.

The Privacy Fix

HOW TO PRESERVE PRIVACY IN THE ONSLAUGHT OF SURVEILLANCE

ROBERT H. SLOAN
University of Illinois Chicago Department of Computer Science
RICHARD WARNER
Chicago-Kent College of Law

CAMBRIDGE
UNIVERSITY PRESS

CAMBRIDGE
UNIVERSITY PRESS

University Printing House, Cambridge CB2 8BS, United Kingdom

One Liberty Plaza, 20th Floor, New York, NY 10006, USA

477 Williamstown Road, Port Melbourne, VIC 3207, Australia

314–321, 3rd Floor, Plot 3, Splendor Forum, Jasola District Centre, New Delhi – 110025, India

103 Penang Road, #05–06/07, Visioncrest Commercial, Singapore 238467

Cambridge University Press is part of the University of Cambridge.

It furthers the University's mission by disseminating knowledge in the pursuit of education, learning, and research at the highest international levels of excellence.

www.cambridge.org
Information on this title: www.cambridge.org/9781108486712
DOI: 10.1017/9781108762168

First published 2021

A catalogue record for this publication is available from the British Library.

Library of Congress Cataloging-in-Publication Data
NAMES: Sloan, Robert H., author. | Warner, Richard, 1946– author.
TITLE: The privacy fix : how to preserve privacy in the onslaught of surveillance / Robert H. Sloan, Richard Warner.
DESCRIPTION: First edition. | New York : Cambridge University Press, 2021. | Includes index.
IDENTIFIERS: LCCN 2021014729 (print) | LCCN 2021014730 (ebook) | ISBN 9781108486712 (hardback) | ISBN 9781108762168 (ebook)
SUBJECTS: LCSH: Privacy, Right of. | Electronic surveillance – Law and legislation. | Electronic monitoring in the workplace – Law and legislation. | Artificial intelligence – Law and legislation. | Electronic surveillance – Government policy. | Self-realization.
CLASSIFICATION: LCC K3263 .S56 2021 (print) | LCC K3263 (ebook) | DDC 323.44/82–dc23
LC record available at https://lccn.loc.gov/2021014729
LC ebook record available at https://lccn.loc.gov/2021014730

ISBN 978-1-108-48671-2 Hardback
ISBN 978-1-108-70821-0 Paperback

Contents

List of Figures *page* viii
List of Tables ix
Preface xi

1 **Surveillance and Self-Realization** 1
The Self and Self-Realization 3
Current Critiques of Surveillance 4
An Overview of the Argument 6
Knowing What Others Will Do 13
Why Privacy in Public Is Essential to Self-Realization 16
Lack of Norms 17
Trust 18
Is This Book Necessary? 19
The Test Case of Artificial Intelligence 21

2 **Artificial Intelligence-Enhanced Surveillance** 22
A Thought Experiment 25
Low Accuracy 26
Decontextualization 28
Data Preparation 30
Explainability and Transparency 35
Feedback Mechanisms 40
Broad-based Predictions 41
Meeting the Threat of AI-Enhanced Surveillance 42

3 **Social Roles, Common Knowledge, and Coordination** 43
Social Roles As a Source of Common Knowledge 45
Common Knowledge 46
Social Roles As Common Knowledge Generators 50

Why Proper Performance of Social Roles Involves Coordination Problems 53
Common Knowledge of the Four-Part Pattern 56
The Examples 59
Completing the "Surveillance Ignored" View 70
Appendix 71
Coordination Games 71
More Than Two Players 75
Coordination Problems 75
The Common Knowledge Solution 76

4 **Coordination Norms** 78

Norms 79
Coordination Norms 82
Examples 85
Informational Norms 89
A World without Informational Norms 90
Not Our World 97
Appendix: Informational Privacy As a Common Pool Resource 99
Natural Resource Common Pool Resources 99
Need, Supply, and Use 100
Subtractiveness 101
Nonexcludability 102
Conclusion 102

5 **Notice and Choice: The Allure and the Illusion** 103

Free and Informed Consent through Informational Norms 104
The Failure of Notice and Choice 109
The Need for Collective Control 115

6 **The Threat of Collapse, The Prospects of Resistance** 117

The Threat of Collapse 118
The Stasi As a Reference Point 125
Making Surveillance Difficult 127
Cases in Which a Party to the Informational Norm Conducts Surveillance 128
Cases in Which a Non-Party to the Norm Conducts Surveillance 131
Resistance Where Relevant Norms Do Not Exist 136
Resistance, Acquiescence, Acceptance 138

7 **Acquiescence** 139

Václav Havel's Greengrocer 139
Acquiescence in "Party to the Norm" Cases 140
Shadow Conformity 148

Acquiescence in "Not a Party to the Norm" Cases 149
Acquiescence Where Relevant Informational Norms Do Not Exist 159
How Common Is Acquiescence? 159

8 **Accept or Take Control?** 160
A Process of Acculturation 160
Party to the Norm 163
Not a Party to the Norm 169
No Norms 171
Time to Take Control 172
Acceptable Tradeoffs 173
A Norm-Creation Model 176
A Test Case 180

9 **Regulating Artificial Intelligence** 181
The Proxy Problem 182
Level Playing Field Fairness 187
A Regulatory Proposal 197
A Role for the Federal Trade Commission 199
Creating an Informational Norm 201

Conclusion 204

Index 205

Figures

3.1 Payoffs for Rock–Paper–Scissors *page* 71
3.2 Driving Game (a coordination game) 72
3.3 Hockey Helmet Game (another coordination game) 73

Tables

4.1 An overview of different norm-governed activities *page* 90
6.1 Initial characterization of "before," resisting, acquiescing, and accepting 121
6.2 Full characterization of "before," resistance, acquiescence, and acceptance 132
7.1 Highlighting "party to the norm" acquiescence 141
7.2 Highlighting "not a party to the norm" acquiescence 150
8.1 Surveillance chart, now highlighting acceptance 163
9.1 Very simple four-attribute model for setting auto insurance premiums 191

Preface

This book grew out of the conviction that society will not resolve critical questions about privacy without an informed discussion. To be adequately informed, that discussion must be a discussion among disparate disciplines, including, at a minimum, computer scientists, economists, lawyers, philosophers, sociologists, and makers of public policy. Part of the experience that informs this book came from our attempt to foster that discussion when coteaching an introductory computer science course. The course was funded in part by a National Science Foundation grant (DUE-1612455), support we gratefully acknowledge. (Of course, any opinions, findings, conclusions, or recommendations expressed in this book are those of the authors and do not necessarily reflect the views of the National Science Foundation.)

We hope that this book will bridge the gaps among these disciplines, and, for that reason, we write in plain English, rather than the jargon of any particular discipline. We emphasize the need to make tradeoffs among complex and competing goals. Our book is a call for reasoned compromise in doing so.

We gratefully acknowledge a considerable debt to the work of Helen Nissenbaum on norms and privacy in public. We are also indebted to her for a comment she made some years ago when we were presenting work from our previous book on privacy. She urged us to give a more central role in our approach to beliefs about what is of value. This book does so by giving pride of place to what people think they ought to do. We also draw importantly on the insights about privacy by the sociologists Christena Nippert-Eng and James Rule. We combine these insights about norms and privacy with work by the philosophers Stephen Schiffer and David Lewis on common knowledge and its role in coordinating group action. We incorporate these diverse sources into a practical proposal for preserving privacy in the onslaught of surveillance.

1

Surveillance and Self-Realization

In *Othello*, Iago manipulates Othello into worrying that his wife Desdemona is unfaithful. Othello declares in response:

> I'll see before I doubt; when I doubt, prove;
> And on the proof, there is no more but this,
> – Away at once with love or jealousy![1]

However, Iago manipulates what Othello sees. In a pivotal scene, he arranges for Othello to eavesdrop on a conversation between Iago and Cassio, one of Othello's lieutenants. The conversation concerns Cassio's mistress, Bianca, but Iago knows that Othello will misinterpret it to be about Cassio's nonexistent affair with Desdemona. Iago's plan is that

> As he [Cassio] shall smile Othello shall go mad;
> And his unbookish [unreflective] jealousy must construe
> Poor Cassio's smiles, gestures, and light behavior
> Quite in the wrong.[2]

Othello does "go mad," and ultimately murders Desdemona.

Businesses and governments embrace their own "I'll see" by employing surveillance technologies that enable a constant and pervasive investigative gaze. They gaze steadily and intently at virtually everyone to learn details about their lives in order to treat them as they see fit.[3] We use "surveillance" through the book for this pervasive investigative gaze. Does this "I'll see" have the same effect as Othello's? Does it undermine the trust on which a variety of relationships and social interactions

[1] William Shakespeare, *Othello*, ed. Stephen Orgel and Russ Mcdonald (Penguin Classics, 2001): Act III, Scene 3, ll. 213–15.

[2] Shakespeare, Act IV, Scene 1, ll. 114–17.

[3] As James Rule notes, modern surveillance practices "share a distinctive and sociologically crucial quality: they not only *collect and record* details of personal information; they are also organized to *provide bases for action toward the people concerned*. Systematically harvested personal information, in other words, furnishes bases for institutions to determine what treatment to mete out to each individual"; James B. Rule, *Privacy in Peril: How We Are Sacrificing a Fundamental Right in Exchange for Security and Convenience* (Oxford University Press, 2007), 14 (original emphasis).

depend? The short answer is "yes." The longer answer explains why, when, and how, and what to do about it. That takes the rest of the book.

Trust may seem like an odd starting point. Noteworthy exceptions aside, discussions of surveillance typically focus on privacy first and trust later, if they get to trust all.[4] In fact, to start with trust *is* to start with privacy. The two concepts are entwined. This is particularly true of the form of privacy that concerns us: informational privacy. Informational privacy consists in the ability to control what others do with information about you. It both *creates and requires* trust, as we argue in the later chapters. Even so, the analogy between contemporary surveillance and Othello's "I'll see" may seem far-fetched. Do people really play Desdemona to the Othello of businesses and governments? Surely, the analogy breaks down with Othello's murder of Desdemona. Surveillance can kill, of course. It does when it leads to lethal drone strikes. However, it poses no death threat to the vast majority.

No threat of *physical* death, that is. It does pose a serious threat to the *self*. Commentators have been sounding the alarm, contending that "the self withers in the searing light of surveillance,"[5] that what survives is not the true self but a fabricated one,[6] that the self transforms into something else entirely – "mere algorithm fodder,"[7] "nodes of information production,"[8] puppets manipulated through "invisible threads."[9] Jean Baudrillard offers one of the more elaborate characterizations:

> We are constantly confronted with the anticipated statistical verification of our behavior, and absorbed by this permanent refraction of our least movements, we are no longer confronted with our own will. We are no longer even alienated . . . Each individual is forced despite himself or herself into the undivided coherency of statistics. There is in this a positive absorption into the transparency of computers, which is something worse than alienation.[10]

The worry is not about a dystopian future. The commentators claim we – all of us – face a *current* threat to the self. Are they right?

4 Exceptions include Helen Nissenbaum, *Privacy in Context: Technology, Policy, and the Integrity of Social Life* (Stanford University Press, 2010); Ari Ezra Waldman, *Privacy as Trust: Information Privacy for an Information Age* (Cambridge University Press, 2018); Woodrow Hartzog, *Privacy's Blueprint: The Battle to Control the Design of New Technologies* (Harvard University Press, 2018); and Neil Richards and Woodrow Hartzog, "Privacy's Trust Gap: A Review," *Yale Law Journal* 126 (2017): 1180–1224.

5 Jeffrey Rosen, *The Naked Crowd: Reclaiming Security and Freedom in an Anxious Age* (Random House Trade Paperbacks, 2005).

6 The seminal source of this claim is Michel Foucault, *Discipline and Punish: The Birth of the Prison*, trans. Alan Sheridan (Vintage Books, 1995), 217. Many have taken up Foucault's claim.

7 Frank Pasquale, *The Black Box Society: The Secret Algorithms That Control Money and Information* (Harvard University Press, 2015), 198.

8 Ronald J Deibert, *Black Code: Inside the Battle for Cyberspace* (McClelland & Stewart, 2011), 63 (noting that "we no longer move about our lives as self-contained beings, but as nodes of information production in a dense network of digital relations involving other nodes of information production").

9 Aleksandr Solzhenitsyn, *Cancer Ward* (Vintage Classics, 2003), 208.

10 Jean Baudrillard, *Jean Baudrillard: Selected Writings*, ed. Mark Poster, trans. Jacques Mourrain, 2nd ed. (Stanford University Press, 2002), 210.

We (the authors) think so. But if you are like us, your daily experience testifies to the opposite. This is not to say that we ignore the fact that stores and office buildings record us on CCTV cameras, that cameras record our movements on city streets (Chicago, where we live, has more than 30,000 cameras feeding video for analysis into a state-of-the-art computer complex), that businesses and governments track online activities, and so on. Yet we have no sense that our selves are withering away, no sense of imminent metaphysical death. Our selves seem to be getting along just fine. We assume you are the same. So exactly what is the threat that surveillance poses to the self? Ubiquitous surveillance profoundly *changes* in the way people relate to businesses, governments, and each other, but why isn't that *just* a change? Why is it a threat? We begin our answer by explaining what we mean by the self.

THE SELF AND SELF-REALIZATION

William James characterizes the relevant concept of the self. He writes,

> I am often confronted by the necessity of standing by one of my ... selves and relinquishing the rest. Not that I would not, if I could, be both handsome and fat and well dressed, and a great athlete, and make a million a year, be a wit, a *bon vivant*, and a lady killer, as well as a philosopher, and a philanthropist, statesman, warrior, and African explorer, as well as a "tone poet" and saint. But the thing is simply impossible ... Such characters may at the outset of life be alike *possible* to a man. But to make anyone of them actual, the rest must be more or less suppressed. So the seeker of his truest, strongest, deepest self must review the list carefully, and pick out the one on which to stake his salvation.[11]

James exaggerates when he suggests that *one* commitment defines who you are.[12] Multiple commitments do:

> We are none of us defined by membership in a single community or form of moral life. We are ... heirs of many distinct, sometimes conflicting, intellectual and moral traditions ...The complexity and contradictions of our cultural inheritance give to our identities an aspect of complexity and even of plurality which is ... essential to them ... [T]he power to conceive of ourselves in different ways, to harbour dissonant projects and perspectives, to inform our thoughts and lives with divergent categories and concepts, is integral to our identity as reflective beings.[13]

You make yourself who you are – you construct your multifaceted identity – by selecting what you will identify with ("stand by") from the possibilities open to

[11] William James, *The Principles of Psychology*, vol. 1 (Dover Publications, Inc., 1890), 309.

[12] It is not at all clear that James actually thought you had to single out one self. As he notes elsewhere, "Properly speaking, a man has as many social selves as there are individuals who recognize him and carry an image of him in their mind ... Nothing is commoner than to hear people discriminate between their different selves of this sort: 'As a man I pity you, but as an official I must show you no mercy; as a politician I regard him as an ally, but as a moralist I loathe him;' etc., etc." James, 1:295.

[13] John Gray, *Post-Liberalism: Studies in Political Thought* (Routledge, 1993), 262–63.

you.[14] Self-realization in this sense figures importantly in moral and political philosophy from Hegel and Mill to Rawls and Raz.[15]

We began the discussion of the self and self-realization to explain why surveillance poses a serious current threat to everyone's self and possibilities for self-realization, but what we have said so far may seem to cut the other way. While surveillance is a pervasive feature of the Internet, social networking, chat, and the like, why doesn't the explosion of online activity testify to a new and rich range of opportunities for self-realization? Where is the threat? It is reasonable to look at existing criticisms of surveillance for the answer. Critiques abound. Don't some adequately explain the danger to the self? The short answer is "no." Those critiques do, however, contain an important theme that we develop in our answer.

CURRENT CRITIQUES OF SURVEILLANCE

Critiques of surveillance take different forms in the case of the government and private business. We begin with the government. Governing effectively requires some degree of surveillance. Enforcing laws, extracting revenues, and predicting compliance require knowing relevant facts about the people over whom the government claims authority.[16] Critiques of governmental surveillance tend to focus on compliance, specifically on uses of surveillance that discourage and prevent behavior of which the government disapproves.[17] Examples include investigative journalists,[18] political dissenters,[19] lawyers representing political activists and dissenters,[20] politicians opposing the policies and goals of those with the power to order surveillance,[21] sustainable energy advocates,[22] environmentalists,[23] animal

[14] There is more than one candidate for the label "concept of the self." In particular, there are "pure ego" or "center" theories. See C. D Broad, *The Mind and Its Place in Nature* (Routledge, 2009), 558ff.; and Colin McGinn, *The Character of Mind: An Introduction to the Philosophy of Mind*, 2nd ed. (Oxford University Press, 1997), 65–70.

For a commitment-based theory of the self, see Richard Warner, *Freedom, Enjoyment, and Happiness: An Essay on Moral Psychology* (Cornell University Press, 1987).

[15] See Georg W. F. Hegel, *The Philosophy of Right* (T. M. Knox, trans., 1967); John Stuart Mill, *On Liberty* (David Bromwich and George Kateb eds., Yale University Press 2003) (1859); John Rawls, *A Theory of Justice* (Belknap Press, 1971) and *Political Liberalism* (Columbia University Press, 1993); Joseph Raz, *The Morality of Freedom* (Oxford University Press, 1986).

[16] Rule, *Privacy in Peril*, 40.

[17] See Robert H. Sloan and Richard Warner, "The Self, the Stasi, and the NSA: Privacy, Knowledge, and Complicity in the Surveillance State," 17 (2016) *Minn. J. Law Sci. Technol.* 347, 380–84.

[18] Heidi Boghosian and Lewis Lapham, *Spying on Democracy: Government Surveillance, Corporate Power and Public Resistance* (City Lights Publishers, 2013), 173–86.

[19] Luis Alberto Fernandez, *Policing Dissent: Social Control and the Anti-Globalization Movement* (Rutgers University Press, 2008).

[20] Boghosian and Lapham, *Spying on Democracy*, 155–72.

[21] Athan Theoharis, *Abuse of Power: How Cold War Surveillance and Secrecy Policy Shaped the Response to 9/11* (Temple University Press, 2011).

[22] Boghosian and Lapham, *Spying on Democracy*, chapter 1.

[23] Boghosian and Lapham, 57.

rights activists,[24] Blacks,[25] Muslims,[26] labor unions,[27] public health practitioners,[28] welfare recipients,[29] parolees,[30] and a diverse collection of types of people the government regards as (possibly) undesirable.[31] Critiques typically claim that some or all of these uses are illegitimate attempts to discourage or prevent activities typically considered permissible in a democratic state. The list is disturbingly long. But most people are not on it. So, how does surveillance harm them now? It may harm them in the future. History demonstrates "the tendency of surveillance systems to . . . expand – to cover more people and more of the lives of the people they cover."[32] That provides ample reason to worry about a future loss of self-realization. However, it does not provide a reason to think your self-realization is threatened now.

We reach the same conclusion when we turn to private sector surveillance.

The private sector critique is diffuse and complex. For our purpose, it is sufficient to list five (not entirely distinct) criticisms, all of which concern the use of surveillance to allocate costs (broadly construed – e.g., being denied employment) and benefits (broadly construed – e.g., being accepted to a top university). The criticisms are that the allocations: (1) discriminate among individuals in unfair ways;[33] (2) result in an unjust distribution of costs and benefits;[34] (3) create a chilling effect on behavior that leads to excessive conformity;[35] (4) lack transparency and accountability;[36] and (5) fail to ensure free and informed consent to the collection

24 Boghosian and Lapham, 140–42.

25 Boghosian and Lapham, 75.

26 Matt Apuzzo and Adam Goldman, *Enemies Within: Inside the NYPD's Secret Spying Unit and Bin Laden's Final Plot against America* (Touchstone, 2014).

27 Theoharis, *Abuse of Power.*

28 Amy L. Fairchild et al., *Searching Eyes: Privacy, the State, and Disease Surveillance in America* (University of California Press, 2007).

29 Christian Parenti, *The Soft Cage: Surveillance in America from Slavery to the War on Terror* (Basic Books, 2004).

30 Parenti.

31 Parenti, 178.

32 Rule, *Privacy in Peril,* 151.

33 Pasquale, *The Black Box Society,* 72.

34 See David Lyon, *Electronic Eye: The Rise of Surveillance Society* (University of Minnesota Press, 1994), and Rule, *Privacy in Peril.*

35 See, for example, Parenti, *The Soft Cage,* 92 ("Ubiquitous but fragmented, commercial surveillance helps make us obedient; it creates consumers with predictable tastes, borrowers who repay their debts, and personality structures acclimated to cooperation with authority"); Boghosian and Lapham, *Spying on Democracy,* 27 ("Distracted by the rush and convenience of information technology, few of us discern that opening a window into our personal transactions helps shape a culture of conformity and normalizes the nefarious business of domestic intelligence gathering"); and Pasquale, *The Black Box Society,* 15 ("In his book *Turing's Cathedral,* George Dyson quipped that 'Facebook defines who we are, Amazon defines what we want, and Google defines what we think.' We can extend that epigram to include finance, which defines what we have (materially, at least), and reputation, which increasingly defines our opportunities").

36 Pasquale, *The Black Box Society,* 61.

and use of data.[37] In all cases, surveillance harms some and helps others. This is hardly surprising. When you allocate costs and benefits, some win and some lose. Discrimination and unfair distribution, for example, harm some but benefit those they favor, and similar remarks hold for excessive conformity, lack of transparency, and free and informed consent. Some individuals and businesses will find ways to exploit those features to their advantage.

So why do commentators contend that surveillance constitutes a current threat to the self? The answer lies in another line of criticism. That criticism focuses on the fact that surveillance creates a massive capacity to know and argues that capacity to know has deleterious effects *independently* of surveillance's use to discourage behavior or to allocate cost and benefits.[38] Before we turn to that point, we provide an overview of the argument we will develop in the chapters that follow.

AN OVERVIEW OF THE ARGUMENT

Our argument divides into four parts:

1. Adequate informational privacy is essential if people are to successfully seek self-realization as they interact in a variety of social roles.
2. Those interactions create and maintain the necessary informational privacy as people conform to shared expectations about the selective flow of information.
3. Conformity to shared expectations about information flow requires complex group coordination facilitated by informational norms.
4. Surveillance creates a massive capacity to know. The existence of that capacity undermines self-realization by undermining the norm-based coordination on which adequate informational privacy depends.

Adequate Self-Realization Requires Adequate Informational Privacy

The philosopher Thomas Nagel paints a compelling picture of the importance of privacy to self-realization. He notes that privacy allows "our inner lives [to] be carried on under the protection of an exposed public self over which we have enough control to be able to identify with it, at least in part." He elaborates:

[37] There are twenty years of criticism. We summarize it in Robert H. Sloan and Richard Warner, "Beyond Notice and Choice: Privacy, Norms, and Consent," *Suffolk University Journal of High Technology Law* 14 (2014): 370.

[38] See, for example, Bruce Schneier, "The Internet Is a Surveillance State," CNN, March 16, 2013, www.cnn.com/2013/03/16/opinion/schneier-internet-surveillance/index.html, and Sandra Fulton, "Senate Report Opens a Window into Hidden World of Data Aggregators," American Civil Liberties Union, December 18, 2013, www.aclu.org/blog/technology-and-liberty/senate-report-opens-window-hidden-world-data-aggregators.

> There is much more going on inside us all the time than we are willing to express, and civilization would be impossible if we could all read each other's minds. Apart from everything else there is the sheer chaotic, tropical luxuriance of the inner life. To quote [the sociologist Georg] Simmel: "All we communicate to another individual by means of words or perhaps in another fashion – even the most subjective, impulsive, intimate matters – is a selection from that psychological-real whole whose absolutely exact report (absolutely exact in terms of content and sequence) would drive everybody into the insane asylum." As children we have to learn gradually not only to express what we feel but also to keep many thoughts and feelings to ourselves in order to maintain relations with other people on an even keel. We also have to learn, especially in adolescence, not to be overwhelmed by a consciousness of other people's awareness of and reaction to ourselves – so that our inner lives can be carried on under the protection of an exposed public self over which we have enough control to be able to identify with it, at least in part.[39]

Nagel rightly emphasizes the role of the "exposed public self" in protecting the inner life, but that is only one of its functions. The "exposed public self" also facilitates a variety of relationships through which people seek self-realization. Self-realization comes not just from the flourishing of the inner self, but from the pursuits of the public self as it interacts with others. You realize yourself as much through the social roles of being a lawyer, doctor, race car driver, chess player, birdwatcher, and so on, as you do through your soliloquies, intimate conversations, and confessions with confidants.[40]

Social roles figure prominently in the chapters which follow, so some further explanation is in order. Social roles are socially recognized patterns of thought and action associated with standards of permitted, expected, or required behavior.[41] By way of illustration, imagine watching birds in a society that does not recognize birdwatching as a social role. Imagine a primitive tribe whose sole use for animals is to hunt and eat them. You are the lone anomaly who spends hours tracking down birds merely to look at them. Although you watch birds, you are not a birdwatcher in the sense that a member of the Audubon Society is. To call yourself a birdwatcher in that sense is not just to say you watch birds; it is also to ascribe to yourself a recognized role. Contemporary societies recognize that people enjoy birdwatching, and the birdwatchers understand themselves and are understood by others as people who enjoy watching birds. In the primitive tribe, your anomalous bird gazing does not fit any recognized pattern of behavior; hence, you lack reference to such a pattern as a way of understanding yourself and explaining yourself to others. Similarly, you cannot be a lawyer except in a society governed by law, practice

39 Thomas Nagel, *Concealment and Exposure: And Other Essays* (Oxford University Press, 2002), 4.

40 Many make the point. See, for example, Raz, *Morality of Freedom*; Richard Sennett, *The Fall of Public Man* (Random House, 1988); David Rosen and Aaron Santesso, *The Watchman in Pieces: Surveillance, Literature, and Liberal Personhood* (Yale University Press, 2013); and Lionel Trilling, *Sincerity and Authenticity* (Harvard University Press, 1972).

41 Talcott Parsons, *The Social System* (Ulan Press, 2012), chapter 6.

medicine unless the society you are in recognizes the practice, be a professional race car driver except in a community that recognizes the sport. The point extends even to being a parent, child, lover, or spouse. Those relationships take on different meanings and definitions in different societies.

A final point about social roles is in order. Recall that we explained them as socially recognized patterns of thought and action associated with standards of permitted, expected, or required behavior. As you pursue self-realization through a variety of social roles, you accept, refine, and modify some or all of the various standards of behavior. The standards become *your* standards, your convictions about what you ought and ought not do. The link between social roles and beliefs about what one ought and ought not do plays a key role for us, and we return to it in Chapter 3.

Conformity to Shared Expectations about the Selective Flow of Information

Interactions in social roles exhibit a feature that impressed the nineteenth-century sociologist of urbanization, Georg Simmel. He saw that interacting people trust each other to respect shared expectations about constraints on the exchange of information.[42] The family holiday dinner is convenient illustration. Imagine a congenial extended family. Everyone shares the goal of a harmonious holiday dinner as they interact in the social role of a family member. Harmony requires a selective flow of information. Things you can say to Aunt Jane should not reach Uncle John's ears and vice versa. Harmony also requires restraint in the ways people use information. For example, in that family, it does not disrupt harmony for Aunt Jane to learn that Uncle John is afraid of heights, but it does undermine harmony when she uses that information to lure John onto the balcony to embarrass him as he trembles and dashes back inside. In the following chapters, we will be concerned not just with where information flows but also with how it is used when it gets there. We will use the phrases "conditions on the flow of information" and "selective flow of information" to cover both where information goes and how it is used. No family member unilaterally can ensure the necessary selective flow and use of information. They must trust each other to conform to the required conditions as they coordinate their efforts to ensure harmony.

Group-created selective flows of information typify interactions in social roles. Waiters do not try to find out if you are married to your dinner partner, nor, if they know you are not, do they announce that your dinner partner is not your spouse. Your pharmacist does not ask if you are happy in your marriage when you pick up your anti-anxiety medication, but your internist may before they prescribe it. Waiters and restaurant patrons, students and teachers, pharmacists and customers, patients

[42] See, for example, Georg Simmel, "The Sociology of Secrecy and Secret Societies," *The American Journal of Sociology* 11 (1906): 468–498.

and doctors, and myriad others observe informational boundaries effortlessly, without thought or explicit negotiation. As the sociologist Nippert-Eng emphasizes:

> At its core, managing privacy is about managing relationships between the self and others . . . privacy . . . [is] a "boundary regulatory process by which a person (or group) makes himself more or less accessible and open to others." When we regulate our accessibility to others . . . we simultaneously regulate our relationships with them.[43]

The process ensures that information selectively shared with others is both private (in being inaccessible to some) and public (in being accessible to others for certain purposes). Following established usage, we call this group-created form of informational privacy *privacy in public*. Talk of privacy in public may seem contradictory. After all, if anything is clear, it is clear that "purely 'private' things are completely inaccessible to others. Purely 'public' ones are completely accessible to others."[44] But how can something be both private and public? The answer is that not all opposites are mutually exclusive. Bankrupt/not bankrupt and pregnant/not pregnant are, but cheap/expensive, for example, are not. Something can be a little cheap, or little expensive; "cheap as possible" and "expensive as possible" are opposite ends of a sliding scale. Private and public are also "sliding scale" opposites. The scale's endpoints are "completely inaccessible to others" and "completely accessible to others."

Interactions in social roles create a complex web of privacy in public as people trust each other to share certain types of information, to refrain from sharing other types, and to use shared information only in certain ways. As the information science professor Helen Nissenbaum notes,

> In medical contexts, it is appropriate to share details of our physical condition or, more specifically, the patient shares information about his or her physical condition with the physician but not vice versa; among friends we may pour over romantic entanglements (our own and those of others); to the bank or our creditors, we reveal financial information; with our professors, we discuss our own grades; at work, it is appropriate to discuss work-related goals and the details and quality of performance.[45]

Nissenbaum (to whom we gratefully acknowledge a considerable debt) has repeatedly emphasized the complex feat of coordination that creates the multifaceted texture of privacy in public.

How does that feat of coordination happen?

Coordination through Informational Norms

It happens through informational norms – in particular, through informational norms that are also *coordination* norms. *Informational norms* are social norms that

[43] Christena E. Nippert-Eng, *Islands of Privacy* (University of Chicago Press, 2010), 22.
[44] Nippert-Eng, 4.
[45] Helen Nissenbaum, "Privacy as Contextual Integrity," Wash. Law Rev. 79 (2004): 138.

constrain the collection, use, and distribution of information. We are concerned with the subset that are also coordination norms. Coordination norms have been extensively studied in game theory, law, and philosophy.[46] They are one instance of a general type of coordination that occurs for a variety of different purposes in a wide range of different situations. Activity under coordination norms is an instance of the "capacity shown, in some form or other, by humans in all cultures to live under rules and values and to shape their behaviour in some degree to social expectations, in ways that are . . . not directly controlled by threats and rewards."[47]

Driving on the right (or, more generally, on the same side of the road as other road users) is a classic example of a coordination norm. As a first approximation, four features make it a coordination norm. We define coordination norms in Chapter 4 by refining and generalizing these conditions:

1. Drivers share the goal of driving on the right for safety and convenience.
2. Each thinks they ought to drive on the right as long as enough others do (there is no safety and convenience point to right-side driving unless enough others also drive on the right).
3. As a result of (2), the following past behavioral regularity exists: enough drivers drive on the right.
4. As a result of (3), the regularity continues to hold in the future, as enough drivers continue to drive on the right.

These conditions make driving on the right a self-perpetuating behavioral regularity. The idea (refined in Chapter 4) is that (1)–(2) ensure that that people will drive on the right as long as enough others do, and (3) and (4) ensure that enough drivers think that enough others will drive on the right. In Chapter 4, we take that to be a hallmark of coordination norms.

Four comments are in order. First, our free use of "ought" may ring false to those who assume that people are entirely self-interested. We reject "the peculiar understanding that rational choice consists only in clever promotion of self-interest."[48] We do not deny that "I ought to do X" may express a resolution to pursue one's self-interest, but it may also express the resolve to act in accord with what you value even when so acting does not advance your self-interest.

Second, we build our account of coordination norms by appealing to connections between thinking one ought to do X and preferring at a given time to do X more than any incompatible action.[49] We focus on the fact that "ought thoughts" can explain

46 See, for example, H. Peyton Young, "The Economics of Convention," J. Econ. Perspect. 10 (1996): 107–8 (providing a game-theoretic explanation of the decision made by individual drivers as to whether to drive on the right or left side of the road).

47 Bernard Williams, *Truth and Truthfulness: An Essay in Genealogy* (Princeton University Press, 2004), 24.

48 Amartya Sen, *The Idea of Justice* (Harvard University Press, 2009), 32.

49 We note that neo-Samuelson explanations of choice appeal to revealed preferences, not "ought thoughts" or other sources of motivation. Amartya Sen has extensively criticized the approach. For

these preferences. For example, when you see Victoria about to immerse herself in the chilly March 1st waters of Lake Michigan as a participant in Chicago's Polar Plunge, it is clear to you that she prefers to do that more than any other incompatible alternative. Otherwise, she would not be wading into the water. When you ask her "Why are you subjecting yourself to that cold water?" you want an explanation for her preference. Victoria provides it by answering "Participating in the Polar Plunge raises money for the Special Olympics, and I think I ought to help do that." We note that thinking one ought to do X does not always yield a preference to do X more than any other incompatible option. For example, suppose that, like Victoria, Victor thinks he ought to participate in the Polar Plunge to raise money for the Special Olympics, but that thought never yields a preference to plunge into the cold water. There are always other things Victor thinks he ought to do that take precedence. Notice, by the way, that we are not saying that *all* preferences arise from thinking one ought to do something. Imagine you think he ought not to take a drink of yellow paint, but you nonetheless experience a whim to take a drink, a whim so strong that you prefer to do so more than any other incompatible action.

The third point concerns the driving-on-the-right example. It may (and indeed usually does) provoke the objection "You're overlooking the fact that the *law* (in right-side countries) requires driving on the right. Isn't the legal regulation the explanation for driving on the right, rather than a coordination norm?" We do not think so. The existence of a law does not ensure conformity to it. United States law requires pedestrians not to cross intersections against either a red light or a "Don't Walk" signal; however, the norm in many cities is to cross against the signal as long as you do not interfere with traffic. Another example is the 1974 US federal law capping speed limits at 55 mph. States had to agree to comply to receive federal funds for highway repair. Motorists rebelled, and states subverted the law by reducing penalties for speeding. The federal government repealed speed limit controls in 1995. As the Nobel Prize–winning political economist Elinor Ostrom notes, "If individuals voluntarily participate in a situation, they must share some general sense that most of the rules governing the situation are appropriate. Otherwise, the cost of enforcement within voluntary activities becomes high enough that it is difficult, if not impossible, to maintain predictability in an ongoing voluntary activity."[50]

Fourth, we have left one question hanging. Why think *informational* norms are examples of *coordination* norms (at least in a wide range of important cases)? After all, not all informational norms are coordination norms. For example, "Say nothing negative about the dead" is an informational norm in some cultures but is not a coordination norm. Unlike driving on the right, one does not need the cooperation

a useful summary and evaluation, see Cyril Hédoin, "Sen's Critique of Revealed Preference Theory and Its 'NeoSamuelsonian' Critique: A Methodological and Theoretical Assessment," *Journal of Economic Methodology* 23 (2018): 349–73. Our goal is not to resolve the issues, just to make our position clear.

50 Elinor Ostrom, *Understanding Institutional Diversity* (Princeton University Press, 2005), 21.

of others to make sure one does not say anything negative about the dead. We devote Chapters 3 and 4 to showing that the informational norms with which we are concerned are also coordination norms.

The Massive Capacity to Know Undermines Self-realization

Surveillance creates a massive capacity to know. We claim that the existence of that capacity severely limits opportunities for self-realization. Adequate self-realization requires adequate privacy in public. The massive capacity to know undermines self-realization by undermining the norm-based coordination on which adequate privacy in public depends. How does it do that? To see the idea, recall the family holiday dinner. Imagine that Mark, a rebellious – and technologically precocious – adolescent has deployed hidden video cameras and microphones to record all the conversations. Voice-to-text transcription software turns the conversations into text and delivers them as texts to the family members' cell phones. To see the effect of the surveillance, compare surveillance-free dinners. In those dinners, the family members knew that their combined adherence to the strictures on information created a harmony-preserving selective flow of information. Mark's surveillance means that the family members can no longer count on creating a *selective* flow of information through their combined adherence to the strictures on information flow, and that prevents realizing the social role of family member since that role requires creating that selective flow through adherence to the strictures. To ensure harmony, they can only say to one another what will be nondisruptive even if all know what was said.

In general, surveillance limits opportunities for self-realization by altering the conditions under which people seek it. In the family holiday dinner example, this happens because Mark's surveillance ensures that he and the rest of the family members *actually know* what the surveillance records. Our general claim is more sweeping: the *mere capacity* to know limits opportunities for self-realization even if no one actually knows what the surveillance captures. Surveillance in the form of a massive capacity to know is a threat we all currently face. To see how the capacity to know creates the threat, note first that, in the holiday dinner example, we described the family members as *knowing* (in the absence of Mark's surveillance) that their combined adherence to the strictures on information flow created a selective flow of information. Mark's surveillance disrupts self-realization by eliminating that knowledge. To see how the mere capacity to know can do the same, we need a deeper understanding of the role knowledge plays in facilitating conformity to informational norms.

We omitted any mention of knowledge in our initial characterization of coordination norms in (1)–(4). The point was to highlight its importance by adding it here. It is the key to seeing how surveillance undermines coordination. It does so by undermining the knowledge essential to coordination. To understand how that happens, we first characterize the role of knowledge in coordination.

KNOWING WHAT OTHERS WILL DO

Driving on the right illustrates the role of knowledge. For convenience, we restate the four conditions. (1) Drivers share the goal of driving on the right for safety and convenience. (2) Each thinks they ought to drive on the right as long as enough others do. (3) As a result of (2), the following past behavioral regularity exists: enough drivers drive on the right. (4) As a result of (3), the regularity continues in the future as enough drivers continue to drive on the right. To see the role of knowledge, ask "How does the 'thinking one ought' in (2) result in the 'enough driving on the right' in (3)?"

Imagine two drivers, Mary and John, have stopped in their respective cars at a four-way intersection. Mary is driving on the right on one cross street; John, on the right on the other. He signals a left turn. As long as he thinks Mary will stay in her lane and hence on her right, John will complete his turn into the lane opposite Mary and thereby continue driving on his right. Similarly, Mary will continue driving on her right as long as she thinks there is no need to evade a not-driving-on-his-right John. A moment later John completes his turn into the lane opposite Mary, as she knew he would do so. But how did she know that? She and John are strangers. The only relevant fact that she knows about him is that he presents himself in the role of a driver, so it is possible, for all she knows, that John is from a left-driving country and will get confused and turn into her.[51] Or, enraged at what he sees as the repressive conformity of modern life, he could have decided to flout convention by driving on the left. Or it could be that he has never driven before in his life, and his no idea that he is supposed to drive on the right. Or ... With a little imagination, one might sketch any number of scenarios in which John drives on the left. The remarkable fact is that Mary does not give these possibilities a moment's thought. Why?

The answer may seem obvious. Isn't it just that Mary *knows* John will continue driving on the right?[52] She looks at him and infers – correctly, we may suppose – that there is an extremely high probability that John will continue driving on the right. The problem is that Mary can know that John will drive on the right without John knowing that she knows that. Likewise, Mary may not know that John knows that she will drive on the right. Focus for the moment on John. Imagine that, if someone asked him whether Mary knew that he would drive on the right, he replied, "I am not sure. She may think that I am from a left-driving country and will get confused and turn into her, or she may think ...," where the dots are filled in with the various possibilities in which John drives on the left. The result is that John hesitates to begin his left turn. He worries that Mary may misinterpret his behavior and begin evasive action by turning into the left lane just as he also turns into it. Suppose similar

[51] Countries that drive on the left include India, Australia, New Zealand, South Africa, the Caribbean, the United Kingdom, Ireland, Malta, and Cyprus, among others.

[52] Some may rightly object that we require too much when we require knowledge. Belief can be enough. (2) will lead to (3) as long as people have adequate reason to believe others will drive on the right. Throughout the book, we will use "know" as shorthand for "know (or have adequate reason to believe)."

remarks hold for Mary. If someone were to ask her whether John knew that she would drive on the right, she would reply, "I am not sure. He may think that I am from a left-driving country and will get confused and turn into him, or he may think . . . ." Like John, Mary hesitates to begin her turn. Coordination fails because of a lack of second-level knowledge. It helps at this point to add subscripts to "know" to keep track of levels of knowledge. The problem is that Mary does not $know_2$ that John $knows_1$ that she will drive on the right, and the same is true of John.

So, should we add a second-level knowledge requirement to our explanation of coordination? For Mary and John, this would mean requiring that Mary $knows_2$ that John $knows_1$ that she will drive on the right, and that John $knows_2$ the same about Mary. However the problem then arises again at the third level of knowledge. Suppose also that John does *not* $know_3$ that Mary $knows_2$ that John $knows_1$ she will drive on the right. Instead, he thinks, "I $know_2$ that Mary $knows_1$ that I will drive on the right, but she does not $know_2$ that I $know_1$ that. She may $think_2$ I $think_1$ she is from a left-driving country and will get confused and drive on the left." The same third-level doubt can arise for Mary. In general, consider any knowledge-level n at which Mary $knows_n$ that . . . $knows_1$ that John will drive on the right, and John $knows_n$ that . . . $knows_1$ that Mary will drive on the right. With enough ingenuity one can construct examples in which coordination fails because one of them fails to $know_{n+1}$ . . . that the other $knows_1$ that he or she will drive on the right.

When driving, no one gives these possibilities serious consideration. Indeed, no one thinks about them *at all* (with the exception of academics driving cars while also thinking about the theory of coordination). To underscore the point, imagine John taking his driving test to renew his driver's license. He explains to the examiner, "I did not take the right of way to turn left because I was worried that the driver on the cross street might not continue to drive on the right." That would be ludicrous. Why? Why do drivers who are strangers to each other never think, "There may be something about the other driver that will lead him or her not to drive on the right?" Why is coordination unhesitating, without explicit thought?

The problem is well known in game theory, and the standard game theory solution is to make the problem disappear by assuming *common knowledge*. Something is common knowledge in a group if everyone in the group knows it, everyone knows that everyone knows it, everyone knows that everyone knows that everyone knows it, and so on ad infinitum. Common knowledge makes the parties transparent to each other in a way that facilitates coordination. Everything is out in the open. There is no possibility of misunderstanding, misinterpretation, doubt, or deception at any knowledge level. Assume, for example, that Mary and John *commonly know* they will drive on the right. That explains their unhesitating coordination since none of the doubts we imagined arise.

We adopt the game theory solution. In Chapter 4, we define coordination norms by requiring the (revised and refined version of) conditions (1)–(4) to be common knowledge. The assumption of common knowledge is more than a game theory artifice. It plays a key role in the coordination that creates privacy in public. As the psychologists Thomas Kyle et al. observe in their groundbreaking study, *The Psychology of Common Knowledge*, "[a]ctors coordinate when they have evidence for common knowledge, and refrain from coordinating when they do not."[53] A central claim of Chapter 3 is that when people present themselves to each other in social roles, the presentations create common knowledge that the people will conform to the norm-imposed strictures on information flow associated with those roles. The common-knowledge-creating function of social roles is a familiar theme in sociology. As sociologists Peter Berger and Thomas Luckmann emphasize in their foundational work, *The Social Construction of Reality*:

> In the common stock of knowledge there are standards of role performance that are accessible to all members of a society, or at least to those who are potential performers of the roles in question. This general accessibility is itself part of the same stock of knowledge; *not only are the standards of role X generally known, but it is known that these standards are known.* Consequently every putative actor of role X can be held responsible for abiding by the standards, which can be taught as part of the institutional tradition and used to verify the credentials of all performers and, by the same token, serve as controls.[54]

Berger and Luckman only note two levels of knowledge: standards are known and it is known that they are known, but we take them to mean that it is also true that it is known that it is known that they are known, and so on.

Appeals to common knowledge in the privacy literature are nonexistent. That lack of attention is of a piece with a general tendency to overlook common knowledge.[55] As Thomas et al. note, given that "much of social life is affected by common-knowledge generators," it is "surprising that the psychology of common knowledge has apparently had so little visibility either in psychology or in everyday life." They urge that "an acknowledgement of the role of common knowledge in enabling coordination can unify and explain a variety of seemingly unrelated and puzzling phenomena,"[56] and note that:

> In recent decades, psychologists have recognized that cooperation is one of the hallmarks of the human species, and that its game-theoretic demands have shaped our emotions, our morality, our social relationships, and our language. Much has been learned about these domains of psychology from a focus on the problem of altruistic cooperation and the mechanisms of reciprocity. We hope that comparable insights are waiting to be discovered by psychologists as they investigate the problem

53 Kyle A. Thomas et al., "The Psychology of Coordination and Common Knowledge," *Journal of Personality and Social Psychology* 107, 4 (2014): 671.

54 Peter L. Berger and Thomas Luckmann, *The Social Construction of Reality: A Treatise in the Sociology of Knowledge* (Anchor, 1967), 73 (emphasis added).

55 Thomas et al., 659 (noting that "despite the fact that common knowledge is fundamentally a psychological phenomenon, little is known about the psychology of common knowledge").

56 Thomas et al., 671.

> of mutualistic cooperation, and the mechanisms of common knowledge are – as we might say – put out there.[57]

We share the same hope with regard to privacy in public.

Our concern in this book is with the role of common knowledge in norm-enabled coordination. In Chapter 4, we discuss that role at length and show that it is essential to adequate privacy in public. Surveillance undermines the common knowledge essential to coordination under informational norms. The consequence is that privacy in public drastically declines, and – we claim – that entails a decrease in opportunities for self-realization. Why is that claim true?

WHY PRIVACY IN PUBLIC IS ESSENTIAL TO SELF-REALIZATION

To begin, imagine a future – say, in 2084 – in which everyone has an implant that connects them to a cloud-based artificial-intelligence complex. The system constructs and updates digital profiles for everyone. Anyone can call up anyone's profile (in a visual display that appears to hover in the air before them). People might refrain from accessing the information, but assume the opposite is true. Everyone – employers, school admissions committees, the Transportation Security Agency, private clubs, hotels, friends, acquaintances, and on – routinely display the dossiers. People still interact in a wide range of social roles, but no one trusts anyone to access, use, and distribute only a selective flow of information. Selves still exist in this world. So, in what sense does surveillance make the self wither?

It does so by reducing the range of opportunities for self-realization. As noted earlier, you make yourself who you are by selecting what you will identify with – "stand by," as William James puts it – from the possibilities open to you. In the 2084 world, the possibilities for what you can "stand by" are severely restricted compared to our current world. To illustrate, consider Roger, who is a birdwatcher, Master Mason of the Scottish Rite of Freemasonry, and a frequenter of drag bars. When Roger meets his fellow birdwatchers, his goal is to relate to them as a birdwatcher, not as a birdwatcher/Mason/frequenter of drag bars. Compare a world without significant surveillance. Roger can exercise his "power to conceive of [himself] in different ways, to harbour dissonant projects and perspectives, to inform [his] thoughts and [life] with divergent categories and concepts" without worrying that his activities will undermine each other.[58] It is possible for Roger to do so even if a fellow birdwatcher knows Roger is a Mason and a drag bar regular. As long as it is common knowledge between the two that they adhere to relevant norms controlling the flow of information, Roger can be confident that he will relate to the birdwatchers just as a fellow birdwatcher. In a world without surveillance, the enclaves of privacy in public are, to use the sociologist Christena Nippert-Eng's apt expression,

57 Thomas et al., 671.

58 John Gray, *Post-Liberalism: Studies in Political Thought* (Routledge, 1993), 262–63, 263.

"territories of the self," wherein "only those aspects of self that we and others deem appropriate are activated and supported at a given time and place."[59] In the 2084 world, there are few, if any, such territories of the self.

Our current world is neither the 2084 world nor the "no significant surveillance" one. Profiles abound in our current world,[60] but they are not as readily accessible to individuals as in the 2084 world. They remain largely in the hands of businesses, governments, and organizations.[61] Individuals realize that businesses, governments, and organizations have a massive capacity to know about them, but they are mostly in the dark about whether and how they use that capacity. We emphasize that the mere existence of the capacity reduces self-realization. This point plays a key role in the book, and it is the insight behind the commentators' claim that surveillance withers the self. As the privacy and security expert Bruce Schneier notes, "[p]sychologists, sociologists, philosophers, novelists, and technologists have all written about the effects of constant surveillance, *or even just the perception of constant surveillance*. Studies show that ... [s]urveillance strips us of our dignity. It threatens our very selves as individuals. It's a dehumanizing tactic employed in prisons and detention camps around the world."[62] Even "just the perception of constant surveillance" reduces self-realization because territories of privacy in public are no longer regions where one can be confident that "only those aspects of self that we and others deem appropriate are activated and supported."[63] Instead, uncertainty displaces confidence. Roger confronts two questions, which he finds it difficult, if not impossible, to answer: *The knowledge question*: "Who knows what about me?"; and *The use question*: "Given that others know some things about me, how will they use that knowledge?" As we explain in Chapters 6–8, people react by resisting surveillance (Chapter 6), acquiescing to it (Chapter 7), or accepting it (Chapter 8). Each option reduces privacy in public and hence reduces opportunities for self-realization.

We propose ensuring adequate privacy in public by maintaining informational norms. The reference to "maintaining" may suggest that we wish to preserve the status quo. That is not our intent. The maintenance process we have in mind allows for (indeed envisions) appropriate transformations of informational norms.

LACK OF NORMS

One may object that we are ignoring half of the problem. Digital devices and the Internet have evolved so rapidly that they have created a wide range of novel

59 Christena E. Nippert-Eng, *Home and Work: Negotiating Boundaries through Everyday Life*, (University of Chicago Press, 1996), 68.

60 See, for example, Bruce Schneier, "Essays: Our Data, Ourselves," *Schneier on Security* (blog), May 15, 2008, www.schneier.com/essays/archives/2008/05/our_data_ourselves.html.

61 Deibert, *Black Code*, 68.

62 Bruce Schneier, *Data and Goliath: The Hidden Battles to Collect Your Data and Control Your World*, (W. W. Norton & Company, 2015), 127 (emphasis added).

63 Nippert-Eng, *Home and Work*, 68.

relationships not governed by any relevant informational norms. Without norm-enabled coordination, there is no effective mechanism to ensure adequate privacy in public and the opportunities for self-realization that it supports. How does our approach of maintaining norms help here? Without any norms in place, there is nothing to maintain. The solution comes in Chapter 8, where the process we propose for maintaining norms is also a process for creating them.

TRUST

We began with trust, but common knowledge has taken center stage. What happened to trust? It is still there, in the form of common knowledge. We equate trust with common-knowledge-created transparency about conformity to norms. This may seem wrong. Isn't it obvious that trust *contrasts* with knowledge? Isn't trust a matter of having faith that something is true when you do *not* know that it is? Those points are obvious on *one* traditional understanding of trust,[64] but there is another tradition on which trusting and knowing are compatible. On this tradition, trust consists of the willingness to act in light of the conviction that one needs *no more* evidence. By way of illustration, suppose Victor is considering lending Mason money based on the evidence he has of his creditworthiness. When Alice offers to provide Victor with additional evidence, he declines, saying "I have enough evidence. I trust that he will repay." Victor's point is that he already knows (has adequate reason to believe) that Victor will repay *and* needs no more evidence. The sociologist Barbara Misztal exemplifies this tradition when she remarks that "Trust always involves an element of risk resulting from our inability to monitor others' behaviour, from our inability to have a *complete* knowledge about other people's motivations."[65] Victor does not have "complete knowledge" of Mason's motivations. He does not have a complete map of all his motivations and of all the varying contingencies that would lead him to repay or not repay. His trust takes the form of his willingness to act without further investigation into those motives and contingencies. In the same way, common-knowledge-created transparency about conformity to norms is a form of trust. Presentations in social roles create common knowledge, and they often do so between complete strangers whose only relevant knowledge of each other is that they present themselves in certain social roles. Such role-based interactions are a constant feature of daily life, and, like Victor, we are convinced that the others will conform to relevant norms, *and* that we need no more evidence.

Some may still wonder why we bother to talk about trust. Couldn't we just talk about knowledge based on role presentations? We could, but we would lose something essential. We would be overlooking the fact that our daily role-mediated

64 See, for example, Adam B. Seligman, *The Problem of Trust* (Princeton University Press, 2000), 21.

65 Barbara Misztal, *Trust in Modern Societies: The Search for the Bases of Social Order* (Polity, 1996), 18–19 (emphasis added).

dependencies on others occur within a web of associations and evaluations, a web that has the concept of trust at its center. Talk of trust keeps those associations and evaluations at center stage. It also underscores the remarkable fact that people confidently predict how complete strangers will act based solely on the fact that they present themselves in a certain role. As the security and privacy expert Bruce Schneier observes,

> Just today, a stranger came to my door claiming he was here to unclog a bathroom drain. I let him into my house without verifying his identity, and not only did he repair the drain, he also took off his shoes so he wouldn't track mud on my floors. When he was done, I gave him a piece of paper that asked my bank to give him some money. He accepted it without a second glance. At no point did he attempt to take my possessions, and at no point did I attempt the same of him. In fact, neither of us worried that the other would . . . Also today, I passed several strangers on the street without any of them attacking me. I bought food from a grocery store, not at all concerned that it might be unfit for human consumption. I locked my front door, but didn't spare a moment's worry at how easy it would be for someone to smash my window in. Even people driving cars, large murderous instruments that could crush me like a bug, didn't scare me.[66]

Trust of strangers in the form of common-knowledge-created transparency is a pervasive feature of daily life.

IS THIS BOOK NECESSARY?

Recent work emphasizes the same point we do: namely, an essential aspect of privacy consists in people's trusting each other to respect shared expectations about the selective flow of information. If that is all we had to say, there would be no reason to write this book. We break new ground with an explanation of how and why trust is essential to privacy in public and an explanation of how and why surveillance undermines trust. But doesn't an explanation already exist in the literature on the role of trust in privacy?

An explanation does indeed exist. We claim that we need a further, deeper explanation. To see why, consider an analogy. Suppose Mary asks her father why the waterwheel turns when the water strikes it. It would not do for her father to answer, "The water makes it turn when it strikes the wheel." Mary can see that much. A more informative answer would be that the wheel can freely turn around its axle, and the weight of the water on one side but not the other makes it turn. If you are going to repair water wheels, you need an explanation of the "free to turn" type. The same point holds for repairing privacy. Current explanations of trust's role in privacy are of the "wheel goes around because the water strikes it" variety. Just as Mary sees

[66] Bruce Schneier, *Liars and Outliers: Enabling the Trust That Society Needs to Thrive* (John Wiley and Sons, 2012), 1.

that the water makes the wheel turn, one can see that trust is essential to privacy. What is not clear is *how and why* trust is essential – not clear enough *in sufficient detail* to figure out how most effectively to preserve privacy in the face of pervasive surveillance. Our explanation emphasizes trust in the form of common knowledge and its role in facilitating the informational-norm-based coordination on which adequate privacy in public depends. We use that explanation as the framework within which to develop our proposal that public policy should preserve and create informational norms. To create such a flow is to create a tradeoff between informational privacy and information processing. The reason is that informational norms implement a selective flow of information that makes some information available to some for some purposes but not to others for other purposes. We use our explanatory framework to address tradeoff issues. Finding a way to make acceptable tradeoffs is an unsolved problem. As the sociologist James Rule notes, "we cannot hope to answer [complex balancing questions] until we have a way of ascribing weights to the things being balanced. And that is exactly where parties to privacy debates are most dramatically at odds."[67] We take it for granted that social and political processes settle the normative questions about what count as acceptable tradeoffs, and we outline a suitable process built around informational norms – one such process. We do not claim it is the only one needed.

To support our claim that a deeper explanation is called for, we consider two recent, excellent books: Woodrow Hartzog, *Privacy's Blueprint: The Battle to Control the Design of New Technologies*,[68] and Ari Ezra Waldman, *Privacy as Trust: Information Privacy for an Information Age*.[69] Hartzog argues for privacy by design. He explains that his "argument boils down to one simple idea: the design of popular technologies is critical to privacy, and the law should take it more seriously. Law and policy makers can do so through recognition and guidance. Lawmakers and courts should better recognize how design shapes our privacy."[70] He notes that "Lawmakers are in a difficult position. If courts and regulators prohibit too much collection, use, or disclosure of information, they will frustrate commerce, free expression, and our ability to freely interact with others. Overregulating design is dangerous. Yet so is ignoring it, and an important balance must be struck."[71] Hartzog does not explain (in any detail) how to strike the required balance. This is not

67 Rule, *Privacy in Peril*, 183. Compare Alan F. Westin, *Privacy and Freedom* (Atheneum Press, 1967), 414 ("If privacy is to receive its proper weight on the scales in any process of balancing competing values, what is needed is a structured and rational weighing process, with definite criteria that public and private authorities can apply in comparing the claims for disclosure or surveillance through new devices with the claims to privacy.").

68 Woodrow Hartzog, *Privacy's Blueprint: The Battle to Control the Design of New Technologies* (Harvard University Press, 2018).

69 Ari Ezra Waldman, *Privacy as Trust: Information Privacy for an Information Age* (Cambridge University Press, 2018).

70 Hartzog, *Privacy's Blueprint*, 7.

71 Hartzog, 6–7.

a criticism. His goal is to draw attention to the importance of privacy by design as a framework for within which courts and regulators can seek an acceptable balance.

In *Privacy as Trust: Information Privacy for an Information Age*, Ari Waldman argues that "Information privacy ... is really a social construct based on trust between social sharers, between individuals and Internet intermediaries, between groups of people interacting online and offline, broadly understood."[72] He investigates how the law can support trust norms, but he does not investigate how to identify and implement the tradeoffs required for securing adequate privacy in public. Again, this is not a criticism. Waldman's goal is to reorient privacy toward trust norms, not to find acceptable tradeoffs. Our contribution is to show how to reach acceptable tradeoffs through a process built around coordination norms.

THE TEST CASE OF ARTIFICIAL INTELLIGENCE

Finding acceptable tradeoffs is the way to prevent our playing Desdemona to the "I'll see" of business and government and instead to ensure that our selves do not wither under an unrelenting investigative gaze but flourish in a world of adequate privacy in public. We turn to that task in Chapter 8. In Chapter 9, we illustrate our approach with the test case of artificial intelligence.

Next, we turn to artificial intelligence in Chapter 2 both to provide background for Chapter 9 and to motivate the consideration of informational norms in Chapters 3 to 7 by illustrating the seriousness and immediacy of the AI-driven surveillance threat. Our ultimate solution is a regulatory one: the preservation and creation of informational norms at least in part through government regulation. We turn to regulation because we assume market solutions are unlikely. Market solutions would require that consumers have the power to influence businesses by changing what they buy in light of sufficient correct information about purchasing options. We take it to be clear that, in the situations which concern us, consumers lack sufficient power and information.

72 Waldman, *Privacy as Trust*, 50.

2

Artificial Intelligence-Enhanced Surveillance

Why would a toothbrush send data to a website? The Oral-B Genius X Rechargeable Electric Toothbrush sends data about a user's brushing practices to Oral-B's servers to help you "brush like your dentist recommends." Oral-B explains that the toothbrush "has a revolutionary Artificial Intelligence technology that enables it to recognize your brushing style and coaches you for your best results every day."[1] The toothbrush connects to your smartphone, and then to the Oral-B servers. Oral-B's Privacy Policy reveals that it collects more than just information about brushing style. It also collects contact information; unique identifiers; government-issued identifiers (such as driver license numbers); financial, biometric, and demographic information; and transaction and commercial information. Transaction and commercial information includes "customer account information, qualification data, purchase history and related records (including returns, product service records, records of payments, credits etc.), records related to downloads and purchases of products and applications, non-biometric data collected for consumer authentication (passwords, account security questions), customer service records."[2] It also collects audio visual information, health information, and "IP address, MAC address, SSIDs or other device identifiers or persistent identifiers, online user ID, encrypted password, device characteristics (such as browser information), web server logs, application logs, browsing data, viewing data (TV, streaming), website and app usage, first party cookies, third-party cookies, flash cookies, Silverlight cookies, web beacons, clear gifs and pixel tags." Oral-B shares this information with "carefully selected partners so that they can send you offers, promotions, or ads about their products and services we believe you may be interested in."[3]

1 "Genius X Rechargeable Electric Toothbrush," Oral-B, https://oralb.com/en-us/oral-b-genius-x-10000-rechargeable-electric-toothbrush/."

2 "P&G Global Consumer Privacy Policy," P&G, March 1, 2021, www.pg.com/privacy/english/privacy_statement.shtml.

3 "P&G Global Consumer Privacy Policy."

Oral-B's information-processing practices may shock, but they should not surprise anybody in the 2020s. Writing in 2013, the authors of a textbook for business students note as a matter of well-established fact that the "past fifteen years have seen extensive investments in business infrastructure, which have improved the ability to collect data throughout the enterprise. Virtually every aspect of business is now open to data collection and often even instrumented for data collection: operations, manufacturing, supply-chain management, customer behavior, marketing campaign performance, workflow procedures, and so on."[4] This development is both the cause and the effect of the fact that "information ... is the fundamental building material of the modern enterprise."[5] A significant part of that "building material" is information about *consumers*. As the business school professor Soshana Zuboff notes,

> Surveillance capitalism unilaterally claims human experience as free raw material for translation into behavioral data. Although some of these data are applied to product or service improvement, the rest are declared as a proprietary behavioral surplus, fed into advanced manufacturing processes known as "machine intelligence," and fabricated into prediction products that anticipate what you will do now, soon, and later.[6]

The information Oral-B collects is an example of Zuboff's "behavioral surplus." An extensive literature details how businesses and governments use that surplus.[7] We focus on the relatively recent use of artificial intelligence to analyze the information.

4 Foster Provost and Tom Fawcett, *Data Science for Business: What You Need to Know about Data Mining and Data-Analytic Thinking* (O'Reilly, 2013), 1.

5 James W. Cortada, *Information and the Modern Corporation* (The MIT Press, 2011), x. Cortada notes that

> Today less than 20 percent of the workers in a computer plant make anything; the rest are accountants, supply-chain supervisors, quality-control specialists, production supervisors, managers, analysts, computer scientists, and engineers. Banks do not have as much cash in their vaults and branches as they did in earlier years; instead, they have digital files that say they have large amounts of money, and they are managing information about how much a particular person or account has, not physically moving coins and paper from one pile to another. And so it goes in one industry after another: hundreds of millions of people working with information. They can do this reasonably well thanks to the existence of computers. Most commentators on information focus on the computers rather than on information, facts, and data. (ix)

6 Shoshana Zuboff, *The Age of Surveillance Capitalism: The Fight for a Human Future at the New Frontier of Power* (PublicAffairs, 2019), 8.

7 See, for example, Ronald J. Deibert, *Reset: Reclaiming the Internet for Civil Society* (House of Anansi Press, 2020); Zuboff, *The Age of Surveillance Capitalism*; Andreas Bernard, *The Triumph of Profiling: The Self in Digital Culture*, trans. Valentine A. Pakis (Polity, 2019); Steffen Mau, *The Metric Society: On the Quantification of the Social* (Polity, 2019); Dan Bouk, *How Our Days Became Numbered: Risk and the Rise of the Statistical Individual* (University of Chicago Press, 2018); Josh Lauer, *Creditworthy: A History of Consumer Surveillance and Financial Identity in America* (Columbia University Press, 2017); David Lyon, *Surveillance after Snowden* (Polity, 2015); Matt Apuzzo and Adam Goldman, *Enemies Within: Inside the NYPD's Secret Spying Unit and Bin Laden's Final Plot against America* (Touchstone, 2014); Luke Harding, *The Snowden Files: The Inside Story of the World's Most Wanted Man* (Vintage, 2014); Glenn Greenwald, *No Place to Hide:*

For convenience, we will use "artificial intelligence" (AI), "machine learning," and "predictive analytics" more or less interchangeably. That is, we are following the business and popular press, which frequently uses the term AI as equivalent to or including machine learning,[8] and we are using "predictive analytics" as more or less synonymous with machine learning.[9] An accurate business-oriented description of machine learning is that it is "the use of mathematical procedures (algorithms) to analyze data. The aim is to discover useful patterns … between different items of data. Once the relationships have been identified, these can be used to make inferences about the behavior of new cases."[10] Artificial intelligence dominates decision-making. That is, it "is being applied to a huge range of problems. In fact,

Edward Snowden, the NSA, and the US Surveillance State (Metropolitan Books, 2014); Beatrice Edwards, *The Rise of the American Corporate Security State: Six Reasons to Be Afraid* (Berrett-Koehler Publishers, 2014); Julia Angwin, *Dragnet Nation: A Quest for Privacy, Security, and Freedom in a World of Relentless Surveillance* (Times Books: 2014); Lori Andrews, *I Know Who You Are and I Saw What You Did: Social Networks and the Death of Privacy* (Free Press, 2013); The Washington Post, *NSA Secrets: Government Spying in the Internet Age* (Diversion Books: 2013); Joel R. Reidenberg, "The Data Surveillance State in the US and Europe," *Wake Forest L. Rev.* 48 (2013): 583–608; Neil Richards, "The Dangers of Surveillance," *Harvard Law Review* 126 1934–1965 (2013): 1934; Robert H. Sloan and Richard Warner, *Unauthorized Access: The Crisis in Online Privacy and Information Security* (Chapman Hall/CRC Press, 2013); Heidi Boghosian and Lewis Lapham, *Spying on Democracy: Government Surveillance, Corporate Power and Public Resistance* (City Lights Publishers, 2013); Simon Chesterman, *One Nation under Surveillance: A New Social Contract to Defend Freedom without Sacrificing Liberty* (Reprint ed., Oxford University Press: 2013); John Gilliom and Torin Monahan, *SuperVision: An Introduction to the Surveillance Society* (University of Chicago Press:2012); Athan Theoharis, *Abuse of Power: How Cold War Surveillance and Secrecy Policy Shaped the Response to 9/11* (Temple University Press: 2011); Ronald J Deibert, *Black Code: Inside the Battle for Cyberspace* (2011); Susan Landau, *Surveillance or Security?: The Risks Posed by New Wiretapping Technologies* (The MIT Press: 2011); James B. Rule, *Privacy in Peril: How We Are Sacrificing a Fundamental Right in Exchange for Security and Convenience* (Oxford University Press, 2009); Luis Alberto Fernandez, *Policing Dissent: Social Control and the Anti-Globalization Movement* (Rutgers University Press: 2008); James Bamford, *The Shadow Factory: The Ultra-Secret NSA from 9/11 to the Eavesdropping on America* (Doubleday: 2008); Jon D. Michaels, "All the President's Spies: Private-Public Intelligence Partnerships in the War on Terror," *Cal. L. Rev.* 96 (2008): 901–66.

8 In computer science, machine learning is generally regarded as a very important subfield of artificial intelligence, not as equivalent. A few might even consider machine learning to be a distinct neighbor subfield to AI.

9 See, for example, Louis Columbus, *Roundup of Machine Learning Forecasts and Market Estimates, 2018*, *Forbes*, www.forbes.com/sites/louiscolumbus/2018/02/18/roundup-of-machine-learning-forecasts-and-market-estimates-2018/ (noting that "61% of organizations most frequently picked Machine Learning/Artificial Intelligence as their company's most significant data initiative for next year").

10 There is no agreement on the precise meaning of predictive analytics and related terms like data mining, machine learning, and AI. See, for example, Steven Finlay, *Artificial Intelligence and Machine Learning for Business: A No-Nonsense Guide to Data Driven Technologies*, 2nd ed. (Relativistic, 2017), 5–16, 27–59 (distinguishing and discussing relationships among machine learning, predictive analytics, data mining, AI, neural nets, and deep learning), and Vijay Kotu and Bala Deshpande, *Predictive Analytics and Data Mining: Concepts and Practice with RapidMiner* (Morgan Kaufmann, 2014), chapter 1 (discussing relations between data mining and predictive analytics).

almost any aspect of life that involves decision making in one form or another."[11] We begin our examination of AI with a thought experiment.

A THOUGHT EXPERIMENT

Imagine that aliens land on earth. They are (or at least appear to be) beneficent aliens who come in peace. One of their first acts is to provide their human hosts with an artificial intelligence system – call it "Alien AI" – for the prediction of individual human actions. The aliens explain that Alien AI is considerably more accurate than human predictions (even computer-assisted predictions), but, they caution, its predictions still have a high error rate in a significant number of cases. Initial tests of the system confirm the aliens' claims. They also reveal that humans have no explanation or understanding of why Alien AI predicts what it does. It appears to involve unknown programming and statistical techniques, and even the best human computer science experts find large parts of Alien AI completely opaque. The aliens draw their human hosts' attention to two additional features:

Broad-based predictions: What happens in virtually any area of one's life (what stores you shop in, what you post on social media, and so on) may serve as input for predictions affecting virtually any other area (what you pay for insurance, whether you get hired, what schools you get in to, and so on).

Data feedback without error correction: Alien AI's decisions affect what happens to people in the future, and that information feeds back into Alien AI as input for subsequent decisions. Alien AI does not, however, have mechanisms that detect and correct its errors.

Despite these concerns, humans – businesses, governments, and individuals – adopt Alien AI systematically in the widest possible range of contexts as a basis for decisions. Unfortunately, data feedback without error correction combines with broad-based predictions to create mistaken and uncorrectable tracks of winners (those whom Alien AI's decisions advantage) and losers (those who are disadvantaged). Losers find it difficult to escape that role, as negative classifications feed data into Alien AI that yields further negative classifications. Social unrest erupts as people react to the massive unfairness of being sorted into winners and losers in ways that are often mistaken and mostly uncorrectable.

We should avoid using Alien AI and systems similar to it. To what extent, then, do human-created systems exhibit low accuracy, opacity, feedback without error

[11] Finlay, *Artificial Intelligence and Machine Learning*. See also Eric Siegel, *Predictive Analytics: The Power to Predict Who Will Click, Buy, Lie, or Die* 293 (Wiley, 2016); Joshua A. Kroll et al., *Accountable Algorithms*, 165 *Univ. Pa. Law Rev.* 663 (2017); Cathy O'Neil, *Weapons of Math Destruction: How Big Data Increases Inequality and Threatens Democracy* (Broadway Books, 2016).

correction, and broad-based predictions? Unfortunately, the answer is that they exhibit those features too often, and to far too great an extent.

We consider each of the features in turn.

LOW ACCURACY

AI systems vary widely in accuracy. Accuracy is a matter of the number of correct versus incorrect predictions.[12] A standard simple definition of accuracy is the percentage (or fraction) of all predictions that are correct. Sometimes we will also want to consider the number of false positives – that is, incorrect predictions that an outcome will occur (or would have occurred if an appropriate action had been taken), and the opposite error, the number of false negatives. AI systems predicting individual human action typically have low accuracy (and hence a high error rate).[13] We offer two very different examples: direct mail advertising and the Chicago Police Department's Strategic Subject List algorithm.[14]

In direct mail advertising, the task is to predict which consumers will respond positively (purchasing, signing up for a credit card, and so on) to a postal mail advertisement. Humans are notoriously poor at identifying positive responders.[15] If, unaided by predictive analytics, a company mails an offer to a list of people with whom it has no prior relationship, the company is doing well if about 10 percent of them respond positively.[16] Using predictive analytics can improve the response rate to 20 or 30 percent.[17] That is still an error rate of 70–80 percent; however, in this case, improved predictive power can translate into increased profitability. If a direct mail marketer finds it profitable to mail with a 10 percent response rate, an improvement to 20–30 percent promises a significant increase in profitability.[18]

12 If we were to ignore false predictions, we could easily design a system to predict with 100 percent accuracy who will be elected US President in 2052. We just predict that everyone will be.

13 See, for example, Steven Finlay, *Predictive Analytics, Data Mining and Big Data: Myths, Misconceptions and Methods* (Palgrave Macmillan, 2014), 6 ("Most predictive models are quite poor at predicting how someone is going to behave"). See, generally, Cathy O'Neil, *Weapons of Math Destruction: How Big Data Increases Inequality and Threatens Democracy* (Broadway Books, 2016) (discussing a number of cases of inaccurate predictions).

14 Andrew Guthrie Ferguson, "The Police Are Using Computer Algorithms to Tell If You're a Threat," *Time*, October 5, 2017, http://time.com/4966125/police-departments-algorithms-chicago/.

15 "Human intuition about customers can often miss important nonobvious segments or not provide the level of granularity that is required for nuanced marketing." John D. Kelleher and Brendan Tierney, *Data Science* (The MIT Press, 2018), 153.

16 Finlay, *Predictive Analytics, Data Mining and Big Data*, 7.

17 Finlay, 143.

18 "In general, the most favorable cases for the use of highly inaccurate predictive systems meet three conditions: (1) humans are even worse at prediction; (2) there is significantly increased benefit from improved prediction accuracy; and (3) the costs of false positives and false negatives are low. The use of predictive analytics in direct mail marketing plausibly fulfils all

The Chicago Police Department's (CPD's) Strategic Subject List algorithm created "a risk assessment score known as the Strategic Subject List or 'SSL.' These scores reflect an individual's probability of being involved in a shooting incident either as a victim or an offender."[19] (The program ended in 2019.[20]) The initial data consists of information about arrests "contained within the CPD data warehouse." Using that data, the algorithm constructs "social networks … to previous homicide victims to predict the likelihood of someone becoming a victim of a homicide."[21] The network is a "co-arrest" network. Chicago uses two types of co-arrests corresponding to two types of links in the network: "A first degree link refers to a relationship between a subject and an individual with whom the subject was previously co-arrested who later became a homicide victim. A second degree link refers to a relationship in which a subject was co-arrested with another person who, in turn, was co-arrested with a later homicide victim." The underlying theory is that the more connections a person has to co-arrested individuals, the more likely they will commit homicide or be a victim of one (depending on the nature of the links).[22]

The Strategic Subject List algorithm "identified less than 1% of homicide victims (3 out of 405)."[23] The case for using such systems is – to say the least – far less clear than the case for predictive analytics in direct mail advertising since the costs of focusing police attention on the wrong people are very high. Unfortunately, "what happens when law enforcement agencies shift their analytic focus from street corners to people is unknown in the world of data-driven policing because there have been few formal evaluations."[24]

three. Credit scoring is another example, because a 20–30% improvement in credit scoring translates into granting 20–30% fewer loans to customers who would have defaulted or 20–30% more loans to good customers who will repay, depending upon how one decides to use the model. To put this in terms of raw bottom line benefit, if a bank writes off $500m in bad loans every year, then a reasonable expectation is that this could be reduced by at least $100m, if not more, by using predictive analytics." (Finlay, 8)

19 "Strategic Subject List – Historical," City of Chicago Data Portal, September 25, 2020, https://data.cityofchicago.org/Public-Safety/Strategic-Subject-List/4aki-r3np. There is only one independent study of the system: Jessica Saunders, Priscillia Hunt, and John S. Hollywood, "Predictions Put into Practice: A Quasi-Experimental Evaluation of Chicago's Predictive Policing Pilot," *Journal of Experimental Criminology* 12, 3 (September 1, 2016): 347–71, https://doi.org/10.1007/s11292-016-9272-0. It studies the "pilot program developed in collaboration between the Chicago Police Department (CPD) and the Illinois Institute of Technology (IIT)" (Saunders, Hunt, and Hollywood, 354). Our discussion concerns that system, which was subsequently developed further.

20 See "Strategic Subject List – Historical." For commentary, see Jeremy Gorner and Annie Sweeney, "For Years Chicago Police Rated the Risk of Tens of Thousands Being Caught up in Violence. That Controversial Effort Has Quietly Been Ended," *Chicago Tribune*, January 24, 2020, www.chicagotribune.com/news/criminal-justice/ct-chicago-police-strategic-subject-list-ended-20200125-spn4kjmrxrh4tmktdjckhtox4i-story.html.

21 Saunders, Hunt, and Hollywood, "Predictions Put into Practice," 354.

22 Saunders, Hunt, and Hollywood, 354.

23 Saunders, Hunt, and Hollywood, 363.

24 Andrew V. Papachristos and Michael Sierra-Alevado, "Policing the Connected World: Using Social Network Analysis in Police-Community Partnerships," Washington, DC: Office of Community Oriented Policing Services, 2018, 22, https://cops.usdoj.gov/RIC/Publications/cops-w0859-pub.pdf.

It is clear that low accuracy is characteristic of systems that attempt to predict individual human action. But *why* is that true? The answer reveals features of predictive analytics that are relevant to its regulation.

DECONTEXTUALIZATION

One important reason is that predictive systems use decontextualized data. An example illustrates what we mean by decontextualization:

> [A person was] doing data entry for a contractor who was developing a tracking system for young people who were under state supervision. The frustration that finally drove her to quit the job was that the architecture of the database didn't allow social service workers to include narrative information about the context of kids' behavior. Simply, the system tracked each student's "success" or "failure" in a number of different programs. So, for example, if students stopped going to an afterschool program because they faced a serious crisis – a death in the family or an apartment fire, for example – a caseworker worker was forced to check a box that reported that they failed to complete the program. Because there was no input box for narrative case notes, there was literally no place in the system to account for the (sometimes pages of) contextual information written in the social workers' reports.[25]

The complaint is that the categories omit the contextual information necessary to understand and explain why the student acted as he or she did.[26] A standard way to explain human action is through narratives that integrate values, purposes, and intentions, together with the context in which they occur, into a meaningful pattern. One could, of course, add a checkbox for "death in the family" or "apartment fire," but that would still fail to capture the values, purposes, and intentions behind the student's reaction to those events. No set of checkboxes, however elaborate, will constitute a narrative integrating context, values, purposes, and intentions into a meaningful pattern.

Contrast AI systems. They make statistical predictions – predictions that people in certain categories have a certain probability of acting in this way or that. Decontextualization is inevitable in statistical explanation. To make statistical predictions about people you look for regularities that hold with some degree of probability for people in certain categories. You abstract away from the enormous variation in individuals' life histories and look for reliable correlations between categories that are independent of the idiosyncratic paths people traced to get into those categories.[27]

25 Virginia Eubanks, *Digital Dead End: Fighting for Social Justice in the Information Age* (The MIT Press, 2011), 95.

26 See generally, Machiel Keestra, "Understanding Human Action: Integrating Meanings, Mechanisms, Causes, and Contexts," in Repko Allen, Szostak Rick, and Newell William (eds.), *Case Studies in Interdisciplinary Research* 201–35 (Sage Publishing, 2011).

27 As one commentator notes, "In social science, as opposed to molecular physics, it is possible to trace individual life histories and, as we may (counterfactually) grant for the sake of the argument, explain

Imagine two scenarios in which you are trying to predict whether Victoria will remain married to Victor once their children graduate from college. In the first, you know that Victoria's publicly observable behavior is typical for a spouse in a twenty-year-long first marriage, and you know that about 40 percent of first marriages end in divorce. Can you predict Victoria's action? Will *she* get divorced? The most the data allow you to do is note that she is in her first marriage and make the statistical prediction that there is a 40 percent chance of divorce for such marriages. Compare this with knowing that Victoria regards her marriage as loveless, places a large disvalue on remaining in loveless relationships, and intends to divorce Victor when their children graduate from college. With that context filled in, you can confidently predict that Victoria will divorce Victor. As we noted when discussing the tracking system for young people under state supervision, you can refine statistical prediction by adding categories (e.g., "regards marriage as loveless"), but you will never produce a narrative that integrates context, values, purposes, and intentions into a meaningful pattern. Statistical prediction will be inaccurate to the extent that those patterns lead to action inconsistent with the prediction.

Our point is not to criticize statistical prediction as inferior to narrative explanations. Statistical explanation is essential. Imagine choosing public policies that affect broad reaches of society. You want to assess the effect on the individuals affected, but the number affected is too large to evaluate narrative explanations of the effect on each individual. The best you can do is divide people into relevant categories and consider the likely effect on individuals in those categories. Statistical prediction for purposes of public policy has a long history. It "was pioneered during the 1660s ... Its purpose, when not confined to the calculation of insurance or annuity rates, was the promotion of sound, well-informed state policy."[28] The vision was that society at last had a tool for making evidence-based predictions about large groups. AI systems have reinvigorated that vision. Computers' capacity to analyze data has raised the hope (or the specter) of processing a massive amount of (decontextualized) information to predict individual action. That hope (or fear) has not yet been realized. Current systems cannot extract information about values, purposes, and intentions from decontextualized data and then reliably predict *an individual's* behavior.[29] While current systems are often somewhat accurate in predicting that

them in terms of determining causal chains. But for the sociological purpose of explaining the overall structure of a society and its changes, this 'historical' or 'dynamical' treatment ... would have to give way to a structural treatment, one form of which is statistics. In order for a statistical treatment to make sense, the overall structures must be invariant with respect to changes in the many detailed histories (of molecules or of people)." Gerd Gigerenzer et al., *The Empire of Chance: How Probability Changed Science and Everyday Life* (Cambridge University Press, 1990), 184.

28 Theodore Porter, *The Rise of Statistical Thinking, 1820–1900*, (Princeton University Press, 1986), 18.

29 As Hannah Fry notes:

> Although AI has come on in leaps and bounds of late, it is still only "intelligent" in the narrowest sense of the word. It would probably be more useful to think of what we've been through as

roughly seventy people in a particular group will behave in a certain way, they cannot reliably predict *which* seventy people, nor whether the number will really be 57, 70, or 76. As Professor Barbara J. Grosz observes about the currently very popular deep-learning approaches to predictive analytics,[30]

> [they] are really good at statistical learning, pattern recognition and large-scale data analysis, but they don't go below the surface. They can't reason about the purposes behind what someone says. Put another way, they ignore the intentional structure component of dialogue. Deep-learning based systems more generally lack other hallmarks of intelligence: they cannot do counterfactual reasoning or common-sense reasoning.[31]

Like Alien AI, actual AI systems have relatively low accuracy rates. That is not surprising given the quite extensive decontextualization of data that occurs in the development of an AI system. Decontextualization occurs as one prepares the data for use in the system.

DATA PREPARATION

Data preparation renders contextual information invisible in five ways: *collection*, *selection*, *cleaning*, *structuring*, and *choice of a model*. The processes typically overlap and interact,[32] but for convenience we treat them as separate and distinct. The processes create the decontextualized "reality" which an AI system uses to make its predictions.[33]

Collection

Data preparation begins with data collection, a starting point that is already a stream of decontextualized data. Much of the information in databases comes from the data

> a revolution in *computational statistics* than a revolution in intelligence . . . [that is] a far more accurate description of how things currently stand. (Hello World, 12)

30 Finlay:

> "Deep" neural networks (Deep learning/Deep belief networks) are very large and complex neural networks (often containing thousands or millions of artificial neurons) which are used for "AI" tasks such as speech recognition and in self-driving cars. [Neurons are the key component] of a neural network . . . a neuron is a linear model whose score is then subject to a (non-linear) transformation. A neural network can therefore be considered as a set of interconnected linear models and non-linear transformations. (*Artificial Intelligence and Machine Learning for Business*, 128–9)

31 Martin Ford, *Architects of Intelligence: The Truth about AI from the People Building It* (Packt Publishing, 2018), 338.

32 Kelleher and Tierney, *Data Science*, 58–59.

33 Kelleher and Tierney, 66 (noting that "With regard to getting the right data for a project, a survey of data scientists in 2016 found that 79 percent of their time is spent on data preparation").

detritus people leave behind. Those leftovers are hardly precise indicators of the contexts of their creation.

To explain why, we first note that data typically divides into content and metadata (i.e., data about the content, such as information about the time of creation or transmission, device used, and so on). The content does not fully (or often even significantly) indicate the relevant context. When communicating content, people *assume* that they and their audiences understand a background that includes the relevant context, values, purposes, and intentions. They do not make that background explicit in the communication, and even a full record of the words and images exchanged would not capture it.

It may seem that metadata, however, captures a great deal of contextual information. Email metadata, for example, can include the sender's name, email and IP address, recipient's name and email address, plus a great deal more.[34] It is indeed true that aggregating metadata can reveal a great deal about people,[35] but it typically does not reveal an explanatory pattern of values, purposes, and intentions. Consider this search metadata for example:

[2018/03/09 18:34:44] abortionfacts.com
[2018/03/09 18:35:23] plannedparenthood.org
[2018/03/09 18:42:29] dcabortionfund.org
[2018/03/09 19:02:12] maps.google.com

The data reveals a concern with abortion, but it does not reveal why. The searcher could be a woman seeking an abortion, a pro-abortion activist, an anti-abortion activist, or an academic researcher. As Shoshana Zuboff notes, you can eliminate some of these possibilities by adding more data (e.g., that the searcher is 60 years old), but no compilation of data, however extensive, will constitute an integrated narrative. In general, data collection practices "render the entire world's actions and conditions as behavioral flows. Each rendered bit is liberated from its life in the social, no longer inconveniently encumbered by moral reasoning, politics, social norms, rights, values, relationships, feelings, contexts, and situations. In the flatness of this flow, data are data, and behavior is behavior."[36]

Selection

One rarely uses all the collected data. One picks and chooses. As the data scientist Steven Finlay explains,

34 Rebecca Greenfield, "What Your Email Metadata Told the NSA about You," *The Atlantic*, 2013, www.theatlantic.com/technology/archive/2013/06/email-metadata-nsa/313842/.

35 Jonathan Mayer, Patricia Mutchler, and John C. Mitchell, "Evaluating the Privacy Properties of Telephone Metadata," *Proc. Natl. Acad. Sci.* 113 (2016): 5536–41.

36 Zuboff, *The Age of Surveillance Capitalism*, 211.

> One feature of Big Data is that most of it has a very low information density, making it very difficult to extract useful customer [or other] insights from it. A huge proportion of the Big Data out there is absolutely useless when it comes to forecasting consumer [or other] behavior. You have to work pretty hard at finding the useful bits that will improve the accuracy of your predictive models.[37]

One selects data that will serve one's predictive goals. One is looking for reliable correlations between categories that are, as we put it earlier, independent of the idiosyncratic paths people traced to get into those categories. Thus, to the extent that collected data is not relevant to the predictive task at hand, one does not include it in the predictive system one is building. This further liberates data "from its life in the social, no longer inconveniently encumbered by moral reasoning, politics, social norms, rights, values, relationships, feelings, contexts, and situations."[38]

Choices made in data collection and selection can create objectionable bias in predictive systems. We consider two examples. One concerns the general use of training data in the machine-learning approach known as supervised learning, which is frequently used in developing predictive systems.[39] The second example is the bail and sentencing algorithm COMPAS. COMPAS fits our definition of supervised learning in that it is a prediction function that was created by using training data and a learning algorithm,[40] but we use the example to illustrate a bias issue that is independent of the nature of the training data.

Supervised learning requires that you have some *training data* available that consists of correctly classified examples of what you want to predict. For example, you want to predict who will default on credit card debt, and you have data from some past cases showing information about particular people who did and did not default on credit card debt. The overall goal is to build a function that takes data about new credit card applicants as input and yields a likelihood of default as output. In supervised learning, you must collect training data, and choose a type of prediction function (e.g., clustering, decision trees, or deep neural nets) for your predictive system. Then, corresponding to each type of prediction function is one or more *learning (or training) algorithm* that converts the training data into a classification or prediction function.[41] As many have pointed out, bias in the

37 Finlay, *Predictive Analytics, Data Mining and Big Data*, 16.

38 Zuboff, *The Age of Surveillance Capitalism*, 211.

39 See, for example, Ford, *Architects of Intelligence*, 18.

40 See Moritz Hardt, Eric Price, and Nathan Srebro, "Equality of Opportunity in Supervised Learning," in *Proceedings of the 30th International Conference on Neural Information Processing Systems (NIPS'16)*, 2016, 3323–31, http://dl.acm.org/citation.cfm?id=3157382.3157469.

41 Typically, one runs a training algorithm on a large *portion* of the training data, and sees how well the resulting prediction function predicts outcome data for the remaining training data. If the predictions are not as accurate as desired, one can repeatedly make various adjustments or try other training algorithms. See, generally, Ethem Alpaydin, *Machine Learning: The New AI* (The MIT Press, 2016), and Andriy Burkov, *The Hundred-Page Machine Learning Book* (Andriy Burkov, 2019).

training data will translate into bias in the predictions made when the algorithm is in use.[42]

A classic example is St. George's Hospital Medical School in London. In the 1970s, it developed a computer program to cull its approximately 2,000 yearly applications down to 500, at which point humans took over. They trained the program on the years of human-rated applications it had in its records. The program developed its criteria from the training data and thereby incorporated the human biases reflected in that data, which reflected a long history of human racial bias in the admissions decisions:[43] "In 1988, the British government's Commission for Racial Equality found the medical school guilty of racial and gender discrimination in its admissions policy."[44]

The judicial bail and sentencing algorithm COMPAS illustrates another source of bias. COMPAS predicts the likelihood that a person convicted of a crime will commit another in the future.[45] However, our point here is that it would be extremely undesirable for a prediction function like COMPAS to exhibit racial bias. Thus, one would hope COMPAS would have the following two features: COMPAS makes equally accurate predictions regardless of race, and it makes false positive and false negative mistakes at the same rate for all racial groups.[46] The problem is that it is mathematically impossible to meet both these conditions if the fractions of people who commit crimes differ among racial groups.[47] This is currently the situation in the United States, where Blacks commit more crimes than whites (a result of centuries of discrimination).[48] The consequence of the choices the COMPAS system made was thus: "black defendants were far more likely than white defendants to be incorrectly judged to be at a higher risk of recidivism, while white defendants were more likely than black defendants to be incorrectly flagged as low risk."[49]

Cleaning and Structuring

Cleaning and structuring are processes by which selected data gets organized, altered, and placed into a database. They are key processes that help construct the database "reality." In discussing cleaning and structuring, we will use this simple

42 O'Neil, *Weapons of Math Destruction*, 115–18.
43 O'Neil, 115–16.
44 O'Neil, 117.
45 Jeff Larson and Julia Angwin, "Bias in Criminal Risk Scores Is Mathematically Inevitable, Researchers Say," *ProPublica*, December 30, 2016, www.propublica.org/article/bias-in-criminal-risk-scores-is-mathematically-inevitable-researchers-say.
46 Fry, *Hello World*, 66.
47 Fry, 66–68.
48 Fry, 66–69.
49 Julia Angwin and Jeff Larson, "How We Analyzed the COMPAS Recidivism Algorithm," *ProPublica*, May 23, 2016, www.propublica.org/article/how-we-analyzed-the-compas-recidivism-algorithm.

example of a traditional relational database, organized as a table of rows and columns:[50]

Owner	Make	Model	Occupation	City	Age
John Smith	Mazda	Miata	Teacher	Chicago	44
Joe Friday	Ford	Fairlane	Police Officer	Los Angeles	39

Each row contains a data set referring to a single item or record, in this case car owners and their car. Each column specifies one *attribute* of an item. In this case, names of owners of cars ("Owner"), "Make," "Model," "Occupation," and "City" are all attributes of the records. The names of the attributes serve as a header row for the table. Other entries indicate the values of attributes; for example, Joe Friday owns a Ford Fairlane, is a police officer living in Los Angeles, and is thirty-nine years old. Nothing in the database reveals the contextually rich narrative that explains why, at age thirty-nine, Friday became a police officer, owns a Ford Fairlane, and lives in Los Angeles.

Structuring puts data in the proper form to include in a database. As Finlay notes,

> Building a predictive system requires structuring the data appropriately: All of the methods used to create predictive models require data to be well structured, and the data must be categorical (e.g. occupation, marital status and gender) or numeric (e.g. age, income and time at address). A predictive model can't be built if the data is not in one of these two formats.[51]

Thus, in our tiny example, Make, Model, Occupation, and City are all categorical, and Age is numerical. Owner is neither, and serves only as an identifier, not as a basis for predictions.

Getting the data in the proper form typically requires cleaning it.

> Data is dirty, filthy, messy stuff. Often it's incorrect, missing or badly formatted, particularly where humans have been involved in creating and/or collecting it. Sometimes numeric data is held as text, or text data is forced into fixed-length fields resulting in some data being truncated, and so on. Consequently, a lot of the time and effort . . . can be spent "cleaning" the data before it's ready to be used.[52]

Cleaning and structuring data may require formatting data, interpreting truncated data, fitting data into fixed length fields, discarding records with missing attributes or making up values for the missing attributes, and correcting or discarding

[50] Abraham Silbershatz, Henry F. Korth, and S. Sudarshan, *Database System Concepts*, 6th ed. (McGraw-Hill Education, 2010).

[51] Finlay, *Predictive Analytics, Data Mining and Big Data*, 162.

[52] Finlay, 162.

information seen as incorrect. Each of those operations may eliminate or alter information. To take just one example, "[i]f unstructured data such as text or images have been considered for inclusion, then suitable text/image analytics will have been applied to extract the useful bits, so as to create a suitable structured representation of that data."[53]

To summarize, cleaning and structuring data *removes context* and frequently also alters or removes some data.

Choice of Attributes

Suppose you want to predict when current car owners will buy another car. You have a wealth of data about current car owners, including their names, the makes and models of their current cars, their ages, occupations, and cities of residence. To the extent that you have reason to think that that information plays a significant role in predicting when an owner will buy another car, you have reason to pick Owner, Make, Model, Occupation, City, and Age as attributes. The choice of variables can have far-reaching consequences. As Catherine O'Neil notes, "Everything that isn't counted as relevant [i.e., is not included as a variable] is then marginalized and rendered invisible to our models."[54]

Our deliberately simple example involves just six attributes, but, as Finlay notes (talking about variables, another term for attributes): "For many projects there are potentially millions of … variables that could be considered – far more than any analytical system can deal with. Therefore an important part of the model-building phase is using business [or other relevant] knowledge to come up with ideas as to what types of … variables one should consider."[55] Choosing which attributes to use and filling in their values for each record in the database constructs the decontextualized database "reality" that serves as the only input to the system's predictions.

EXPLAINABILITY AND TRANSPARENCY

In computer science, an AI system is explainable if, roughly speaking, one can provide a human-understandable explanation of why it makes any particular prediction.[56] The computer science literature contains many similar but subtly distinct variations on this

53 Finlay, 167.

54 Cathy O'Neil, *On Being a Data Skeptic* (O'Reilly Media, 2013), 6.

55 Finlay, *Predictive Analytics, Data Mining and Big Data*, 164.

56 See, for example, Mark G. Core et al., "Building Explainable Artificial Intelligence Systems," in *AAAI*, 2006, 1766–73; David Gunning and David W. Aha, "DARPA's Explainable Artificial Intelligence (XAI) Program," *AI Magazine*, 40(2) (2019): 44–58, https://doi.org/10.1609/aimag.v40i2.2850; and Wojciech Samek, Thomas Wiegand, and Klaus-Robert Müller, "Explainable Artificial Intelligence: Understanding, Visualizing and Interpreting Deep Learning Models," *ArXiv:1708.08296 [cs.AI]*, (2017), https://arxiv.org/abs/1708.08296.

basic definition.[57] For our purposes, we will say that a decision system is *explainable* if one can produce a human-understandable explanation of why any given decision was reached in terms of only the training data used, the kind of decision function, and the particular inputs for that decision. Note that we use "explain" and "explanation" in the standard dictionary sense of "an account that gives a reason." We use "explainable" and "explainability" for the *computer science concept* of being able to provide a human-understandable explanation of why a system makes any particular prediction. Some kinds of predictive systems are typically explainable – for example, decision trees. One can readily characterize the output in general terms: for example, "Our system will predict that the twenty-something will go to the movies if their parents are visiting, otherwise play tennis if it's sunny and not windy, go to the movies if it's sunny, windy, and they don't have much money, and ..." And, once a prediction is made, a human-understandable explanation of why that prediction was made for that particular input data is typically readily available. On the other hand, deep neural nets and support vector machines, for example, usually involve sufficiently complex decision functions that they are not explainable.

Regulating AI systems requires more than explainability. In at least some cases, it requires some degree of *transparency*. The problem is that legal scholars "have argued for twenty years that automated processing requires more transparency, but it is far from obvious what form such transparency should take."[58] We define a notion of transparency that fits with our concern about the regulation of AI systems. To motivate and explain that notion, we start with what 'transparent' means. Physical objects are transparent when you can see through them, and things like motives, plans, ambitions, and so on are transparent when they are easy to detect. Now, imagine a regulator confronted with a complex predictive system. The regulatory task is to ensure that the system's predictions stay within certain parameters. To accomplish that task, the regulator needs the system to be transparent enough that the regulator can easily detect relevant features of how the system generates its predictions. The way a regulator detects those features is through an *adequate* explanation of how it generates its predictions. The adequacy of an explanation depends on the purposes the explanation serves. "The battery is dead" may be an adequate explanation to the tow truck driver of why your car will not start, but it will not be an adequate explanation for the mechanic who is dealing with the problem. The mechanic wants to know why the battery died. Is there, for example, a problem with the electrical system that drains the battery? As we argue below, regulatory purposes can require explanations that incorporate information *not* contained in the training or input data. Thus, we define *transparent for a regulatory purpose* as follows:

57 See generally Alejandro Barredo Arrieta et al., "Explainable Artificial Intelligence (XAI): Concepts, Taxonomies, Opportunities and Challenges toward Responsible AI," *ArXiv:1910.10045 [cs.AI]*, (2019). http://arxiv.org/abs/1910.10045.

58 Joshua A. Kroll et al., "Accountable Algorithms," *University of Pennsylvania Law Review* 165 (2017): 633–705.

A predictive system is *transparent for a regulatory purpose (r-transparent)* when regulators have an explanation, adequate for that purpose, of why it yields the predictions it does.

Note that construction of an explanation adequate for a regulatory purpose may require incorporating information that is not in the training or input data.

An example illustrates the definition. Suppose Sally defaults on a $50,000 credit card debt. When the credit card company begins collection procedures, she declares bankruptcy. Roger also defaults on a $50,000 credit card debt and declares bankruptcy. Sally, a single mother, incurred her debt to pay for lifesaving treatment for her eight-year-old daughter. Roger incurred his debt through compulsive gambling, an addiction which has resisted years of attempted cures. Suppose that postbankruptcy Sally is a good credit risk. Her daughter is well, with no further expenses expected; she is earning a good income that considerably exceeds her expenses; and she is debt free. Roger, however, remains a poor risk. A credit scoring system, however, predicts that both Sally and Roger are poor credit risks. Is it fair that the predictive system incorrectly burdens Sally with a low credit rating for saving the life of her daughter? Many, including us, will think not, but we defer that argument to Chapter 9. Our question here is: What do you need to know about the predictive system to answer the fairness question – no matter how you ultimately answer it?

Explainability will typically not be enough. Assume the credit scoring system is explainable. That is, there is a human-understandable explanation of predictions in terms only of the training data, input data, and decision function. Now, suppose the training data includes information about who filed for bankruptcy but not any information about healthcare or gambling expenditures. Hence, the system does not distinguish between gambling bankruptcies and healthcare bankruptcies, and neither will explanations meeting our definition of explainability. Thus, in this example, explainability does not provide the information relevant to answering the fairness question. The point is not confined to the Sally/Roger example. Judgments about fairness are highly contextual. They vary as the relevant context varies (the earlier state supervision tracking system is an example). You can include more relevant information in the training data, but you can still reproduce a Sally/Roger-type example by adding facts that are not in the training data. As an influential article on transparency notes about the problem: "It is possible to build a wide variety of definitions of fairness into a wide variety of data analysis and classification systems, at least to the extent that a definition of fairness is known or can be approximated in advance," but the requirement that the definition of fairness be known in advance is a serious limitation: "There are no bright-line rules that allow the designer or operator of a machine-learning system to guarantee that the system's behavior is compliant with antidiscrimination laws … [F]airness must be determined contextually and often must be reviewed ex post."[59]

59 Kroll et al., 689.

Fairness questions arise more widely than the Sally/Roger example may suggest. That example involves the *incorrect* prediction that Sally is a poor credit risk, but fairness questions arise in cases of *correct* predictions as well. Imagine an earlier point in Sally's life. Her daughter has recovered, but Sally has not yet secured the job that pays enough that her income considerably exceeds her expenses. Given all the available evidence, it is not yet clear what path her life will take – continued financial difficulties, or financial security. In these circumstances, Sally is not (yet) a good credit risk, but is it fair that she labors under a poor credit rating as a result of saving her daughter's life? The low credit rating means that credit card companies can avoid the risk of extending her credit, but it limits Sally's ability to manage her expenses at a critical time. A higher credit rating expands her ability to manage her expenses while imposing the risk of default on the credit card companies that extend her credit. Which option is fairer?

The notions of explainability and r-transparency combine to yield four possibilities. Surveying the possibilities provides a useful overview of the regulatory landscape for predictive systems.

Not Explainable and Not R-Transparent

Alien AI is neither explainable nor r-transparent since even the best computer experts cannot explain how it reaches its predictions. Unfortunately, human predictive systems are typically similarly opaque. Information about how databases of training data are constructed – what is in them and what was omitted – is rarely available. Businesses routinely guard databases as trade secrets, and even when the database is available, you typically do not know what data was discarded or altered in the processes of collection, selection, cleaning, and structuring.

Consumer scoring systems are an example. The systems generate a numerical ranking that purports to predict an individual's value to a business, government, or organization.[60] Credit scoring systems are just one example. In addition to systems that score the value of a consumer for a business, there are, for example, financial and risk scores, fraud scores, identity and authentication scores, health scores, smart grid and energy scores, tax return scores, and police, transportation, safety scores.[61] As one commentator notes,

> [a] growing number of companies, including banks, credit and debit card providers, insurers and online educational institutions are using these scores to choose whom

60 See, for example, Natasha Singer, "Electronic Scores Rank Consumers by Potential Value," *The New York Times*, August 18, 2012, www.nytimes.com/2012/08/19/business/electronic-scores-rank-consumers-by-potential-value.html. In general, a "model's predictions are almost always represented by a single number – a score": Steven Finlay, *Predictive Analytics in 56 Minutes* (CreateSpace Independent Publishing Platform, 2015), 4.

61 Pam Dixon and Bob Gellman, "The Scoring of America: How Secret Consumer Scores Threaten Your Privacy and Your Future," *World Privacy Forum*, April 2, 2014, www.worldprivacyforum.org/2014/04/wpf-report-the-scoring-of-america-how-secret-consumer-scores-threaten-your-privacy-and-your-future/.

to woo on the Web. These scores can determine whether someone is pitched a platinum credit card or a plain one, a full-service cable plan or none at all. They can determine whether a customer is routed promptly to an attentive service agent or relegated to an overflow call center.[62]

Some scoring systems lack explainability.[63] Concerns about explainability can arise because the scoring systems may use classification algorithms such as clustering with poor explainability. Clustering is used to sort consumers into "similarly behaving" groups.[64] A "significant weakness of clustering [models] . . . is their complexity and 'black box' nature. You can't tell by looking at these types of model what variables contributed significantly to the model score and which did not."[65] As mentioned, the training data will almost certainly be guarded as a trade secret. As we note below, it is possible for a system to lack explainability but still be r-transparent. That possibility is realized, however, only when someone provides what r-transparency requires: an adequate explanation for a specific regulatory purpose of why the system yields the predictions it does. As far as we know, no one has yet provided such an explanation for a consumer scoring system.

Explainable but Not R-Transparent

The Sally and Roger example illustrates this possibility. Other cases are subtler. Suppose, for example, that doctors use an explainable decision tree system to detect drug interactions. Imagine that the training data was all from white male patients, and there is at least some reason to suspect the drug interactions in question may vary by race and gender. This would thereby be another example of an explainable system that is not r-transparent. Imagine instead that the training data came from a diverse set of patients and that any differences in drug interaction correlated with race and gender are captured in the decision tree. This system is then both explainable and r-transparent.

Not Explainable but R-Transparent

Our regulatory proposal in Chapter 9 illustrates this possibility. We show how an unexplainable system can still be r-transparent. There can be good reason

62 Singer, "Secret E-Scores."

63 Not all scoring systems lack explainability. Some, if not all, of the major credit reporting agencies will offer explanations of your credit rating that meet our definition of explainable.

64 O'Neil, *Weapons of Math Destruction*, 145: "[Scores] carry out thousands of 'people like you' calculations. And if enough of these 'similar' people turn out to be deadbeats or, worse, criminals, that individual will be treated accordingly."

65 Finlay, *Predictive Analytics, Data Mining and Big Data*, 124.

to use unexplainable systems, and this possibility means that they are not beyond the insight into them necessary for sensible and effective regulation.

Explainable and R-Transparent

The Sally/Roger example could also illustrate this possibility, assuming an explanation sufficient for r-transparency. In the Sally/Roger case, that explanation raises doubts about the fairness of the system's predictions. Ideally, one hopes for systems where r-transparency confirms the fairness of their predictions.

FEEDBACK MECHANISMS

Another issue with AI systems is *feedback*. There are two questions: "Does the system have a mechanism for error correction?" and "Do the classifications and predictions of the system have consequences that create information that feeds back into the data on which the system bases future classifications and predictions?"

Without error correcting feedback, a predictive system "can continue spinning out faulty and damaging analysis while never learning from its mistakes."[66] If, for example, Amazon's predictive systems "started recommending lawn care books [primarily] to teenage girls, the clicks would plummet." In this case, monitoring click rates provides error-correcting feedback, and "the algorithm would be tweaked until it got it right."[67] Unfortunately, many predictive systems lack error-correcting feedback. In many cases there is no way to determine what would have happened if someone who was allocated a "bad" outcome based on a system's prediction had gotten the "good" outcome instead. To be concrete, suppose a business uses a predictive system to decide which callers to route to a series of voice prompts, and which to a person. The business is unlikely to be able to determine whether it consigned a potentially valuable customer to an infuriating series of voice prompts, and even if it did, it is unlikely to have a way to enter that information in an error-correcting way into the scoring system to which the vendor does not allow the necessary access (in order to protect trade secrets). Additional examples of systems that lack error correcting feedback include teacher rating systems,[68] judicial sentencing algorithms,[69] predictive policing systems,[70] *US News and World Report* rankings of colleges and universities,[71] and prehiring screening systems.[72]

Now turn to the question of whether a system's classifications and predictions have consequences that create information that feeds back to create additional predictor data. This is typical of "[m]achine-learned models for recommendation,

66 O'Neil, *Weapons of Math Destruction*, 7.
67 O'Neil, 6–7.
68 O'Neil, 7.
69 O'Neil, especially chapters 1 and 2.
70 O'Neil, especially chapters 1 and 2.
71 O'Neil, 53–4.
72 O'Neil, 110.

ranking, and spam detection all [of which] become obsolete unless they are regularly infused with new data."[73] Data feedback, especially when combined with lack of error correction and broad-based predictions, creates mistaken and uncorrectable tracks of winners and losers.

BROAD-BASED PREDICTIONS

Like Alien AI's predictions, the predictions of actual AI systems are typically broad-based in the sense that events in virtually any area of one's life can figure in predictions about virtually any other area. The reason is an extensive use of proxy variables (proxies). You use proxies when you cannot directly measure the things relevant to the predictions you would like to make. Suppose, for example, a teacher is interested in the length of time students pay attention in class. She cannot directly measure paying attention, so she uses proxies: taking notes, looking at material displayed on the board, and so on. AI systems make extensive use of proxies.[74]

The use of proxies raises questions of fairness. We asked earlier whether it was fair to burden Sally with a lower credit rating for saving her daughter's life. Widespread use of proxies raises such questions across the board. Imagine your good deeds, innocent amusements, regretted mistakes, and so on. In a proxy-driven AI system that sets insurance premiums, those activities may affect your car insurance premium. The more predictive systems use proxies from various different parts of a person's life, the more a negative classification by one system can lead to a negative classification by another. This can make it quite difficult to recover from financial or personal difficulties, as lower ratings in some areas generate lower ratings in others.[75] As one commentator notes, "as more of our life is quantified . . . proxy judgments can get more esoteric yet more intrusive. Better prediction can lead to subtler and more nefarious discrimination."[76]

AI systems compound the fairness problem inherent in the heavy use of proxies to the extent that their decision functions are not public and comprehensible.[77]

73 Alekh Agarwal et al., "Making Contextual Decisions with Low Technical Debt," *arXiv:1606.03966 [cs.LG]*, (2016): 1, http://arxiv.org/abs/1606.03966.

74 O'Neil, *Weapons of Math Destruction*, chapters 8 and 9.

75 For a detailed discussion of examples, see Michelle Gilman, "Poverty Lawgorithms: A Poverty Lawyer's Guide to Fighting Automated Decision-Making Harms on Low-Income Communities," *Data & Society*, September 2020, https://datasociety.net/library/poverty-lawgorithms/.

76 Seth Stephens-Davidowitz, *Everybody Lies: Big Data, New Data, and What the Internet Can Tell Us about Who We Really Are* (Dey Street Books, 2017), 262.

77 To require public comprehensibility would be to require more than either explainability or r-transparency, and would sometimes raise issues of gaming the system, trade secrets, or both. Explainability requires only that a post hoc explanation of a particular decision can be given, not that individuals being classified know a priori the important factors contributing to the decision function in general. R-transparency refers only to what regulators should be able to determine for a given purpose. In Chapter 9, we propose a regulatory system which is based on r-transparency and which we suggest yields sufficient public comprehensibility.

You do not have a suitably detailed picture of what factors contribute to the system's predictions – apart, perhaps, from the general knowledge that people in higher socioeconomic classes tend to get predictions that favor them more than people in lower classes. Your lack of knowledge makes it difficult to take steps to avoid predictions that have adverse consequences. You are gambling without knowing what bets you are placing.[78]

MEETING THE THREAT OF AI-ENHANCED SURVEILLANCE

Human-created predictive systems are objectionable to the extent that they share the features that characterize Alien AI: low accuracy, opacity, lack of error correction, and broad-based predictions. We meet the threat in the same way we meet the threat of pervasive surveillance generally – by preserving and creating norms. AI-enhanced surveillance complicates that task by requiring the regulation of a complex mathematical construction that may lack explainability and transparency. We divide our explanation of how to respond into two parts. First, we explain why pervasive surveillance – with or without AI – threatens privacy in public, and we show how to maintain and create norms in response. Second, we show how to apply that approach to AI-enhanced surveillance.

78 The analogy is not perfect. Unlike most gambling, in AI-driven surveillance you do have some control over the outcomes since they depend on your individual attributes, and you have some control over them. You just don't know which values of those attributes are good and which bad.

3

Social Roles, Common Knowledge, and Coordination

In a coffee shop, your "Small coffee, please" conveys information that your server seeks to acquire, and the server's response indicates what you want to know – his or her willingness to fulfill your request. The example illustrates a fact that impressed the sociologist Erving Goffman: "When an individual enters the presence of others, they commonly seek to acquire information about him."[1] The coffee shop illustrates another important feature: *social roles* mediate the information exchange. In the coffee shop example, the roles are customer and server. We focus here on such role-mediated exchanges of information. Our discussion in this chapter divides into five parts.

(i) We show that people's presentation of themselves in social roles creates the common knowledge that they will conform to standards of thought and behavior associated with those roles.

Some will rightly object that presentations in a social role do not always create knowledge (let alone common knowledge). People can use those presentations to deceive. The *Othello* example from Chapter 1 illustrates the possibility. In the past, Iago was Othello's reliable lieutenant, and, on that basis, Othello assumes that the present-day Iago is loyal and trustworthy. In fact, he hates Othello and exploits his trust to deceive him. As he announces early in the play,

> In following [Othello], I follow but myself.
> Heaven is my judge, not I for love and duty,
> But seeming so, for my peculiar end [of deceiving Othello],
> . . .
> I am not what I am.[2]

We ignore the possibility of using social roles to deceive. We take it for granted that duplicity is the exception and focus on the typical nondeceptive cases.

1 Erving Goffman, *The Presentation of Self in Everyday Life* (Anchor, 1959), 1.

2 William Shakespeare, *Othello*, ed. Stephen Orgel and Russ Mcdonald (Penguin Classics, 2001): Act I, Scene 1, lines 57–64.

(ii) We explain how social roles create common knowledge.
Our explanation goes well beyond the typical explanation of common knowledge as "the recursive belief state in which A knows X, B knows X, A knows that B knows X, B knows that A knows X, ad infinitum."[3] That defines common knowledge but does not explain how it arises. The explanation of how social roles give rise to common knowledge is the key to seeing how surveillance's massive capacity to know impairs or eliminates social roles' ability to create common knowledge. Our explanation will leave one open question: Why have social roles evolved to give rise to common knowledge? Does common knowledge solve some problem typically present in interactions through social roles? There is such a problem, one typically known as a coordination problem.

(iii) We introduce the notion of a coordination problem.
A coordination problem is a situation "in which each person wants to participate in a group action but only if others also participate."[4] The social role interactions that concern us involve coordination problems. Common knowledge takes center stage because it greatly facilitates solving coordination problems.

(iv) We explain why social role interactions involve coordination problems.
We show that social role interactions involving the exchange of information typically involve coordination problems. The family holiday dinner from Chapter 1 illustrates the idea. We argue that the family faces a coordination problem. Members want to participate in the group action of creating a harmony-preserving selective flow of information, but only if enough others do so too.

(v) We offer six examples of how common knowledge solves the coordination problems that typify social role interaction.
We discuss these examples in this chapter. They exhibit the variety of ways in which common-knowledge-facilitated coordination creates privacy in public. We describe the examples as if widespread surveillance were *not* a significant factor – a more or less accurate mid-twentieth-century description – roughly from the 1950s to the 1980s. Seeing how norm-enabled coordination created privacy in public during that 1950s–1980s timespan helps us understand how contemporary surveillance later undermines it. The 1950s starting point is not a time before *any* surveillance, or even the start of surveillance: of course, surveillance has a long history before 1950.[5] We choose the 1980s for the end of the period of analysis because the changes in surveillance from the mid-1980s to 2020 have been so rapid and extensive that they

3 Kyle A Thomas et al., "The Psychology of Coordination and Common Knowledge," *Journal of Personality and Social Psychology* 107, 4 (2014): 657–76, 657: https://doi.org/10.1037/a0037037.

4 Michael Suk-Young Chwe, *Rational Ritual: Culture, Coordination, and Common Knowledge* (Princeton University Press, 2013), 3.

5 Christian Parenti, for example, begins his history of surveillance in the United States with the eighteenth-century surveillance of slaves: Christian Parenti, *The Soft Cage: Surveillance in America From Slavery to the War on Terror* (Basic Books, 2004).

make a dramatic qualitative difference. We complete our "surveillance ignored" view in Chapter 4, in which we show that each example is an instance of a coordination norm. This approach may seem backward. Why not first define coordination norms and then turn to the examples? Because it is the examples that breathe life into the general definition. They motivate the definition and illuminate its significance.

SOCIAL ROLES AS A SOURCE OF COMMON KNOWLEDGE

Social roles generate common knowledge. This point is implicit in the following passage (quoted in Chapter 1) from sociologists Berger and Luckmann:

> In the common stock of knowledge there are standards of role performance that are accessible to all members of a society, or at least to those who are potential performers of the roles in question. This general accessibility is itself part of the same stock of knowledge; not only are the standards of role X generally known, but it is known that these standards are known. Consequently every putative actor of role X can be held responsible for abiding by the standards, which can be taught as part of the institutional tradition and used to verify the credentials of all performers and, by the same token, serve as controls.[6]

We highlight two points.

The first is that there are "standards of role performance." The standards that concern us constrain information exchanges, as in the family holiday dinner example. However, in explaining how social roles generate common knowledge, we first focus on standards for social role performance generally. A reported interaction at a Starbuck's provides a good example.[7] When a pregnant woman picked up the caramel macchiato she had ordered, the server said, "Oh, it's for you. Do you want me to make a decaf?" When the woman replied, "No, thanks," the sever continued, "No, I should because caffeine is bad for the baby." When the woman assured him (correctly) that the one caramel macchiato she had a day posed no threat to her unborn child, the server began a five-minute sermon on why it was right for him to intervene with "It's bad for the baby so that's why I'm saying it." A bystander, who posted an account of the incident on Twitter, criticized the server for violating the standards for role performance:

> [The customers are] there to buy your product. They're not there to instantly receive the wisdom of your refined judgment. Unless they ask whether the Dark Roast is better than the Pike. However strongly you might feel about a particular

6 Peter L. Berger and Thomas Luckmann, *The Social Construction of Reality: A Treatise in the Sociology of Knowledge* (Anchor, 1967), 73.

7 Chris Matyszczyk, "A Starbucks Customer Ordered a Simple Coffee. Then the Barista Went Too Far," *Inc.com*, June 1, 2019, www.inc.com/chris-matyszczyk/a-starbucks-customer-ordered-a-simple-coffee-then-barista-went-too-far.html.

> issue – their clothes, a chocolate stain on their face, their MAGA hat – you're there to . . . [provide] a simple service.

A Starbucks spokesperson tried (with astonishing implausibility) to characterize the comments as proper performance: "We have reason to believe that this was truly a misunderstanding, and the worker was trying to clarify the customer's order."

How do the bystander and the spokesperson know what the standards are? They draw on "the common stock of knowledge" of standards of role performance. This is the second point we highlight:

> In the common stock of knowledge there are standards of role performance that are accessible to all members of a society, or at least to those who are potential performers of the roles in question. This general accessibility is itself part of the same stock of knowledge; not only are the standards of role X generally known, but *it is known that these standards are known.*[8]

We add that not only is it known that the standards are known, the standards are common knowledge. At least among "those who are potential performers of the roles in question," it is known, known that it is known, known that it is known that it is known, and so on ad infinitum.

This appeal to common knowledge faces two problems. One concerns common knowledge generally. The other concerns social roles specifically. We consider each in turn.

COMMON KNOWLEDGE

Common knowledge might seem impossible. Consider the claim that Alice and Bob commonly know something. That is, they know, know they know, know they know they know, and so on ad infinitum. The "ad infinitum" is the problem. It appears to mean that Alice and Bob know the following *infinite* sequence. We add subscripts to keep track of knowledge levels:

First level:	Alice $knows_1$ that so-and-so. Bob $knows_1$ that so-and-so.
Second level:	Alice $knows_2$ that Bob $knows_1$ that so-and-so. Bob $knows_2$ that Alice $knows_1$ that so-and-so.
Third level:	Alice $knows_3$ Bob $knows_2$ that Alice $knows_1$ so-and-so. Bob $knows_3$ Alice $knows_2$ that Bob $knows_1$ so-and-so.

.
.
.

8 Berger and Luckmann, *The Social Construction of Reality*, 73 [italics added].

How do Alice and Bob take this infinite series of steps?

The answer is that they don't. What they do have – and all they need – is the *capacity* to generate any finite sequence of successive levels of knowledge. In practice, common knowledge among people does not require generating the entire infinite sequence. An example from the game theorist Michal Chwe illustrates the idea. During a ball game in 1996,

> baseball fans at Cleveland's Jacobs Field [looked] up to see an airplane pulling a banner advertising anonymous HIV testing. Obviously the irony here is the airing of such a sensitive issue as AIDS publicly and even festively on a bright sunny day at the ballpark ... [The underlying purpose is that] I would be more likely to get an HIV test if I knew that doing so was not unusual, but I wouldn't find this out through everyday conversation; at the ballpark, looking up at the plane, however, it is obvious to all that everyone is seeing the same thing.[9]

The display of the banner creates the capacity to know, know they know, know they know they know, and so on, to any arbitrary level. Two features explain why. The first is that seeing the banner was sufficient for knowing that anonymous testing was available. The second is that it was "obvious to all that everyone is seeing the same thing." That is, everyone knows_2 that everyone who sees the banner knows_1 anonymous testing is available. These two features make the banner a *common knowledge generator*. A common knowledge generator (for X) is a situation meeting two conditions:

(**G 1**) The situation ensures that all members of a group G know_1 X.
(**G2**) The situation ensures that all members of G know_2 that all members of G experience the situation and as a result come to know_1 X.[10]

The banner example is compelling. It does seem obvious that common knowledge is created. However, that example does not fully explain *how* the fulfillment of (G1) and (G2) creates common knowledge. Our explanation has two parts. We show how (G1) and (G2) together create the capacity to generate any arbitrary initial subsequence of the infinite sequence of knowledge levels, and then we explain why having only that capacity is enough to count as having common knowledge. One does not need to actually generate any part of the infinite sequence.[11]

To see how (G1) and (G2) create the capacity, suppose Alice and Bob are strangers to each other who happen to be sitting together in the stadium. Start with Alice. There are two relevant background facts. First, Alice is paying attention to the banner overhead, and she has normal perceptual abilities. The consequence is that she sees that the banner announces that anonymous testing is available.

9 Chwe, *Rational Ritual*, 41.
10 The notion of a common knowledge generator is implicit in Stephen Schiffer, *Meaning* (Oxford University Press, 1972), 32–35, and in David K. Lewis, *Convention* (Harvard University Press, 1969), 56.
11 Our explanation parallels the explanations in Schiffer and in Lewis.

Second, she has normal reasoning abilities, so she infers from the banner (and the surrounding context) that the banner's message is true: anonymous testing really is available. The same points hold for Bob. So, we have:

Alice knows_1 that anonymous testing is available.
Bob knows_1 that anonymous testing is available.

Now, how can they get the second level? That is the point at which:

Alice knows_2 that Bob knows_1 that anonymous testing is available.
Bob knows_2 that Alice knows_1 that anonymous testing is available.

Start with Alice. She reasons – suppose, for the moment, that she explicitly reasons – her way to knowing_2 that Bob knows_1. She reasons as follows: "*Anyone* paying attention to the sign knows that anonymous testing is available, as long as the person has normal perceptual and reasoning abilities. I see Bob paying attention to the sign, and so I can conclude he sees it – as long as I assume he has normal perceptual and reasoning abilities. That is a reasonable assumption given that Bob got himself to the stadium, found his seat, and is watching the game. So, I can conclude that Bob knows_1 that anonymous testing is available. For me to reach that conclusion is for me to know_2 that Bob knows_1 that anonymous testing is available."

Bob reasons in the same way about Alice to his conclusion that he knows_2 that she knows_1. Thus:

Alice knows_2 that Bob knows_1 that anonymous testing is available.
Bob knows_2 that Alice knows_1 that anonymous testing is available.

Alice and Bob get to their third-level knowledge by reasoning about their reasoning at the second level. Alice reasons: "At the second level, I reasoned from the fact that I saw Bob looking up at the sign to the fact that I know_2 that Bob knows_1 anonymous testing is available. Bob will have done the same: at the second level he will have reasoned about me the way I reasoned about him. He will have seen me paying attention to the sign, and he will have realized that I have normal perceptual abilities. On that basis, he will – assuming he has normal reasoning abilities – have reasoned to *his* conclusion that he knows_2 that I know_1 that anonymous testing is available. Can I assume that Bob has normal reasoning abilities? His appearance and behavior make that assumption reasonable. So, I know that Bob reasoned to *his* conclusion that he knows_2 that I know_1 that anonymous testing is available. Thus, I know_3 that Bob knows_2 that I know_1 that anonymous testing is available."

Bob will reason in the same way that he knows_3 that Alice knows_2 that Bob knows_1 that anonymous testing is available. Thus:

Alice knows_3 that Bob knows_2 that Alice knows_1 that anonymous testing is available.
Bob knows_3 that Alice knows_2 that Bob knows_1 that anonymous testing is available.

Alice and Bob can get to any arbitrary higher level the way they get from the first level to the second and from the second to the third: by reasoning about their reasoning at the level below. For any level n, Alice reasons about Bob's $n - 1$ level reasoning to reach the conclusion that Alice knows$_n$ Bob knows$_{n-1}$ . . . that they see the sign, and Bob reasons in the same way to reach the conclusion that Bob knows$_n$ Alice knows$_{n-1}$ . . . that they see the sign.

We do not claim that Alice and Bob really carry out this reasoning. The reasoning represents what they *could* do.[12] Seeing the banner gives them the *capacity* to explicitly reason their way to higher levels of knowledge. They may not, and indeed, they probably do not, use that capacity when they see the banner at the ball game. Alice and Bob may not reason at all. Each may just think, "We both see the banner" while implicitly realizing that, as (G1) requires, seeing the banner was sufficient for knowing that anonymous testing was available, and implicitly realizing, as (G2) requires, that everyone knows$_2$ that everyone who sees the banner knows$_1$ anonymous testing is available.

That is enough for them to have common knowledge. As long as they have the capacity to generate the sequence, they need not actually do so to have common knowledge. Thomas et al. provide empirical support.[13] They offer evidence for the claim that "common knowledge has its own representation, it need not contain multiple levels of embedded knowledge; it could consist of a single mental symbol which means, 'We have common knowledge.'" Building on Thomas et al., we take the "mental symbol" to indicate the existence of a common knowledge generator. Notice that there is nothing unusual about having a finite representation of an infinite sequence. Suppose 10-year-old Johnny says, "If you start with one and count one number at a time, you can go on forever." Johnny knows a finite set of facts that entail that, starting from 1, the operation of adding the number 1 to each number can in principle be repeated arbitrarily many times. We will take it for granted that people have the capacity to recognize a wide range of common knowledge generators and form a "mental symbol which means, 'We have common knowledge.'" What else would you expect from reflective beings for whom thinking about thinking is routine?

Eye contact is another good example. Imagine that Mason sees Briana, an old acquaintance. Mason stares at her, hoping to remember her name before she sees him. Unfortunately, Briana sees him before he remembers. As soon as that happens, Mason realizes it would be pointless to pretend he did not see her because there is now common knowledge that they see each other. Common knowledge exists because appropriate versions of (G1) and (G2) hold:

[12] We characterize the capacity by exhibiting what they could do under idealized conditions with no limits on time, memory, or reasoning ability. That is the sense in which we can generate the infinite sequence of natural numbers, add any two numbers no matter how large, and so on. The proper characterization of our ability to count and to add is given by exhibiting what we can do with limitations removed. We are indebted to Steven Wagner for helpful discussions of these points.

[13] Thomas et al., "The Psychology of Coordination and Common Knowledge," 660.

(G1) When Mason and Briana see their open-eyed heads facing each other, each knows$_1$ that they see each other.
(G2) Each knows$_2$ that when two people see with their open-eyed heads facing one another, they know$_1$ that they see each other.

(G1) and (G2) mean that Mason and Briana have the capacity to generate "know$_n$ know$_{n-1}$ . . . know$_1$" sequences for any level n.[14] That capacity makes them *transparent* to each other as far as eye contact goes. Everything is out in the open, so there is no possibility of misunderstanding, misinterpretation, doubt, or deception at any knowledge level. If a question of misunderstanding, misinterpretation, doubt, or deception arises at any knowledge level, they have the capacity to generate the knowledge required to settle the question.

SOCIAL ROLES AS COMMON KNOWLEDGE GENERATORS

Social roles work in the same way as the banner over the stadium. People "fly a banner" when they present themselves to one another in social roles. Those presentations serve as common knowledge generators that create common knowledge of conformity to standards of proper performance. We begin with an example.

During a visit to Philadelphia, Mason goes to Geno's Steaks and stands in line to order a genuine Philly Cheesesteak. When he gets to the order window, proper performance of the role of a Geno's customer requires that he specify which of six Cheesesteak options he wants. He must specify one of three types of cheese (Cheese Whiz,[15] American, or provolone) and whether he wants onions. His "order should sound something like this: 'Could I please have a whiz with' (meaning Cheese Whiz with onions). If he doesn't want onions, he can simply say, 'whiz without.' His other options are 'American with (without)' or 'Provolone with (without).'"[16] Mason's saying "Could I please have a whiz with" makes it common knowledge between Mason and the server that Mason wants a Cheesesteak with Cheese Whiz (the traditional option) and onions. What gives the utterance that power? Mason and the server's presentations in the roles of Geno's customer and Geno's server. We claim that the presentations are common knowledge generators. That is, they fulfill these conditions:

(G1) The presentations result in Mason and the server knowing$_1$ that Mason and the server will conform to their respective roles.
(G2) The presentations ensure that Mason and the server know$_2$ that they know$_1$ that they will conform to the respective roles.

[14] Putting aside limitations of time and memory.

[15] Cheese Whiz is a processed cheese spread sold by Kraft Foods and widely used on cheesesteaks in Philadelphia.

[16] genosteaks_admin, "How to Order a Philly Cheesesteak," *Geno's Steaks* (blog), April 11, 2018, www.genosteaks.com/order-philly-cheesesteak/.

Given (G1) and (G2), the role presentations display a message, just like the banner over the stadium. In this case, the message is "I conform to the standards of role performance." Putting aside the possibility of deception (as we are), each can infer that the other does conform.

How do presentations in social roles have the power to fulfill (G1) and (G2)?

Creating Knowledge$_1$ That People Will Conform

How do those presentations result in Mason and the server knowing$_1$ that they will conform to their respective roles? Relevant background knowledge is the key. In the anonymous testing example, the relevant background knowledge was that Alice and Bob had normal perceptual and reasoning abilities. Similarly, we assume parties interacting in social roles have normal perceptual and reasoning abilities, and we need to add that the parties have enough background knowledge to be able to recognize relevant social roles and know the standards associated with those roles.

How do you get the ability to recognize social roles and knowledge of the standards associated with them? Through explicit instruction and observation.[17] Ordering at Geno's illustrates both. You can learn by explicit instruction how to order at Geno's. A knowledgeable friend could tell you. Or, you could learn by observation as you stand in line and see the ritual of the proper way to order acted out again and again in front of you. You act in the ways you have seen others act and note what works and correct what does not. In general, from early childhood on, explicit instruction and observation account for a wide range of background knowledge about social roles and their associated standards of performance.[18] This background knowledge explains the fulfillment of (G1): a person's presentation in a social role results in people knowing$_1$ that the person will conform to the standards of that role.

Creating Knowledge$_2$ of Knowledge$_1$ of Conformity

Common knowledge also requires the second-level knowledge that everyone knows$_2$ that everyone knows$_1$. How might that happen in the Geno's Steaks case? In theory, via any combination of explicit instruction and observation. We start with explicit instruction.

Suppose every school in the United States taught the proper way to order at Geno's. The instructional process would be a common knowledge generator:

(G1) Everyone (everyone who went to school and paid enough attention) would know$_1$ how to order at Geno's.

(G2) Everyone would know$_2$ that everyone comes to know$_1$ how to order at Geno's.

[17] See, for example, Talcott Parsons, *The Social System* (Ulan Press, 2012), chapter 6, and Bruce J. Biddle, *Role Theory: Expectations, Identities, and Behaviors* (Academic Press, 1979), 7.

[18] Parsons, *The Social System*, chapter 6.

However, schools don't teach the proper way to order at Geno's (not even in Philadelphia), and how to order at Geno's is not common knowledge among those educated in the United States.

Compare knowing that George Washington was the first president of the United States. That is common knowledge, and the explanation is that schools teach it in a process that is a common knowledge generator. First, consider students in the same classroom. Explicit instruction ensures that (G1) everyone (that is, everyone who went to elementary school and paid enough attention) knows$_1$ Washington was the first president. Observation by the students of the explicit instruction ensures that (G2) everyone in the classroom knows$_2$ that everyone knows$_1$ Washington was the first president. There are many examples in which people acquire common knowledge communally, as for all the students in one classroom. Indeed, Chwe contends that some of the best examples of

> social processes that generate common knowledge … turn out to be "public rituals," such as public ceremonies, rallies, and media events. Public rituals can thus be understood as social practices that generate common knowledge … A public ritual is not just about the transmission of meaning from a central source to each member of an audience; it is also about letting audience members know what other audience members know.[19]

Now, what about students who do not share a classroom? How do they know$_2$ that students in other schools know$_1$ that Washington was the first president? By knowing that elementary education is sufficiently standardized that all students learn who was the first president. Chwe offers interesting examples of how people who are not observing each other still come to know$_2$ that others know$_1$. One of his examples is Super Bowl advertising, which, because of its enormous audience, he calls the "best common knowledge generator in the United States."[20] Anyone in that audience who pays attention to the advertising knows$_1$ the advertising content, *and* knows$_2$ that anyone who is paying attention knows$_1$. The 2018 Super Bowl Groupon advertisement, for example, portrayed the wealthy as having a disdain for small business and implied that anyone who did not use Groupon shared that disdain. The goal was to make it common knowledge that not using Groupon was tantamount to disdain for small business. In general, in any culture, various forms of explicit instruction ensure that, across a wide range of things, every knows$_2$ that everyone knows$_1$ certain things. The Groupon message (the wealthy disdain small business) is an example of a *narrative*: "a story or representation used to give an explanatory or justificatory account."[21] Broadcasts of narratives may be far more diffuse than a Super Bowl advertisement. They can consist of a combination of traditional media articles,

19 Chwe, *Rational Ritual*, 3–4.

20 Chwe, 45.

21 Robert J. Shiller, *Narrative Economics: How Stories Go Viral and Drive Major Economic Events* (Princeton University Press, 2020), xi.

email newsletters, blog postings, online articles, and the like. From political discourse to advertising to teaching, narratives are a powerful device for changing minds and behavior.[22]

Observation is another source of second-level knowledge. Suppose Noah, a student, does not know that George Washington was the first president. However, he sees another student answer "Who was the first president of the United States?" with "George Washington." Later on, when Noah is asked who the first president was, he tries out the answer "George Washington" and has his response acknowledged as correct. In this way, Noah comes to know$_1$ that Washington was the first president, *and*, just as in the stadium, he knows$_2$ that everyone who pays attention to such question-and-answer sequences knows$_1$ that Washington was the first president.[23]

In the case of social roles, it is routine to come to know$_2$ that people know$_1$ about a role through observation. Children observing their parents interacting with their friends, first-year graduate students attending a graduate seminar, and travelers visiting a foreign country learn norms of interaction through observation. Indeed, it is "the major way in which roles are taught . . . [P]ersons are exposed to experiences that would lead them to form similar expectations for their own and others' roles, and these in turn lead them to exhibit or encourage appropriate role behavior."[24]

Now that we have discussed how people come to have common knowledge about social roles, we move on to how, for the social roles of most interest to us in this book, people also come to have common knowledge that someone presenting themselves in a particular role will conform to its performance requirements.

WHY PROPER PERFORMANCE OF SOCIAL ROLES INVOLVES COORDINATION PROBLEMS

We have positioned common knowledge center stage because it plays a key role in solving the coordination problems that arise in information exchanges in social role interactions. We first define coordination problems by refining our earlier characterization of them as situations "in which each person wants to participate in a group action but only if others also participate."[25] We then explain how coordination problems arise in social-role-mediated exchanges of information. Our notion of a coordination *problem* is a generalization of the game theory notion of a coordination *game*, as we explain in the appendix to this chapter.

22 See Shiller, *Narrative Economics*; Frederick W. Mayer, *Narrative Politics: Stories and Collective Action* (Oxford University Press, 2014); Dennis Chong, *Collective Action and the Civil Rights Movement* (University of Chicago Press, 1991); and Hans Hansen, *Narrative Change: How Changing the Story Can Transform Society, Business, and Ourselves* (Columbia Business School Publishing, 2020).

23 Compare Chwe, *Rational Ritual*, 25.

24 Biddle, *Role Theory*, 282.

25 Chwe, *Rational Ritual*, 3.

Coordination Problems Defined

We explain coordination problems by appeal to two other concepts: group-action goals, and dominant preferences.

Group-action goals. A group-action goal is a goal that cannot be realized by one individual acting alone. The goal of meeting your friends at the opera is a *group-action* goal. The goal of combing your hair is not. Sometimes the distinction between group-action goals and other goals can depend on framing, since, for example, the goal of going to the opera is not necessarily a group-action goal: it is not if you frame it as going by yourself, it is if you frame it as going with others. Some group-action goals require action by *all* members of a group – for example, meeting your three buddies to play contract bridge (which requires exactly four players). Some require action only by *enough* members of the group – for example, meeting at least three of your poker buddies to play poker, which is pleasant as long as you have at least four.

Dominant preference. One dominantly prefers something if one prefers it more than one prefers other options one has that conflict with its realization. Note that one dominantly prefers something in a particular context at a particular time. Aunt Jane, for example, loves to gossip, but during the holiday dinner she prefers to forego gossip to contribute to family harmony.

Coordination problems defined. We define a *coordination problem* for a group as a situation where there is a *group-action goal* that each member of the group shares and, moreover, *dominantly prefers* to realize.[26]

We note one important implication of the dual requirements of group-action goal with a dominant preference. Individuals' behavior may be *conditional*: even though someone has a dominant preference to attain the group-action goal, they may behave in the way needed to obtain it only *as long as they know (have adequate reason to believe) enough others do so too.* To illustrate, consider Aunt Jane and the family holiday dinner. Jane highly prizes both gossip and family harmony. She will forego gossip at the holiday dinner to contribute to family harmony as long as she knows enough others will conform to harmony-creating constraints. If she thinks the group effort required for harmony is not going to happen, she cannot regard her own conformity as contributing to that nonexistent group effort, so she will gossip. To illustrate further, compare Roger, who is also at the dinner. He always does everything he reasonably can to minimize what others know about him and what he knows about them. So, even if he believes the others will not observe the harmony-creating constraints, he will do so, but he will not do so *in order to contribute to a group effort of conformity to the harmony-creating constraints*. As long as he believes that group effort will not happen, he cannot see his conformity as contributing to it.

[26] See, for example, Chwe, 3.

The problem is to achieve the coordination that realizes the group-action goal given that people will try to achieve the goal only if enough others do so too. Chapter 1's example of Mary and John illustrates the problem. They are stopped in their respective cars at a four-way intersection. They share the group-action goal of driving on the right, and they both dominantly prefer to realize that goal – as long as the other joins in realizing the goal. Their problem is to arrive at common knowledge that each will drive on the right.

Why Coordination Problems Arise in Social Role Interactions

We consider social roles involving interactions among people sharing a group-action goal (so a coordination problem could potentially arise) *and* whose proper performance involves selective information flow. We claim coordination problems frequently arise in such social-role-mediated exchanges of information. We use the holiday dinner example to illustrate why.

Proper performance of the role of a family member at the dinner has two requirements. The first is that one thinks one ought to act so as to realize the relevant group-action goal: in this example, family harmony. To be more precise about the "thinks one ought" requirement, each family member thinks they ought to do so *as long as enough others do so too*. Here, "enough" is enough to realize the group-action goal – harmony, in our example. Harmony, and other group-action goals, may not always require that all conform. The necessary number will vary with the context. Consider the disaffected adolescent who deviates from proper performance. He thinks he ought to violate the strictures on information flow to make the family confront the conflicts he thinks they ignore, so he announces what the rest want hidden. Depending on the exact family dynamics, his behavior may or may not change the other family members' behavior, and possibly will not destroy the dinner's harmony. We are of course not claiming this is a realistic description of families in general – just of the one we are imagining.

Fulfilling the "thinking one ought" requirement means the "shared goal" requirement for the existence of a coordination problem is met. The family members share the group-action goal of harmony in the sense that they share thinking that they ought to try to realize that goal as long as (enough) others also do.

The second requirement for proper performance of the family member role is that – at appropriate times – one dominantly prefers to conform to the strictures on information flow to realize the group-action goal of family harmony. We first explain the rationale for the requirement and then turn to the reason for the "at appropriate times" requirement. The idea behind the requirement is that proper performance is *performance*. It is not enough just to think one ought. When the time comes to perform, one must form the dominant preference to do what one thinks one ought to do. A variant of the disaffected adolescent example illustrates the rationale. This time, imagine he values family harmony and *does* think he ought to conform to the strictures on information flow. However, he also has a conflicting "ought" thought. He also thinks he ought to force the family to confront the conflicts the strictures conceal. The second thought outweighs the first, and so he violates the strictures. That is the opposite of what proper performance requires.

There are two reasons for the "appropriate times" qualification. First, one dominantly prefers something in a particular context at a particular time. For example, at the holiday dinner, Aunt Jane dominantly prefers to conform to the conditions on information flow (and so forego gossip), but only as long as she knows enough others will conform to harmony-creating constraints. If the context were different – if she thought not enough would conform – she would dominantly prefer to gossip instead. Second, it would be implausible in information exchange cases to represent proper performance as *always* requiring adherence to the strictures on information flow. Suppose, for example, Uncle John takes a low daily dose of Viagra. Everyone knows that, but the strictures on information flow require that no one talk about it – unless it is appropriate to do so in the circumstances. It is appropriate to do so when John has sudden heart-related pain in his chest. The paramedics are about to give him nitroglycerin (which should not be combined with Viagra), when Roger stops them just in time by yelling from across the room "He's on Viagra."

Since the family members fulfill the "dominant preference" requirement and the group-action goal requirement, there is a coordination problem. What makes the problem a *problem* is the nontrivial task of coordinating behavior to realize the goal of harmony. Aunt Jane, for example, will refrain from gossiping, but only if she knows that enough others will also adhere to the conditions on the flow of information. How do the family members ensure that each of them knows the others will conform to the conditions?

They solve the problem by creating relevant common knowledge. Specifically, their presentations to each other in the role of family member at a holiday dinner make four facts common knowledge. This four-part pattern is characteristic of cases in which presentations in social roles create common knowledge that solves a coordination problem. After describing the four-part pattern in the holiday dinner example, we offer six more examples. In Chapter 4, we define coordination *norms* by generalizing from those examples.

COMMON KNOWLEDGE OF THE FOUR-PART PATTERN

To explain how common knowledge arises in the holiday dinner example, we show how the presentations in the role of a family member function as common knowledge generators. Recall the definition for a situation being a common knowledge generator:

(G1) The situation results in all members of a group G knowing$_1$ X.

(G2) The situation ensures that all members of G know$_2$ that all members of G experience the situation and as a result come to know$_1$ X.

For the family holiday dinner, we will instantiate (G1) and (G2) as follows:

(G1) The presentations result in each family member knowing that the four conditions hold.
(G2) The presentations result in each family member $knowing_2$ that the presentations result in each family member $knowing_1$ that the four conditions hold.

To see that these versions of (G1) and (G2) hold, we introduce and then consider each of the four conditions separately. Roughly speaking, the first two conditions state that the existence of the coordination problem is common knowledge.

First, conditionally thinking one ought. As required by proper role performance, family members think they ought to conform to certain conditions on the flow of information as a means to realizing the group-action goal of a harmonious dinner as long as enough others also conform.

Explicit instruction and observation ensure that (G1) holds. The family members explain the strictures on information flow to children and to those who exchange information that threatens harmony. First-time adult attendees may figure out the strictures by observation. If not, family members explain to them as well. They note that proper performance requires that one think one ought to abide by the strictures to realize the group-action goal of family harmony. Of course, they are unlikely to say explicitly "Proper performance requires thinking one ought to realize the group-action goal of harmony," but they do use words broadly to that effect. Instruction and observation result in each family member knowing that family members think they ought to conform to certain strictures on the flow of information to realize the group-action goal of a harmonious dinner as long as (enough) others also conform. Thus, (G1): The presentations result in each family member knowing that family members think they ought to conform to the strictures on the flow of information to realize the group-action goal of a harmonious dinner as long as (enough) others also conform.

(G2) is fulfilled because instruction and discussion function like the banner over the stadium. In the case of the banner, it was "obvious to all that everyone is seeing the same thing."[27] It was obvious because people who saw the sign know others in the stadium also saw it. Similarly, at the dinner, members who receive instruction can infer that others are instructed in the same way with the same result, and people who observe conformity to the strictures see others observing the same. Thus, it is "obvious to all" that each family member thinks – and hence knows that he or she thinks – that he or she thinks they ought to conform to certain strictures on the flow of information to realize the group-action goal of a harmonious dinner as long as (enough) others also conform. Thus, (G2) holds: The presentations result in each family member $knowing_2$ that the presentations result in each family member $knowing_1$ that they ought to conform to certain strictures on the flow of information to realize the group-action goal of a harmonious dinner as long as (enough) others also conform.

[27] Chwe, 41.

Second, a dominant preference. Family members dominantly prefer at appropriate times to conform to the strictures on information flow to realize the group-action goal of a harmonious dinner provided (enough) others also conform to those strictures.

The argument for common knowledge in this case is the same as for the first condition. Proper performance of the role of a family member requires both that one thinks one ought to act so as to realize the relevant group-action goal *and* that one dominantly prefers to do so (at appropriate times). Explicit instruction and observation ensure that (G1) and (G2) hold for the second condition.

Third, enough conform. The following behavioral regularity exists: enough family members conform to the strictures on information flow.

The third condition follows – almost – from the second. Other things being equal, people who dominantly prefer to act in a certain way will do so – or at least attempt to do so. A star soccer player likely dominantly prefers to score a goal, but may attempt to do so and miss. More radically, if other things are not equal, the preference may not translate into action at all. When Mason is playing golf, imagine he dominantly prefers to hit his ball onto the green, but as he steps up to do so, he pulls a muscle and must stop playing. It easy for the family members to detect when other things are not equal. Family members who normally contribute to the flow of conversation would not be doing so. Similarly, failed attempts to conform to the strictures would reveal themselves in the disharmony they cause.

How do the family members commonly know that enough family members conform to the strictures? Through observation. (G1) holds because each family member knows by observation that enough family members conform. (G2) holds because each family member sees the family members seeing the others. Thus, (G2): each family member knows$_2$ that the family members seeing the others know$_1$ that enough members conform to the strictures.

Fourth, continuing conformity. Family members continue to conform to the strictures on information flow at future dinners. Fulfillment of this condition is not inevitable even given fulfillment of the first three. Imagine the family has grown tired of the strictures on information flow, but they agree to conform to them one last time at the holiday dinner coming up. The first three conditions are fulfilled but not Condition (4). So when is Condition (4) fulfilled?

When past conformity can be good evidence of future conformity. To see how, suppose the family members have participated in eleven holiday dinners in a row. On the morning of the twelfth time, as Victoria walks into the dinner, she asks herself, "Am I going to conform to the conditions on information flow?" As she considers the question, she looks at the others and thinks, "Given their past participation, I know they are going to conform to the conditions," and, since, at appropriate times, she dominantly prefers to conform, she conforms. The others conform for the same reason Victoria does. The pattern repeats itself indefinitely until one or more of the following occurs. (i) They (enough of them) stop thinking they ought to conform to the conditions on information flow as long as enough others do. (ii) They stop dominantly preferring (at appropriate times) to do so. (iii) Past participation is no longer good evidence of future participation (e.g., it is common knowledge among them that most family members find the conditions on information flow too confining). In Chapter 4 we show that such self-perpetuating patterns are coordination norms.

How can the family members have common knowledge that the fourth condition holds? They could reason their way to it. Consider Victoria again. She reasons: "All the family members will realize, as I did, that past conformity is good evidence of future conformity, and since, like me, they dominantly prefer to conform given that enough others do, I can conclude that they will conform." Thus, to the extent that family members approximate Victoria's reasoning, (G1) holds: Each family member will reason his or her way to the conclusion that the family members will conform. To see that (G2) holds, start with Victoria. She reasons: "The family members will realize that the family members will reason their way to the conclusion that the family members will conform. So each family member will know_2 that the family members know_1 that the family members will conform." To the extent that family members approximate Victoria's reasoning, (G2) holds: each family member knows_2 that each family member reasons his or her way to knowing_1 that the family members will conform.

THE EXAMPLES

We offer six more examples. Each is an instance of the four-part pattern. We characterize them by drawing on "the common stock of knowledge [which includes] ... standards of role performance that are accessible to all members of a society, or at least to those who are potential performers of the roles in question."[28] The value of the four-part pattern is that it subsumes diverse forms of thought and action under one illuminating explanatory perspective. Illustrating that point is the reason for giving six examples. A number of scholars discuss similar patterns, including Nobel Prize–winning political economist Elinor Ostrom and her followers,[29] political scientist Dennis Chong,[30] game theorists Michael Chwe[31] and Thomas Schelling,[32] and philosophers/game theorists David Lewis,[33] Christina Bicchieri,[34] and Edna

28 Berger and Luckmann, *The Social Construction of Reality*, 73.

29 Elinor Ostrom, "Collective Action and the Evolution of Social Norms," *The Journal of Economic Perspectives* 14 (2000): 137–58.

30 Chong, *Collective Action and the Civil Rights Movement*, and Dennis Chong, *Rational Lives: Norms and Values in Politics and Society* (University of Chicago Press, 2000).

31 Chwe, *Rational Ritual*.

32 Thomas C. Schelling, *Micromotives and Macrobehavior*, Revised edition (W. W. Norton & Company, 2006).

33 David K. Lewis, *Convention*.

34 Cristina Bicchieri, *Norms in the Wild: How to Diagnose, Measure, and Change Social Norms* (Oxford University Press, 2016).

Ullmann-Margalit.[35] In addition, while not specifically focused on patterns such as the four-part pattern, a number of other scholars provide ample evidence that people solve the specific type of coordination problem that arises in social interactions that involve the exchange of information. They include communications theorist Helen Nissenbaum[36] and sociologists Erving Goffman,[37] Irwin Altman,[38] and Christena Nippert-Eng,[39] as well as the Chicago Symbolic Interactionists and their successors.[40]

The explanation of how common knowledge arises is the same in each example as it is for the holiday dinner, so we do not repeat that explanation.

Restaurants

Imagine Mason eats in a small trattoria. He goes hoping for a pleasant break from the rest of his life, for an experience as disconnected as possible from that life. He does not want them to know, for example, that he is the CEO of an international business. His concern is not just that the knowledge could change the way they relate to him and open the door to further questions. He does not even want to have to *think* about whether it *might* do that. He wants to play the role of "customer they know very little about." He succeeds. The waiters confine their interactions to the standard pleasantries and to taking and fulfilling his order. What explains his success? Role presentations that ensure that each part of the following four-part pattern is common knowledge.

(1) *Thinking one ought*. Mason and the restaurant[41] think they ought to conform to conditions on the exchange of information as a means to realizing the group-action goal of meeting customers' restaurant needs (as long as enough others do).[42]

35 Edna Ullmann-Margalit, *The Emergence of Norms* (Oxford University Press, 2015).

36 Helen Nissenbaum, *Privacy in Context: Technology, Policy, and the Integrity of Social Life* (Stanford University Press, 2010).

37 Tom Burns, *Erving Goffman* (Routledge, 2014).

38 Irwin Altman, *The Environment and Social Behavior: Privacy, Personal Space, Territory, Crowding* (Brooks Cole, 1975).

39 Christena E. Nippert-Eng, *Islands of Privacy* (University of Chicago Press, 2010).

40 Alex Dennis, Rob Philburn, and Greg Smith, *Sociologies of Interaction* (Polity, 2013).

41 Does it make sense to refer to the *restaurant*? Why not refer to the server or the restaurant owner? They can exchange information, but what sense does it make to talk about restaurants – inanimate business entities – exchanging information? It makes sense in the same way that it makes sense to talk about the Supreme Court following the precedent in one of its 100-year-old decisions. The Justices who compose the Supreme Court have changed many times over that 100-year period, but we see the decision as a decision of the Court even though any particular decision is the product of the votes of particular Justices. Similarly, restaurant staff come and go and owners change, but it serves our purposes to see the restaurant as engaging in information exchanges even though any given exchange is the result of interactions with particular staff and owners.

42 See Chris Schonberger, "The 20 Most Annoying Things Servers Do at Restaurants: Overshare about Their Day, Their Job, or Their Life Beyond The Restaurant," *First We Feast*, January 17, 2013, http://firstwefeast.com/laugh/the-20-most-annoying-things-servers-do-at-restaurants/s/overshare-about-their-day-their-job-or-their-life-beyond-the-restaurant/ (noting that "Restaurants are awkward. But we also all know how to play this game, so don't . . . talk about how you are actually a marine biologist and you're getting ready to move to Alaska to study whales – or, worse still, tell a sob story about how

The conception of proper role performance specifies the conditions and requires conformity to them. Following Nissenbaum, we take it for granted that proper performance of social roles typically requires a role-specific selective flow of information. Notice that as we have formulated the group-action goal for the restaurant example, conditions on information exchange arise entirely from the conditions on the social roles, *not* from the nature of the group-action goal. We defined that goal as meeting customers' restaurant needs. An alternate definition that builds privacy protection into the goal is meeting customers' restaurant needs while meeting conditions on the exchange of information. Then we could see the conception of proper role performance as specifying those conditions. The two approaches are equivalent. We have opted for the first.

It may still seem like we mischaracterized both the exchange of information and the group-action goal. To begin with the exchange of information: why did we describe Mason as exchanging information with *the restaurant*? For two reasons. One is that customers do exchange information with restaurants when they make reservations, pay, and fill out surveys, and exchanges with waiters are exchanges with the restaurants that employ them, especially to the extent that the waiters share information in staff meetings and the like. The other reason is that contemporary surveillance makes the exchange of information between consumers and businesses a focal point of concern, as we discuss in Chapters 6 through 9. Five of our six examples involve such exchanges.

Turning to the group-action goal, why did we formulate the goal in terms of customers' (plural) needs? Why would a customer think he or she ought to help meet other customers' needs? Because restaurants set their menus and policies to meet customers' needs generally. Restaurants use information from customers to set menus and devise policies. Mason's trattoria, for example, uses his menu choices as input to designing future menus, his reservation patterns as input to setting waiter and chef schedules, and his payment patterns as input to what range of credit and debit cards to accept. The result is a ready-made deal for customers. They arrive and order. They do not need to negotiate the details about menu options, serving hours, or payment. The convenience explains the willingness of customers to contribute to the general pool of information.

We note two additional points. First, role-specific restrictions do not require absolute compliance. Customers and waiters, for example, may exchange other information, but those exchanges are limited unless the relationship expands to

another table stiffed you on a tip. Keep it professional, and we promise to not drag you into our arguments and ask you to arbitrate. The less we know about each other, the better"). See also John Mariani, "What Your Favorite Restaurants Know about You," *Eat Like a Man* (blog), November 8, 2011, www.esquire.com/food-drink/restaurants/a11616/great-restaurant-service-110811/; Katie Van Syckle, "The Waitressing Life: The Honor of a Second-Class Profession," *The Atlantic*, August 26, 2011, www.theatlantic.com/business/archive/2011/08/the-waitressing-life-the-honor-of-a-second-class-profession/244176/. The same appears to be true of some customers: see "Why Fine Dining Is Still Important," *DiRōNA* (blog), April 30, 2019, https://dirona.com/why-fine-dining-is-still-important/.

include other social roles such as acquaintances or friends. Second, the boundaries of "restaurant needs" are quite indeterminate, but, through most of the twentieth century, that did not matter much since the customers were the main source of the restaurant's information about them, and thus they could draw the boundaries the way they wanted. That allowed Mason to realize his aim of being the customer they know little about.

(2) *Dominant preference*. In typical restaurant interactions, customers and restaurants dominantly prefer, at appropriate times, to conform to the conditions on information exchange as a means to realizing the group-action goal of meeting the customers' restaurant needs.[43]

(3) *Enough conform*. As a result of (1) and (2), the following past behavioral regularity exists: enough diners and restaurants conform to the conditions on information exchange to succeed in realizing the group-action goal of meeting customers' restaurant needs.

(4) *Continued conformity*. The regularity continues in the future. Customers and restaurants continue to exchange information primarily in order to realize the group-action goal of meeting the customer's restaurant needs as long as they know enough others also do so. In the future, as long as "thinking one ought" translates into a dominant preference for the group-action goal, restaurants and customers will (exceptional circumstances aside) continue to exchange information as a means to realizing the group-action goal of meeting the customer's restaurant needs.

This does not mean that the pattern of interaction is set in stone. Changes in the behavioral pattern may lead to changes in common knowledge that in turn lead to changed conceptions of proper role performance. For example, increasingly in the United States, waiters ask, "Have you dined with us before?" if they do not recognize you. The question is part of a script many restaurant managers give to waiters.[44] If the answer is negative, the waiter is supposed to go over key points about the menu. (That may even be useful in some restaurants, such as those "that serve small plates that require a football-play diagram to put together."[45]) If enough customers

[43] Condition (2) requires that one dominantly prefer to conform *as a means to realizing the shared group-action goal of meeting customers' restaurant needs*. The italicized requirement is to rule out certain cases that do not really fit the pattern with which we are concerned. Suppose Mason thinks he ought to conform to conditions on the exchange of information as a means to realizing the group-action goal of meeting customers' restaurant needs, but also has the conflicting thought that he ought to rebel against social norms by violating the conditions. He enters the restaurant having decided to rebel, but then he sees that one of his good friends is his server, and, as a result, he dominantly prefers to conform to the conditions. He does not, however, dominantly prefer to do so as a means to realizing the group-action goal, but as a means to not upsetting his friend.

[44] The Salty Waitress, "Ask the Salty Waitress: Why Do Servers Ask If You've Been to the Restaurant Before?," *The Takeout*, June 20, 2019, https://thetakeout.com/why-do-servers-ask-if-youve-been-to-restaurant-before-1835658668.

[45] The Salty Waitress.

acquiesce in the practice long enough, waiters will ask the question, and customers will expect the question and respond. Those changed expectations and responses can change the conception of the proper role of a waiter and a customer, and explicit instruction and role modeling can lead to it being common knowledge that the proper role of a waiter includes asking the question, and the proper role of the customer includes responding truthfully.

Restaurants are an example of the purchase of consumer goods and services – retail sales, for short. Another example of a typical retail transaction is in order. We return to it (and the restaurant example) in Chapter 7 when we discuss whether and how surveillance has altered the conception of proper role performance for retail customers.

Retail Sales

When Victoria enters a wine shop, she takes it for granted that the store will not request information about her liver function, record the kind of clothes she is wearing, record whether she is in the store with her spouse or another companion, or analyze her buying patterns to predict her sexual orientation. When she consults the store about a party she is planning, she assumes that it will not publicize the party details. The store complies with her assumptions, and it does so without explicit negotiation or discussion. This will happen even if Victoria has never visited that store before and she and it are complete strangers to each other. What explains this effortless coordination? Victoria and the store coordinate effortlessly because the role presentations of customer and retailer make the following conditions common knowledge.

(1) *Thinking one ought*. As in the restaurant case, retailers and customers think they ought to conform to conditions on the exchange of information as a means to realizing the group-action goal of meeting customers' retail needs as long as (enough) others also conform. This may provoke the reaction "You're being naïve about retailers." To see the reason for that reaction, assume (very plausibly) that it was inconsistent with twentieth-century constraints on proper role performance for retailers to collect information about their customers for the purpose of determining their sexual orientation. Suppose, however, that the wine retailer, Michael, was convinced that he could maximize profits by distinguishing between straight and LGBTQ customers. To gather the relevant information, he engaged his customers in what appeared to be causal conversation. If Michael's profits increased as a result, and his customers never discovered what he was doing, why would Michael have thought he ought not to collect that information? There are three reasons.

First, as long as Michael had internalized the requirements of proper role performance, he would have thought he ought to exchange information primarily to realize the group-action goal of meeting customers' retail needs as long as (enough) others do. As the sociologist Bruce Biddle notes, socialization leads one to develop a "self-concept that is composed of (among other things) a set of role expectations for him or herself as he or she assumes various identities and enters different contexts."[46] Second, mid-twentieth-century technological limitations could make the analysis too difficult. Excel, for example, was first released in 1985, and even if Michael had it and was an expert in its use, he may have been unable to extract sufficient data from the conversations. Third, we assumed Michael's customers never discovered what he is doing, but systematic differences in the way Michael treated customers could have revealed that he was distinguishing among them by presumed sexual orientation. Michael's profits would have dropped if enough offended customers stop buying from him. The risk of loss could have kept Michael from attempting to collect and use the information.

Now, why do *customers* think they ought to conform? Consider Victoria. Provided she has internalized the requirements of proper role performance, she will, like Michael, think that she ought to exchange information to realize the group-action goal of meeting customers' retail needs. She will have an additional self-interested reason to conform arising from the fact that she allots a relatively small amount of time to purchasing wine. She wants to purchase suitable wine within that time and return to pursuing her other goals. She knows the store will process some range of personal information, but – like consumers generally, we assume – what she primarily cares about is whether the benefits of disclosing information outweigh the privacy cost. She prefers to spend as little time as possible on determining whether that is true. She gets what she wants by conforming to a pattern in which retailers process consumer information primarily in ways that meet consumer retail needs.

(2) *Dominant preference*. Retailers and customers dominantly prefer, at appropriate times, to realize the group-action goal of exchanging information in ways that meet customers' retail needs.

(3) *Enough conform*. As result of (1) and (2), this past behavioral regularity exists: enough retailers and customers conform to the conditions on information exchange as a means of realizing the group-action goal.

(4) *Continued conformity*. The regularity continues in the future. As long as "thinking one ought" continues to combine with a dominant preference for the group-action goal, retailers and customers will (exceptional circumstances aside) continue to exchange information primarily in order to realize the group-action goal of meeting customers' retailer needs.

The next example does not involve buying and selling.

Students and Professors

Students and professors in large universities share a commitment to grading students primarily in light of their relevant academic achievements, not in light of students' previous academic records, honors, punishments, or extracurricular aspects of their

[46] Biddle, *Role Theory*, 7.

personalities.[47] To minimize the influence of such irrelevant factors, students and instructors combine to limit what instructors know about students. Limiting information is a group-action goal. Professors must limit what they tell other professors and the university about the students they know, and students must limit their disclosures of what they know about other students.

Suppose William walks into his professor Sarah's office during her office hours. It is the first week of the semester, and William is one of more than 100 students in Sarah's class. All that Sarah knows about William is that he is a student in the class, and, as it happens, all that William knows about Sarah is that she teaches the class. Even in this case of strangers, role presentations make our four conditions common knowledge.

(1) *Thinking one ought*. Students and professors think that they ought to conform to conditions on information flow as a means to realizing the group-action goal of limiting bias in grading as long as (enough) others also conform.

(2) A *dominant preference*. Students and professors dominantly prefer, at appropriate times, to conform to the conditions on information flow as means to realizing the group-action goal.

(3) *Enough conform*. As a result of (1) and (2), this past behavioral regularity exists: enough professors and students conform to the conditions on information flow as a means to realizing the group-action goal.

(4) *Continued conformity*. The regularity continues in the future as enough students and professors conform to the conditions on information flow as a means to realizing the group-action goal.

The hallmark of the student/professor example is a commitment to fair grading. The next example involves a different commitment: the commitment of investigative journalists (journalists who investigate and disclose government wrongdoing) to journalism as a political watchdog.

Investigative Journalists

Investigative journalists aim at a selective flow of information. They make information public that the government wants secret, and they conceal information the government wants to know (the identity of their sources). Creating this selective flow of information exposes journalists to significant risks. The *New York Times* reporters

47 Our evidence for the claims in this section is anecdotal. It is drawn from a combined experience of nearly 100 years as students and teachers in large universities. Students and teachers we have informally asked about the claims acknowledge their accuracy. Outside the large university context, the claims require qualification. For an interesting approach to empirically investigating the existence of norms generally, see Yan Shvartzshnaider et al., "Learning Privacy Expectations by Crowdsourcing Contextual Informational Norms," in *The Fourth AAAI Conference on Human Computation and Crowdsourcing (HCOMP 2016)*, 2016, http://yansh.github.io/papers/HCOMP/.

James Risen and Eric Lichtblau are good examples. In mid-2004, they were ready to publish a story exposing the NSA's warrantless eavesdropping, but the George W. Bush administration pressured the *Times* into delaying publication for fifteen months – until Bush was reelected. The investigation and publication exposed them to the (far from insignificant) harassment of government surveillance, the risk of imprisonment for refusal to disclose a source, and the threat of prosecution under the Espionage Act.[48] Why do investigative journalists run such risks? There are two parts to the answer.

One part is a commitment to using journalism as a political watchdog:[49] "Journalism has an unusual capacity to serve as watchdog over those whose power and position most affect citizens. The Founders recognized this to be a rampart against despotism when they ensured an independent press; courts have affirmed it; citizens rely on it."[50] A well-established tradition sees informed public deliberation and government accountability as central to most conceptions of democracy. Historical evidence confirms that it is unwise to rely solely on the government to voluntarily disclose evidence of its own wrongdoing.[51] The second part of the answer is that a coordinated collective effort by journalists counterbalances the risks journalists run.[52] When the government pursues an investigative journalist, they do not attack just that journalist; they also attack a long, widespread tradition of using identity-protected sources to reveal government wrongdoing. Journalists (and editors and media owners) respond by organizing public opinion and funding legal battles. Preserving and defending the tradition is a group-action goal. No journalist can unilaterally create the tradition of using identity-protected sources to reveal government wrongdoing, nor can he or she effectively organize public opinion and fund legal battles.

How does an investigative journalist know that he or she does not act in isolation when revealing government wrongdoing and protecting a source's identity? How does the journalist know that other journalists – journalists who may be strangers, unknown

48 See Rahul Sagar, *Secrets and Leaks: The Dilemma of State Secrecy* (Princeton University Press, 2013), 105, 154.

49 Commissioner for Human Rights, "Ethical Journalism and Human Rights" (Council of Europe, November 8, 2011), https://wcd.coe.int/ViewDoc.jsp?id=1863637#P252_37545.

50 Leighton Walter Kille, "Committee of Concerned Journalists: The Principles of Journalism," Journalist's Resource, November 26, 2009, https://journalistsresource.org/tip-sheets/foundations/principles-of-journalism/.

51 Sagar, *Secrets and Leaks*, 2.

52 Barton Gellman, *Dark Mirror: Edward Snowden and the American Surveillance State* (Penguin Press, 2020), 249, quoting former FBI Director James Comey's response to Gellman's interview question about whether the FBI could seize an investigative journalist's – actually Gellman's – materials:

> "They could say, 'We're searching for evidence of a crime, so we should be able to get a search warrant to recover this, just like we could if it was in a storage locker.' It's in the journalist's computer. Technically you could, but . . . that would eventually become public and the world would be on fire. It's the norms, practices, traditions, culture, and external pressure that would be brought to bear by the journalists. Not just journalists but by the community."

and unnamed – will, perhaps at considerable risk, preserve and protect the tradition? The answer is that presenting oneself as an investigative journalist creates common knowledge of the four conditions listed below. The role presentations are most effective in a culture that recognizes and values the role of journalists as "essential checks on government and partners in ensuring a healthy democratic debate,"[53] so we focus on a period from the end of McCarthyism in 1956 to the beginning of the Bush administration in 2001 (a time period that includes the Pentagon Papers and the associated landmark First Amendment case *New York Times* v. *Sullivan*).

(1) *Thinking one ought*. Proper role performance requires journalists to think they ought to reveal government wrongdoing while protecting the identity of sources as a means to realizing the group-action goal of maintaining investigative journalism as an effective political watchdog, as long as (enough) other journalists also reveal wrongdoing and protect sources.

(2) *Dominant preference*. Investigative journalists dominantly prefer, at appropriate times, to reveal wrongdoing while protecting the identity of sources as a means to the group-action goal.

(3) *Enough conform*. As result, in part, of (1) and (2), this behavioral past regularity exits: enough investigative journalists reveal government wrongdoing while protecting the identity of sources as a means to the group-action goal.

At least, enough did prior to 2001. We began with the example of Lichtbau and Risen to underscore the importance of the legal and political culture to the success of coordinated efforts to offset the risks. That culture changed with George W. Bush and Obama. After Lichtbau and Risen's story was published in 2006, Risen was "pursued by both the Bush and Obama administrations in a six-year leak investigation," in which Risen faced the threat of years in prison.[54] That is part of the story of the later chapters of how surveillance can undermine the coordination that creates privacy in public.

(4) *Continued conformity*. The behavioral regularity continues in the future as enough journalists continue to reveal government wrongdoing and conceal the identity of sources to succeed in realizing the group-action goal of maintaining investigative journalism as an effective political watchdog.

Note that, unlike the restaurant and retail sales examples, the proper performance in the journalist case does not require exchanging information with a business or the government. The family holiday dinner is similar. Other examples include

53 Human Rights Watch and ACLU, "With Liberty to Monitor All: How Large-Scale US Surveillance Is Harming Journalism, Law and American Democracy," July 2014, www.aclu.org/sites/default/files/assets/dem14-withlibertytomonitorall-07282014.pdf.

54 "James Risen Prepared to 'Pay Any Price' to Report on War on Terror Amid Crackdown on Whistleblowers," *Democracy Now!*, October 14, 2014, www.democracynow.org/2014/10/14/james_risen_prepared_to_pay_any.

relationships with friends, colleagues, seminar participants, members of clubs (sailing, bridge, and chess, for example), acquaintances who frequent the same bars and restaurants, and so on. Selective information flow is a hallmark of our interactions with others.[55] In general, one can divide information exchanges in which proper performance requires exchanging information with a business, government, or organization, and cases in which proper performance requires only exchanges among individuals. The distinction looms large when we turn to the impact of surveillance in Chapters 6 to 9.

The next example returns to market relations and information exchange with a business, but this time outside the context of a consumer's purchase of a retail good or service.

Employers and Job Applicants

Employers and applicants share the group-action goal of determining whether the applicant is a good fit for the job. Proper performance of their respective roles requires that one think one ought to conform to conditions on the exchange of information as a means to realizing that goal, and that (at the appropriate times) one dominantly prefers to conform to those conditions. The group-action goal and associated conceptions of proper performance exist alongside conflicting goals for applicants. Applicants have an incentive to withhold unfavorable information as well as to limit even favorable or neutral information to keep aspects of their lives private from a potential employer. The conflicting goals complicate the solution of the coordination problem, but it is still solved through social-role-generated common knowledge of the following conditions.

(1) *Thinking one ought.* Employers and applicants think they ought to conform to conditions on the exchange of information as a means to realizing the group-action goal of determining whether the applicant is a good fit for the job as long as (enough) others also conform.

The reference to "good fit" introduces considerable indeterminateness. This is not to deny that there are clear cases. No one would object to providing references from past employers, providing a resume, being interviewed, and, where relevant, providing certifications of expertise. Applicants might well object to being asked how much red meat they eat, how much alcohol they consume, and where they would rate themselves on a scale from generally depressed to generally cheerful. Your internist

[55] Selective secrecy is a focal point of Nippert-Eng's portrayal of privacy in *Islands of Privacy*. She notes that "Secrecy is a means to an end, a process in which we actively work to manage our private matters . . . perhaps the most significant aspect of secrets is their selectively shared nature. There are secrets with and secrets from, intentionally disclosed to and concealed from specific individuals at specific times and in specific ways. Simultaneously inclusive and exclusive, secrets are quite effective at achieving social boundary work, an excellent measure of the social distance between individuals." Nippert-Eng, *Islands of Privacy*, 24.

can properly ask such questions, but many will regard them as out of bounds for employers. State and federal laws do prohibit a wide range of inquiries, including inquiries about race, sex, national origin, religion, age, disability, and whether the applicant has children.[56] The restrictions are easy to circumvent, however. Employers can simply ask questions that allow them to infer what they cannot ask directly: for example, "When did you graduate from high school/college?" as a way to infer age, or, as long as it is arguably job related, "What is your experience with such-and-such age group?" as a way to discover if the applicant has children. In addition, employers can ask job applicants to waive privacy rights.[57] The upshot is that employers have considerable power to obtain information. Even so, in the mid-twentieth century it could be difficult for employers to discover, for example, that Alice was a single mother with a sick child if she did not disclose that, and the same is true for a wide range of other "undesirable" traits.

(2) *Dominant preference.* Employers and applicants dominantly prefer, at appropriate times, to conform to the conditions on the exchange of information as a means to realizing the group-action goal of determining fitness for employment. Here too there may be some indeterminateness, because even applicants who share the general group-action goal may not have a dominant preference to give certain information to employers.

(3) *Enough conform.* As result, in part, of (2), this past behavioral regularity holds: enough applicants and employers conform to the conditions on information flow to succeed in realizing the group-action goal of determining the applicants' fitness for employment.

(4) *Continued conformity.* The regularity holds in the future as enough employers and applicants adhere to the conditions on the flow of information as a means to realizing the group-action goal of determining fitness for employment.

Health Insurers

Health insurers need information about the incidence of morbidity and mortality across different segments of the general population. In many countries, governments providing health insurance (or healthcare) need the information to calculate their budgets. Private health insurers need it to correlate premiums with risks. Obtaining this information for the purposes of setting budgets and premiums is a group-action goal. The group of people seeking or using insurance – call them all *insureds* – are an essential source of that information. No one individual can supply all the necessary information. Further, no one insurance company or government agency can make

56 Mathew W. Finkin, *Privacy in Employment Law*, Fifth edition (Bloomberg Law, n.d.).

57 There are limits. Applicants can consent to credit checks under federal law, but state law may prohibit checks even with employee consent. "Use of Credit Information in Employment 2011 Legislation," National Conference of State Legislatures, December 19, 2011, www.ncsl.org/research/financial-services-and-commerce/use-of-credit-information-in-employment-2011-legis.aspx.

sure that other companies and agencies use the information primarily for setting premiums and calculating budgets. Subject to an important qualification below, we take proper performance of the respective roles to require that insureds and insurers think they ought to exchange information primarily in order to realize the group-action goal, and that they dominantly prefer (at appropriate times) to do so.

Insureds and insurers solve the coordination problem through social-role-generated common knowledge of the following conditions:

(1) *Thinking one ought*. Insurers and insureds think they ought to conform to conditions on the exchange of information as a means to realizing the group-action goal of setting budgets and premiums as long as (enough) others also conform.

This may not be true for insureds in the twenty-first-century United States, which invests almost one-fifth of its gross domestic product in health but "delivers worse health outcomes than any other developed country, all of which spend on average about half what we do per person."[58] We turn to that issue in Chapter 7. Notice that what is at issue is whether people think they ought to exchange information *in order to realize the group-action goal*. They may not think that and still think they ought to exchange information with insurance companies. You need to exchange information to obtain health insurance, and going without health insurance in the United States has a very large downside.

(2) *Dominant preference*. Health insurers and their insureds dominantly prefer, at appropriate times, to conform to the conditions on information exchange.

(3) *Enough conform*. As result of (1) and (2), this past behavioral regularity exists: enough insurers and insureds conform to the conditions on information exchange to succeed in realizing the group-action goal of setting budget and premiums

(4) *Continued conformity*. The regularity continues in the future as enough insurers and insureds continue to exchange information as means to realizing the group-action goal.

COMPLETING THE "SURVEILLANCE IGNORED" VIEW

Myriad instances of the four-part pattern create a complex web of privacy in public. That web implements contextually varying tradeoffs between the value of privacy and the benefits of processing information as selective flows of information make some – but only some – data publicly available. To provide the background for assessing the impact of surveillance, we described the creation of privacy in public assuming that there was little or no surveillance of parties' interaction in social roles. We complete that description in Chapter 4.

[58] Elisabeth Rosenthal, *An American Sickness: How Healthcare Became Big Business and How You Can Take It Back* (Penguin Books, 2018), 3.

APPENDIX

Our notion of a coordination *problem* is a generalization of the game theory notion of a coordination *game*. We first explain what a coordination game is, then we turn to coordination problems.

COORDINATION GAMES

By a **game**, we mean a game in which everybody has complete information about the situation, and everybody moves simultaneously. Rock–Paper–Scissors is an example. Two players simultaneously show a hand signal for one of Rock, Paper, or Scissors; the winner is determined according to the rules, “Rock breaks scissors; scissors cut paper; paper covers rock.” It is traditional to show a two-player game’s outcomes in a two-dimensional table, with one player’s choices being the rows and the other player’s choices being the columns.

For Rock–Paper–Scissors we have:

Each cell of the table in Figure 3.1 gives the outcome for the corresponding choices of row and column, with the number in the lower left showing what the row chooser receives, and the number in the upper right showing what the column chooser receives. We call these the payoffs. Let us say that the payoff to a player will be 0 for a tie, +1 unit for a win, and –1 unit for a loss.

Thus, if both players make the same choice, then the game is a tie and each player gets 0, so the table has a pair of 0s in the corresponding entry. Compare the case in which the row chooser picks Rock and the column chooser Scissors; the rules say the row chooser is the winner (“Rock breaks Scissors”), so the entry in the cell of the

	Rock	**Paper**	**Scissors**
Rock	0 0	+1 –1	–1 +1
Paper	–1 +1	0 0	+1 –1
Scissors	+1 –1	–1 +1	0 0

FIGURE 3.1 Payoffs for Rock–Paper–Scissors

table that is in the Rock row and the Scissors column has +1 for the row chooser in the lower left and –1 for the column chooser in the upper right.

Coordination Problems

Game theory is best known for modeling games of pure conflict, such as Rock–Paper–Scissors. Such games are often called **zero-sum** games, because whatever one player wins, the other loses, and their combined winnings add to zero. However, game theory can equally well describe games of perfect cooperation, called **coordination games**, such as choosing which side of the road to drive on.

To keep things simple, we describe the Driving Game for only two players, each of whom chooses which side of the road to drive on: either Left or Right. For this game, the payoff is +10 to each player if they both drive on the same side of the road, and 0 otherwise. We show the payoffs in table form in Figure 3.2.

Observe that the payoffs for the Driving Game are exactly the same as those for a coordination norm: Each player prefers Right *as long as the other player chooses Right*, and each player prefers Left *as long as the other player chooses Left*. In fact, both drive on Right and drive on Left are coordination norms in the game and in practice, Right being the norm in the United States and Canada (among other places), and Left being the norm in England and Australia (among other places).

As a first approximation, let us say a game is a coordination game if:

1. there are at least two different actions; and,
2. when a player chooses an action, she prefers that action to all others as long as the other player chooses that action.

For example, in the Driving Game, Left and Right are the two actions that show that the Driving Game is a coordination game. Each player prefers Left as

	Left	**Right**
Left	10 10	0 0
Right	0 0	10 10

FIGURE 3.2 Driving Game (a coordination game)

long as everyone else chooses Left, and prefers Right as long as everyone else chooses Right. The "prefers as long as everyone else does" in the definition of a coordination *game* parallels the "think one ought to conform as long as everyone else does" in the definition of a coordination *norm*.

Not all coordination games are as simple as the Driving Game. As a second example, we revisit the case of hockey helmets. We assume that the hockey players preferred, all other things being equal, having the protection of wearing a helmet to playing without a helmet. However, we also assume that players preferred having the small advantage in games from playing helmetless against helmeted opponents to playing a game in which both teams were helmetless and greatly preferred playing a game in which both teams were helmeted to playing at a small disadvantage. In such a case, the payoffs might be those shown in Figure 3.3.

Again, this game has two possible ways for the players to choose the same action: one where everybody wears a helmet, and one where everybody plays helmetless. Consider first the row chooser in the Hockey Helmet Game. If he believes the other payer is going to wear a helmet, then the row chooser is going to get one of the payoffs from the left column of the table in Figure 3.3. So the row chooser's payoff will be 10 for choosing Helmet but only 5 for choosing Helmetless. Thus, he wants to choose Helmet as long as the other player does. On the other hand, if the row chooser believes the column chooser will choose Helmetless, then the payoff is going to be one of the payoffs from the right column of the table. In this case the row chooser's payoff will be 0 for choosing Helmet, and 3 for choosing Helmetless. Since 3 is better than 0, the row chooser wants to choose Helmetless – as long as the other player does. The same analysis holds for the column chooser: the column chooser will prefer Helmet as long as the other player chooses Helmet, and will prefer Helmetless as long as the other player chooses Helmetless.

	Helmet	**Helmetless**
Helmet	10 10	5 0
Helmetless	0 5	3 3

FIGURE 3.3 Hockey Helmet Game (another coordination game)

Equilibria

In the Driving Game and the Hockey Helmet Game, it can happen that (1) the players choose the same action (Right, or Helmet, for example), and (2) each prefers that choice as long as the other also chooses it. Game theory has a technical term for such situations: a Nash equilibrium.[59]

Let's call the rule a player uses to choose his move his *strategy*. For our purposes, we need to consider only *pure strategies*, consisting of single-action rules like "Choose Rock" or "Choose Scissors," though in general mixed strategies, such as "Choose Rock with probability 25 percent, Paper with probability 25 percent, and Scissors with probability 50 percent" would also be allowed. We call a list containing one strategy for each player a **strategy profile.** So if Alice and Bob are playing Rock–Paper–Scissors, and Alice's strategy is "Choose Scissors" and Bob's is "Choose Rock," then the strategy profile would be "Alice, Choose Scissors; Bob, Choose Rock."

A strategy profile is a **Nash equilibrium** if each player, knowing the strategies of all other players, prefers his own strategy to any other possible strategy. From here on, we will often drop the "Nash" and use the term "equilibrium" to mean a Nash equilibrium. In the Driving Game, there are two equilibria: both players choosing Left, and both players choosing Right. After all, in that game, each player wants to drive on the same side of the road as the other players. That is, if the Row chooser knows that the Column chooser is picking Right, then the Row chooser will be better off (get a higher payoff) picking Right, and if the Column chooser knows that the Row chooser is picking Right, then the Column chooser will be better off picking Right. The same argument holds for Left, and the same argument holds for both Helmet and Helmetless for the Hockey Helmet Game.

The general importance of Nash equilibria is that they are equilibria in the dictionary sense of being in a steady state. Rational players who have correct expectations about one another's strategies will always choose (the same) equilibrium strategy profile.

Equilibria also allow us to make our definition of a coordination game more precise. A *game is a coordination game if it has at least two different equilibria where both players choose the same action and no equilibria with players choosing different actions.* Thus, both Driving and Hockey Helmets are coordination games.

Rock–Paper–Scissors is an example of a game that is *not* a coordination game. Indeed, it has no equilibria with pure strategies. For instance, if the Row chooser picks Rock, then the Column chooser would be best off picking Paper, but in that case the Row chooser would be best off picking Scissors. The

[59] Named after its inventor, John Nash, who received the Nobel Prize in economics for this work, and who was the subject of the movie A *Beautiful Mind*.

situation is similar if the Row chooser picks either Paper or Scissors instead of Rock. (Rock–Paper–Scissors does have an equilibrium using mixed strategies. That equilibrium occurs if each player picks one of Rock, Paper, or Scissors randomly.)

MORE THAN TWO PLAYERS

The notion of a game in general, and a coordination game in particular, and associated concepts such as equilibria extend from two players to three, four, or any finite number of players in a mathematically straightforward way. However, at some point, the precise mathematical model of coordination games becomes less useful for understanding real-world situations. As the number of participants grows into the hundreds, or the millions, it's implausible that *everybody* will choose the same action, so a game-theoretic model showing equilibria only if everybody chooses the same action is less useful. This is not surprising. Game theory is intended to crisply model situations with relatively few players: two, four, and perhaps one or even two dozen.

Nevertheless, the lessons from studying coordination games with even two players are informative for large real-world cases, as long as we remember that the "all players" choose the same action condition will become "almost all players" or "enough players." This is in fact the case for both of our examples: Driving and hockey helmets. In the United States, *almost* everybody drives on the right *almost* all the time, but an average of 269 fatal wrong-way driving crashes occur each year.[60] That number would surely be orders of magnitude higher if there was no agreement about which side of the road to drive on. In the NHL, when the helmet mandate first came into effect, long-time NHL players could opt out, and some did. It's a famous piece of hockey trivia that in the mid-1990s, there was one NHL player, Craig MacTavish (known as "MacT") who still played without a helmet.[61]

COORDINATION PROBLEMS

Now we show the connection between coordination *games* and our definition of coordination *problems* for a group. Recall that our definition of a coordination problem requires two things:

1. There must be a group-action goal shared by all the members of the group.

[60] Mahdi Pour-Rouholamin et al., "Current Practices of Safety Countermeasures for Wrong-Way Driving Crashes," in *Transportation Research Board 94th Annual Meeting*, Washington DC, 2015.

[61] Sal Barry, "Helmet Holdouts: The Last Players Not to Wear Helmets in the NHL," *The Hockey News on Sports Illustrated*, www.si.com/hockey/all-access/helmet-holdouts-the-last-players-to-wear-helmets-in-the-nhl.

2. Everyone in the group must have a dominant preference to achieve that group-action goal.

For simplicity's sake, we will restrict attention to group-action goals that require action by all. The group-action goal alone doesn't say anything about *relative* utilities, only that everybody in the group has positive utility for some outcome. You may have a group-action goal of going to the opera with your best friend, in the sense that it is something you would derive positive utility from. However, you may also have goals of going to a ballgame with your spouse and of staying home by yourself the same night as the opera, and one of those goals may have a higher utility for you than going to the opera.

The dominant preference requirement means precisely that you have higher utility for going to the opera with your best friend on that night than for any competing activity such as going to the ballgame with your spouse or staying home alone.

That still doesn't guarantee that the situation is accurately modeled by a coordination game. The missing piece is that you have higher utility for taking some action that *conflicts* with the group-action goal in the case where the group-action goal will not be realized because of the actions (or lack of action) of other participants. That is, you are in a situation where your utility payoff is higher if everybody acts to realize the group-action goal than if others act to realize the group-action goal and you do not, *and* your utility payoff is higher if nobody acts to realize the group-action goal than if everybody else except you acts so as not to realize the group-action goal.

To make this concrete, assume that you and a friend have a group-action goal of meeting at a party, and that you both dominantly prefer to meet there. Assume that each of you also likes staying home alone pretty well, and that each of you would really dislike going to the party by yourself. This situation is a coordination game: If your friend goes to the party then you would prefer to be at the party too (because of the dominant preference). If your friend does *not* go to the party, then you would prefer not to go either.[62]

THE COMMON KNOWLEDGE SOLUTION

Common knowledge "solves" the coordination problem because it allows everybody to know that they all have a dominant preference, meaning that they will all choose to act to realize the group-action goal. The common knowledge of the shared group-action goal of a harmonious dinner together with the common knowledge of everybody's dominant preference for that goal allows the family members at our holiday dinner to choose the better Nash equilibrium of all

[62] In fact, this is a famous coordination game called the Assurance Game, which we will discuss in the next chapter.

contributing to the selective flow of information that yields family harmony, instead of the worse Nash equilibrium where the discussion shatters the family's harmony.

In fact, the first two conditions of our four-part pattern of common knowledge solve the game-theoretic coordination game that we have presented in this appendix, which would model a *single* family dinner. The reason we need the third and fourth conditions is that our real concern is with *repeated* games. All our examples, from the holiday dinner to credit rating to investigative journalism, play out repeatedly. Game theory *does* include extensive study of repeated games, but that is beyond the scope of this appendix.

4

Coordination Norms

How important is the four-part pattern? The preceding chapter makes it look fundamental. It portrays the pattern as drawing a contextually varying boundary between the private and the public, and, as the philosopher Thomas Nagel notes, the "boundary between what we reveal and what we do not, and some control over that boundary, is among the most important attributes of our humanity."[1] However, from the perspective of the 2020s, the pattern can look like a historical idiosyncrasy. It flourished with the nineteenth-century rise of urbanization and persisted – it may appear – only until the rise of pervasive surveillance eliminated or transformed it. From this perspective, our endorsement of the four-part pattern may look as out of step with the times as Justus Möser's eighteenth-century critique of the rise of international market economies. Möser lived in what was then the tiny independent state of Osnabrück (now a German city). He saw international markets as "destroying the particular culture of Osnabrück."[2] Cheaper imported goods undermined the traditional guilds and created "new needs that could not be fulfilled by the traditional economy of the region."[3] He lamented the impact on the self: "For Möser the real self was the socially encumbered self, the self based on status, on historical and regional particularity, and on property. It was a self whose prime virtue was honor."[4]

The forces of change swept away the world Möser hoped to preserve, and his laments provided little guidance for life in the world that emerged. Does the four-part pattern face a similar fate? We think not. The pattern creates privacy in public as people guide their actions in light of what they think they ought to do. We take it for granted that this is desirable. We avoid Möser's mistake by not assuming that we should preserve *past* patterns. We argue for adaptive change that ensures adequate privacy in public.

The next step in the argument is to show that the four-part pattern is an instance of a special kind of norm: a coordination norm. Seeing the pattern as a coordination

[1] Thomas Nagel, *Concealment and Exposure: And Other Essays* (Oxford University Press, 2002), 4.
[2] Jerry Z. Muller, *The Mind and the Market: Capitalism in Western Thought* (Anchor Books, 2003), 84.
[3] Muller, 84.
[4] Muller, 91.

norm links it to the large body of work on such norms. That work includes game theory studies;[5] the work of the philosophers Stephen Schiffer,[6] David Lewis,[7] Edna Ullmann-Margalit,[8] and Christina Bicchieri;[9] and the extensive empirical studies of the Nobel Prize–winning political economist Elinor Ostrom and those inspired by her.[10] Ostrom and her followers demonstrate the descriptive and explanatory power of coordination norms – and hence of the four-part pattern – in contexts concerned with framing effective public policy. Thus, we propose that coordination norms take center stage in any adequate response to pervasive surveillance. The first step in putting them there is to note that coordination norms are a subspecies of norms in general. We use "norms" for the general concept, and "coordination norms" for the subspecies.

NORMS

There are norms in various groups about manners, dating, littering, speaking in seminars, how to dress, showing anger, when, how, and with whom to express affection, how loudly to speak in public, when to use contractions, when to purchase insurance, when to use the salad fork, and on and on. We discuss three examples in more detail. In contrast to the later examples of coordination norms, none of the three examples involve a group-action goal. After the examples, we will give our definition of norms.

Birdwatching

Suppose all the members of a birdwatching group follow the American Birdwatching Association's guideline that one should "avoid stressing birds or exposing [birds] to danger, [and] exercise restraint and caution during observation, photography, sound recording, or filming."[11] Each member of the group adheres to the guideline at least in part because each believes that they ought to do so. Adhering to the guidelines is an individual rather than a group-action goal. No member needs

5 See, for example, Thomas C. Schelling, *Arms and Influence: With a New Preface and Afterword*, Revised edition (Yale University Press, 2008).
6 Stephen Schiffer, *Meaning* (Oxford University Press, 1972).
7 David K. Lewis, *Convention* (Harvard University Press, 1969).
8 Edna Ulhmann-Margalit, *The Emergence of Norms* (Oxford University Press, 1977).
9 Cristina Bicchieri, *Norms in the Wild: How to Diagnose, Measure, and Change Social Norms* (Oxford University Press, 2016).
10 See, for example, Elinor Ostrom, *Governing the Commons: The Evolution of Institutions for Collective Action* (Cambridge University Press, 1990); Elinor Ostrom, *Understanding Institutional Diversity* (Princeton University Press, 2005); Charlotte Hess and Elinor Ostrom, "Ideas, Artifacts, and Facilities: Information as a Common-Pool Resource," *Law and Contemporary Problems* 66, 1 (April 1, 2003): 111–46.
11 "ABA Code of Birding Ethics," American Birding Association, www.aba.org/aba-code-of-birding-ethics/.

the cooperation of the others to ensure that they do not stress birds and to exercise restraint and caution. (There is of course a related group-action goal: the goal of birdwatchers' coordinating their individual activities to minimize the stress they collectively cause birds.)

Code of Silence

Assume (what may not in fact be true[12]) that Mafia members adhere to *omertà*: the code of silence. The code requires complete lack of cooperation with law enforcement. To break the code is to incur extreme dishonor. Sarah is a Mafia member, and, when arrested, she refuses to cooperate because she thinks she ought to avoid dishonor. Like exercising birdwatching restraint, Sarah's individually adhering to *omertà* is not a group-action goal. She would observe the code even if most others did not.

Supreme Court Attire

The United States Supreme Court requires that attorneys observing oral arguments wear appropriate attire out of respect for the Court: "Male attorneys shall wear a coat and a tie. Female attorneys shall wear comparable attire (suit, dress, or dress slacks with matching jacket)."[13] When the attorney James observes oral arguments, he wears a suit and tie because he thinks he ought to out of respect for the Court. James can realize that goal even if other attorneys do not comply with the attire requirements.

What do these examples have in common? In each, there is a social role – birdwatcher, Mafia member, attorney. Proper performance requires that one thinks one ought to realize a certain goal, and that one dominantly prefers (at appropriate times) to do so. As people act on those preferences, they create a behavioral regularity that holds in the relevant group – birdwatchers don't disturb birds, Mafia members don't cooperate with police, attorneys dress appropriately for the Supreme Court. Such social-role-generated regularities in behavior are norms.

A behavioral regularity in a group generated by a social role is a *norm* when (and only when):

1. As proper performance of the social role requires, people in the group both think they ought to realize the goal, and dominantly prefer (at appropriate times) to do so; and
2. As a result of (1), the behavioral regularity holds in the group.

12 Celestine Bohlen, "As Code of Silence Cracks, Mafia Changes Rules," *The New York Times*, October 11, 1995, www.nytimes.com/1995/10/11/world/as-code-of-silence-cracks-mafia-changes-rules.html.

13 "Bar Members Seating," Supreme Court of the United States, n.d., www.supremecourt.gov/visiting/visitorsguidetooralargument.aspx.

We emphasize that we have defined when a *social-role-generated* regularity is a norm. The standard notion of a norm is broader. As Bicchieri notes, "a shared, common understanding of what a social norm is can be traced across all fields: *a norm refers to a behavior that is collectively approved or disapproved in a group or population, and is enforced by sanctions.*"[14] We add a reference to social roles and drop explicit reference to collective approval or disapproval. Instead, we refer to what people think they ought to do. Reference to collective approval or disapproval is implicit, however, since you expose yourself to collective approval or disapproval if you fail to do what you and the rest of a group think you ought to. However, not every case of collective approval or disapproval is tied to social roles, so our definition is narrower than the standard conception. We opted for our narrow definition because it picks out the cases we will later compare and contrast with coordination norms. We note in passing that we also do not refer to sanctions. While they are a significant feature of many cases, they are not so in all cases. Consider a lone birdwatcher, for example. It is easy for a lone birdwatcher to violate the norm of nondisturbance without fear of a sanction. Lone birdwatchers conform because they think they ought to, not because someone will impose sanctions.[15]

Norms generally are interesting and important, but we narrow our focus to the special subclass of coordination norms. Our immediate goal is to show that

[14] Cristina Bicchieri, "Norms, Conventions, and the Power of Expectations," in *Philosophy of Social Science: A New Introduction*, ed. Nancy Cartwright and Eleonora Mantuschi (Oxford University Press, 2014), 209 (emphasis in the original). Our notion of a norm is also similar to the notions discussed in the law and economics literature. We differ in explicitly referring to social roles, and in our appeal to people's beliefs about what they ought to do. In contrast, the recent literature explains conformity as the result of self-interested actors avoiding the costs of nonconformity. "One approach assumes that people care only about their (material) well-being, and relies on repeated game models to explain how they cooperate or refrain from violating social norms . . . [A second] approach assumes that people care about something else aside from material goods – esteem, status, conformity, or some such thing": Eric A. Posner, "Introduction," in *Social Norms, Nonlegal Sanctions, and the Law*, ed. Eric A. Posner (Harvard University Press, 2007). Richard McAdams, a proponent of the second approach, notes that "by a norm I mean a decentralized behavioral standard that individuals feel obligated to follow, and generally do follow . . . [to gain the esteem of others], or because the obligation is internalized, or both": Richard McAdams and Eric A. Posner, "The Origin, Development, and Regulation of Norms," in *Social Norms, Nonlegal Sanctions, and the Law* (Harvard University Press, 2007), 101. The emphasis on "feeling obligated" would appear close to our view that people conform because they think they ought to; however, McAdams explains "feeling obligated" in terms of the costs of nonconformity – thus: "Without internalization, one obeys the norm to avoid external sanctions . . . After internalization, there is yet another cost to violating a norm: guilt. The individual feels psychological discomfort whether or not others detect her violation" (McAdams and Posner, 144). McAdams still conceives of people as self-interested agents seeking to avoid costs they regard as unacceptable. We take it to be clear that people are not merely self-interested agents. For an excellent overview of various ways to define norms, see Gerry Mackie et al., "What Are Social Norms? How Are They Measured?," Working Paper (UNICEF, 2014), https://prevention-collaborative.org/resource/what-are-social-norms-how-are-they-measured/.

[15] For an argument that norms need not involve sanctions, see Cristina Bicchieri, *The Grammar of Society: The Nature and Dynamics of Social Norms* (Cambridge University Press, 2005).

Chapter 3's four-part pattern is an instance of the more general pattern of coordination norms.

COORDINATION NORMS

We offered a preliminary definition of coordination norms in Chapter 1. We refine that definition by generalizing from Chapter 3's examples of the four-part pattern. In those examples, parties interact in social roles in ways that create a selective flow of information. To characterize the general pattern of a coordination norm, we keep the reference to social roles but understand those roles more broadly to include roles that, like the Supreme Court attire example, do not involve the exchange of information. Take those away from Chapter 3's four-part pattern, and we have this left:

> A behavioral regularity in a group generated by a social role is a *coordination norm* when (and only when) it is common knowledge among the members of the group that, with regard to a group-action goal G:
>
> 1. As proper performance of the role requires,
>   a. each thinks they ought to conform to the regularity as a means to realizing G as long as enough others also conform (where enough is enough to realize G);
>   b. each dominantly prefers, at appropriate times, to conform to the regularity as a means to realizing G.
>
> 2. As a result of (1), the following past regularity holds: enough of the parties have conformed to the behavioral regularity as a means to realizing G.
>
> 3. As a result of (2), the regularity continues to hold in the future as (enough of) the parties conform to it as a means to realize G.

The *three* conditions of the definition capture the *four*-part pattern by virtue of the fact that the first condition has two parts.

Schiffer, Lewis, and Bicchieri offer broader definitions that do not refer to social roles. Bicchieri, for example, defines a "social norm" (a coordination norm in our terms) this way: "A social norm is a rule of behavior such that individuals prefer to conform to it on condition that they believe that (a) most people in their reference network conform to it (empirical expectation), and (b) that most people in their reference network believe they ought to conform to it (normative expectation)."[16] Our key difference from Bicchieri is that our definition explicitly refers to the "rules of behavior" that concern us: namely, requirements of proper performance associated with social roles. A minor difference from Bicchieri is that our definition states "enough others" where hers has "most."

[16] Bicchieri, *Norms in the Wild*, 35.

To illustrate the definition, suppose five acquaintances – Alice, Bob, Charlie, Dan, and Eve – each promise to participate in Chicago's Polar Plunge as long as the others do so too. Polar Plunge participants dive into the icy waters of Lake Michigan in March to raise money for the Special Olympics. For the five acquaintances, proper performance of the social role of promisor requires that each think they ought to dive in as long as the rest do, and it also requires that, when the time comes, each dominantly prefers to take the dive. It is not proper performance to lose one's nerve at the last moment. It follows that the five acquaintances face a coordination problem. There is a group-action goal that each shares (by virtue of each thinking they ought to realize the goal as long as the rest do), and which each (at appropriate times) dominantly prefers to realize.

We explain how the exchange of promises serves as a common knowledge generator that creates common knowledge of (1)–(3). For convenience, we begin by recalling the conditions for the existence of a common knowledge generator.

Common Knowledge Generators

A common knowledge generator is a situation meeting two conditions:

(G1) The situation results in all members of a group G knowing X.
(G2) The situation ensures that all members of G know that all members of G undergo the situation and as a result come to know X.

For the Polar Plunge, we fill out (G1) and (G2) as follows:

(G1) Their presentations to each other as having promised to take the Polar Plunge result in their knowing that (1)–(3) hold.
(G2) Their presentations to each other as having promised to take the Polar Plunge result in their $knowing_2$ that they $know_1$ (1)–(3).

To see that these versions of (G1) and (G2) hold, we consider (1)–(3) in turn, starting with (1).

Condition (1)

Imagine Alice, Bob, Charlie, Dan, and Eve all promise to take the Polar Plunge. The act of their each promising in the presence of the others ensures that (G1) holds: a group member's seeing and hearing the exchange of promises results in that member's knowing that each group member thinks they ought to dive in to realize the group-action goal of their all doing so as long as all or most of the others dive in, and that each group member dominantly prefers (at the appropriate time) to dive in. (G2) also holds: since each group member sees the others seeing and hearing the exchange of promises, each $knows_2$ that group members $know_1$ each thinks they ought to dive in to realize the group-action goal of their all doing so as long as all or most of the others dive in, and, as a result, each dominantly prefers (at the appropriate time) to dive in.

Condition (2)

(G1): each knows by observation that the rest dive in.
(G2): each $knows_2$ that the others see the others dive in and so $knows_1$ that the rest dive in.

Condition (3)

Now we divide the Polar Plunge example into two variants. In the first, the five acquaintances agreed, when they promised, that their dive would be a one-time thing. They would never do it again. In this case, the fourth condition is not fulfilled. It is not common knowledge (and indeed not true) that

> (3) as a result of (2), the regularity continues to hold in the future as enough of the parties conform to it in order to realize G.

In the second variant, they promise to participate in all Polar Plunges for the foreseeable future.

We represent the group members as reasoning their way to common knowledge of Condition (3). As we noted in Chapter 3, people rarely engage in detailed explicit reasoning. Our point is that the five acquaintances *could* do so if the question arose of whether they should continue thinking they ought to participate. They have the answer in hand even if they never need to produce it. Imagine the group members have participated in several Polar Plunges one after the other without exception, and assume that the past participation is good evidence of participation in the future. (G1) holds because each group member will reason as follows: "Each of us realizes that past conformity is good evidence of future conformity, so, since we know that we all dominantly prefer to participate at appropriate times, each of us knows that we will participate." (G2) holds because each will reason this way: "Each of us realizes that each of us will reason in the (G1) way above to the first-level knowledge that we will participate, so each of us $knows_2$ that each of us $knows_1$ that we will participate."

Fulfillment of the third condition makes participation in the Polar Plunge a self-perpetuating regularity. Suppose they have all participated eight times in a row. On the morning of the ninth time, Alice, thinking of the icy water that awaits, asks herself, "Am I going?" She answers, "Yes, I ought to participate as long as the rest do, and, given their past participation, I know they will participate again." As she stands on the shore and looks at the cold water, she asks herself, "Am I really getting in that cold water?" As she considers the question, she looks at the others and thinks, "Given their past participation, I know they are going to dive in," and, since she dominantly prefers to dive in as long as the rest do, she dives in. The others dive in for the same reason Alice does. The pattern repeats itself indefinitely until one or more of the following occurs: (i) They (enough of them) stop thinking they ought to participate. (ii) They stop dominantly preferring (at appropriate times) to do so. (iii) Past participation is no longer good evidence of future participation (e.g., it is common knowledge among them that every year their doctors express increasing concern about the wisdom of their participation). It is this self-perpetuating pattern we are calling a coordination norm. In short, a coordination norm is a social-role-generated, common-knowledge-facilitated, self-perpetuating regularity in behavior. Schiffer,[17] Lewis,[18] and Bicchieri[19] give similar definitions (Schiffer and Lewis call what they define a "convention").

The definition may prompt the objection "What is the point? You have made a few refinements, but basically all you have done is give the four-part pattern from Chapter 3 a different name." We claim we have done more than just rename it. Explicitly defining coordination norms reveals that the pattern is an instance of a more general pattern one finds in a wide variety of human activities studied by political economists, game theorists, and sociologists. The connections demonstrate the descriptive and explanatory power of coordination norms and their importance for framing effective public policy.

In Chapter 1, we illustrated coordination norms with reference to the example of driving on the right. Here we offer three more examples. In each there is a relevant group-action goal, but, unlike the Chapter 3 examples, the goal is *not* one whose realization ensures a selective flow of information. The noninformation-flow examples of this chapter show that Chapter 3's information-flow examples are special cases of a broader pattern.

EXAMPLES

Elevators

You are about to enter an elevator in which others are already present. Where will you stand? The pattern is well known.[20] Alone, you may stand anywhere. Two people align roughly horizontally facing forward with each nearer to a sidewall

[17] Schiffer, *Meaning*. Schiffer simplifies and revises Lewis's definition in David K. Lewis, *Convention*. Schiffer and Lewis communicated extensively about such issues in the late 1960s and 1970s (Schiffer, personal communication).

[18] In addition to *Convention*, see David K Lewis, "Languages and Language," in *Language, Mind, and Knowledge*, ed. Keith Gunderson, vol. VII, Minnesota Studies in the Philosophy of Science (Minnesota University Press, 1975), 3–35.

[19] Bicchieri, *Norms in the Wild*, 65–66.

[20] "Where People Stand in Elevators," *Nationwide Lifts Blog* (blog), December 15, 2015, www.home-elevator.net/blog/commercial-elevators/where-people-stand-in-elevators/; "Elevator Proxemics," *Weird Universe*, August 30, 2016, www.weirduniverse.net/blog/comments/elevator_proxemics.

than they are to each other. Three people form a triangle; four, a square, and a fifth person stands in the middle. If more enter, they distribute themselves in the available spaces. Why do people do this? Because they are maximizing their distance from the person nearest to them.[21] The point is to strike a balance between two potentially conflicting goals: using elevators – even crowded ones – when they come, and minimizing the feeling of being crammed into a small space.[22] Balancing using elevators and minimizing the feeling of being crowded is a group-action goal. Maximizing their distance from one's nearest neighbor is the means elevator riders adopt for realizing that goal. Thus, proper performance of the social role of an elevator rider requires both that one thinks one ought to be a nearest-neighbor-maximizer as a means to realizing the goal of maximizing use while minimizing the feeling of being crowded, and that, at appropriate times, one dominantly prefers to maximize one's distance from one's nearest neighbor.

Elevator riders realize the group-action goal by creating relevant common knowledge of (1)–(3) through presenting themselves to each other as elevator riders.

1. As proper performance of the role requires,
   a. riders think they ought to maximize the distance from their nearest neighbor as a means to realizing the group-action goal as long as enough others are also nearest-neighbor-maximizers.[23]
   b. riders dominantly prefer at appropriate times to maximize their distance from their nearest neighbor as a means to realizing the group-action goal.
2. As a result of (1), the following past behavioral regularity exists: enough riders maximize their distance from their nearest neighbor as a means to realizing the group-action goal.
3. As a result of (2), the regularity continues to hold in the future as enough riders continue to maximize their distance from their nearest neighbor as a means to realizing the group-action goal.

Sadly (in our opinion), this pattern may be disappearing. We do not know of any relevant studies, but our observations during our own elevator use in 2019 suggested that many enter elevators while absorbed in their phones and pay little attention to

[21] We believe that you try to find the best compromise between maximizing distance and not standing outside others' field of vision, but, for simplicity, we ignore the visual field requirement. How has the COVID-19 pandemic affected the norm as of this writing? There are two ways to look at the situation. One is that a modified version of the norm now holds: namely, that one should be no closer than six feet to one's nearest neighbor, where the total number of people in the elevator does not exceed the new, much smaller maximum allowed by pandemic rules. The other is that a new "maintain the specified distance for at most the specified number of occupants" norm has replaced the "maximize your distance from your nearest neighbor" norm.

[22] "Elevator Proxemics."

[23] Writing in November of 2020, we note that the global pandemic has put this norm on hold – or perhaps changed the understanding of "nearest neighbor" to "one of the allowed number of riders who is at least six feet away."

where they stand. If the global pandemic had not disrupted elevator use, and if over a long enough period of time enough elevator users failed to maximize their distance from their nearest neighbor, it would have stopped being common knowledge that users maximize that distance, and the pattern would have ceased to exist, even without the interference of the pandemic.

The Alanya, Turkey Inshore Fishery

In the 1970s, overfishing at the Alanya, Turkey inshore fishery was depleting fishing stocks and leading to intense competition that raised costs and sometimes even led to violent conflict.[24] Hence, "[e]arly in the 1970s, members of the local cooperative began experimenting with an ingenious system for allotting fishing sites to local fishers."[25] After ten-plus years of trial and error, they devised a system of allotting fishing sites. A lottery at the beginning of the fishing season assigned each fisher an initial area, and fishers then rotated to a different spot each day. The rotation ensured an equitable distribution of the quality spots. On the days a fisher is assigned one of the better fishing spots, they will "exercise that option with certainty ... Consequently, an effort to cheat on the system by traveling to a good spot on a day when one is assigned to a poor spot has little chance of remaining undetected."[26]

Fishers adhering to the lottery system is a group-action goal, and proper performance of the role of Alanya fisher requires that one thinks one ought to fish in one's allotted spot in order to realize that goal (as long as enough others join in its realization), and that, at appropriate times, one dominantly prefers to fish only in one's allotted spot.[27] Fishers create common knowledge of (1)–(3) as they present themselves in the role of member of the cooperative.

1. As proper performance of the role requires,
   a. each thinks he ought to fish in his allotted spot as a means to realizing the group-action goal as long as enough others do so too;
   b. each dominantly prefers (at appropriate times) to fish in his allotted spot as a means to realizing the group-action goal.
2. As a result of (1), the following past behavioral regularity exists: enough fishers fish in their allotted spots as a means to realizing the group-action goal.

[24] "The list of fishing locations is endorsed by each fisher and deposited with the mayor and local gendarme once a year at the time of the lottery. The process of monitoring and enforcing the system is, however, accomplished by the fishers themselves as a by-product of the incentive created by the rotation system" (Ostrom, *Governing the Commons*, 19).

[25] Ostrom, 19.

[26] Ostrom, 20.

[27] Fishers sometimes did not fish at all on the days when they were allocated a poor fishing spot. Our "appropriate times" qualification allows for this possibility.

3. As a result of (2), the regularity continues to hold in the future as enough fishers continue to fish in their allotted spots as a means to realizing the group-action goal.

Alanya is not an isolated example. As Ostrom notes, "The case of the Alanya inshore fishery is only one empirical example of the many institutional arrangements that have been devised, modified, monitored, and sustained by the users of [a natural resource] to constrain individual behavior that would, if unconstrained, reduce joint returns to the community of users."[28] The work of Ostrom and her followers shows that coordination norms govern a wide variety of situations.

One drawback of the Alanya example is that the cooperative "is a relatively small operation. Many of the approximately 100 local fishers operate in two- or three-person boats."[29] Our ultimate goal is to show how to create and preserve coordination norms on at least a national scale. To this end, the next example shows how a combination of advertising and legal enforcement created an antilittering coordination norm in the United States.

Littering

In the early 1950s, despite a widespread desire for a cleaner environment, almost everyone in the United States littered.[30] The problem was that a clean environment was a group-action goal. As long as most people littered, people unilaterally taking the time and effort to use waste receptacles would not make the environment cleaner. This changed during the 1950s through the 1970s as a result of an intensive antilittering advertising campaign combined with legal liability.[31] The "don't be a litterbug" slogan of the highly effective advertising campaign implied that if you littered you were an insect.

Enough people using waste receptacles is a group-action goal, and by some time in the 1960s, proper performance of the role of civic-minded citizen required that one think one ought to not to litter in order to realize the group-action goal, and that, as a result, at appropriate times, one dominantly prefers not to litter. People create common knowledge of (1)–(3) as they present themselves in the role of a civic-minded citizen.[32]

28 Ostrom, *Governing the Commons*, 20–21.

29 Ostrom, 19.

30 See, for example, Bradford Plumer, "The Origins of Anti-Litter Campaigns – Mother Jones," *Mother Jones*, May 22, 2006, www.motherjones.com/politics/2006/05/origins-anti-litter-campaigns/.

31 See Heather Rogers, *Gone Tomorrow: The Hidden Life of Garbage* (The New Press, 2005). Rogers is rightly critical of the political motives behind the antilittering campaign.

32 Bastin Tony Roy Savarimuthu et al., "Social Norm Emergence in Virtual Agent Societies," in *Declarative Agent Languages and Technologies VI* (International Workshop on Declarative Agent Languages and Technologies, Springer, 2008), 18–28, https://doi.org/10.1007/978-3-540-93920-7_2.

1. As proper performance of the role requires,
   a. each thinks that they ought to not to litter as a means to realizing the group-action goal as long as enough others do;
   b. each dominantly prefers at appropriate times not to litter as a means to realizing the group-action goal.
2. As a result of (1), the following past behavioral regularity exists: enough do not litter as a means to realizing the group-action goal.
3. As a result of (2), the regularity continues to hold in the future as enough continue not to litter as a means to realizing the group-action goal.

By the 2000s, littering had become a problem again.[33] This would not have occurred if relevant social role presentations had made (1)–(3) common knowledge, so a plausible explanation is that cultural change altered the conception of a civic-minded citizen in such a way that people no longer created such common knowledge when they presented themselves to each other in that role.

In general, common-knowledge-enabled coordination norms facilitate coordination across a broad range of interactions in social roles.

INFORMATIONAL NORMS

Our concern is with the special subcase of coordination norms illustrated by the Chapter 3 examples. Those examples are instances of *informational* coordination norms: coordination norms that govern the selective flow of information as people interact in social roles. We will call them informational norms for short. Helen Nissenbaum singled out informational norms for study in her seminal 2004 article "Privacy as Contextual Integrity." She notes that there are norms that

> circumscribe the type or nature of information about various individuals that, within a given context, is allowable, expected, or even demanded to be revealed. In medical contexts, it is appropriate to share details of our physical condition or, more specifically, the patient shares information about his or her physical condition with the physician but not vice versa; among friends we may pour over romantic entanglements (our own and those of others); to the bank or our creditors, we reveal financial information; with our professors, we discuss our own grades; at work, it is appropriate to discuss work-related goals and the details and quality of performance.[34]

We reformulate the definition of a coordination norm specifically for the case of *informational* coordination norms:

[33] Rogers, *Gone Tomorrow*.

[34] Helen Nissenbaum, *Privacy as Contextual Integrity*, 79 *Wash. Law Rev.* 119, (2004): 120–21.

A behavioral regularity in a group generated by a social role is an *informational coordination norm* when (and only when) it is common knowledge among the members of the group that, with regard to a group-action goal G:

1. As proper performance of the role requires,
   a. each thinks they ought to conform to role-specific conditions on information flow as a means to realizing G as long as enough others also conform;
   b. each dominantly prefers, at appropriate times, to conform to role-specific conditions on information flow as a means to realizing G.
2. As a result of (1), the following past regularity holds: enough of the parties have conformed to the role-specific conditions on information flow as a means to realizing G.
3. As a result of (2), the regularity continues to hold in the future as (enough of) the parties continue to conform to role-specific conditions on information flow as a means to realize G.

For convenience, from here on we will use "informational norm" for "informational coordination norm."

The examples we discussed in Chapter 3 are all informational norms in the sense just defined. Table 4.1 organizes the examples of informational norms we have discussed so far. We also include in italics our examples of noninformational coordination norms.

TABLE 4.1 *An overview of different norm-governed activities*

Commercial		
Buyer/seller	Professional	Noncommercial
Starbucks	Students/professors	Holiday dinner
Geno's steaks	Investigative journalists	*Elevators*
Restaurants	*Alanya Fishery*	*No littering*
Retail sales		*Same-side driving*
Employers and applicants		
Health insurance		

A WORLD WITHOUT INFORMATIONAL NORMS

We propose that social and political action should preserve, restore, and create a network of acceptable informational norms sufficient to ensure adequate privacy in public. It lends support to this proposal to imagine a world *without* informational norms. This would be a world without the complex web of privacy in public we alluded to in Chapters 1 and 2, without the opportunities for self-realization it creates, and without the tradeoffs it implements. Coordinating information exchanges with others would still be possible, but it would be highly problematic.

How does one imagine a world without informational norms? We do so by using Assurance Games, a well-known game theory model of cooperation. Assurance Games are a species of coordination problem. Up to this point, the general notion of a coordination problem was all we needed, but Assurance Games are an excellent model of the type of coordination in social role interactions, and are particularly useful in contrasting coordination with and without relevant common knowledge. We first consider Assurance Games in general, rather than those specifically involved in information exchanges in interactions in social roles. We show how solving Assurance Games becomes problematic without relevant common knowledge. We then show that the same is true for the Assurance Games involved in the exchange of information in social roles.

Assurance Games

The Assurance Game gets its name from the way in which its outcome depends on what each player thinks the other will do.[35] Suppose, for example, that Victor and Victoria are discussing by cell phone whether to meet at the opera later in the evening or to each stay home alone. Before they decide, their phone batteries run out, and they have no other way to communicate. They both really like to go to the opera with someone, and both really dislike going to the opera alone. They both have, and know they both have, the following preferences in the following order. (1) Attend the opera together. (2) Stay home alone while the other does too. (3) Stay home alone while the other goes to the opera. (4) Go to the opera while the other does not.

The Assurance Game consists of two players with similar preferences.[36] (While precise definitions vary, the crucial thing is that the top preference is for both players

35 The game goes by a variety of names besides Assurance Game. Others are Trust Dilemma, Coordination Game, and Stag Hunt. William Poundstone, *Prisoner's Dilemma* (Doubleday, 1992), 219. "Stag Hunt" is perhaps the most used name. It harks back to Rousseau's description of the stag hunt dilemma (the translation uses "deer" instead of "stag"): "Was a deer to be taken? Every one saw that to succeed he must faithfully stand to his post; but suppose a hare to have slipped by within reach of any one of them, it is not to be doubted but he pursued it without scruple." Jean-Jacques Rousseau, *A Discourse Upon the Origin and the Foundation of the Inequality among Mankind* (Dover Publications, 2004), 29–30. We use "Assurance Game" to emphasize the role of knowledge – or lack of it – in determining what the players do. For a discussion of the importance of the Assurance Game to analyzing social coordination, see Brian Skyrms, *The Stag Hunt and the Evolution of Social Structure* (Cambridge University Press, 2004), chapter 1.

36 In addition, the parties are unable to communicate, and each chooses without observing or otherwise learning about the choice of the other. These assumptions, and the joint knowledge of one another's preferences, are the classic assumptions of game theory. See, generally, Kevin Leyton-Brown, *Essentials of Game Theory: A Concise, Multidisciplinary Introduction* (Morgan and Claypool Publishers, 2008); Martin J. Osborne and Ariel Rubinstein, *A Course in Game Theory* (The MIT Press, 1994).

to make a particular choice, in this case, going to the opera, and the bottom preference is to make that choice when the other player makes the opposite choice, here staying home.[37]) But exactly what are the preferences about? They do not always involve operas and homes. To generalize, think of going to the opera as *cooperating* in the attempt to meet at the opera, and staying home as *defecting* from the coordination needed to meet at the opera. For appropriate specifications of cooperation and defection, an Assurance Game consists of two parties with these preferences: (1) cooperate when the other cooperates; (2) defect when the other defects; (3) defect when the other cooperates; (4) cooperate when the other defects. What will Victor and Victoria do? If they had relevant common knowledge the answer would be easy. Suppose their presentations to each other in the role of friend make it common knowledge between them that they would both go to the opera. Then they would go.

Common knowledge makes solving Assurance Games simple. Without it, solutions are harder to come by. To see why, focus on Victoria (similar remarks hold for Victor). What she will do depends in part on how much she values her options. We will describe the relative values using a scale of 10 to –10. This is the beginning of a small bit of mathematical precision that is a useful and harmless idealization. It is useful because allows us to derive crisp results easily and clearly. It is harmless because the results remain valid – more or (importantly, it turns out) less – for the unidealized reality. Suppose, then, that Victoria rates meeting Victor at the opera (i.e., cooperate/cooperate) at 5. On the other hand, she regards going to the opera when Victor does not (i.e., cooperate/defect) as a disaster, so she rates that –10. Staying home alone when Victor also does (i.e., defect/defect) is 3; while staying home when Victor goes to the opera (i.e., defect/cooperate) is 1. The 3 versus 1 difference represents the value Victoria places on coordinating with Victor. Given these valuations, should Victoria go to the opera or stay home?[38] We answer the

[37] The game theory literature is not completely consistent on terminology. Some definitions give other orders or indifference between outcomes (2) and (3), and some make distinctions between "Stag Hunt" and "Assurance Game" based on this sort of difference. Perhaps the most common definition has our second and third preferences reversed, with equality between them also allowed. The crucial point is that both outcomes where the two players do the same thing form Nash equilibria, with one of those two outcomes having a higher payoff than all other payoffs. See, for example, Samuel Bowles, *Microeconomics: Behavior, Institutions, and Evolution* (Princeton University Press, 2003): 43.

[38] If Victor and Victoria played out this scenario on a regular basis, then in game theory terminology we would have a repeated game rather than a one-shot game. For repeated games, game theory predicts that the players will settle into one of the two Nash equilibria, either both going to the opera or both staying home, and then remain in that equilibria. See, for example, Evelyn C. Fink, Scott Gates, and Brian D. Humes, *Game Theory Topics: Incomplete Information, Repeated Games and N-Player Games* (Sage Publications, Inc, 1998). For our one-shot case, the player's dilemma is whether to go to the opera, intuitively aiming for the payoff-dominant best possible outcome of going to the opera together, or to stay home, avoiding the risk of going to the opera when the other stays home. For the seminal technical treatment of this issue, see John C. Harsanyi, "A New Theory of Equilibrium Selection for Games with Complete Information," *Games and Economic Behavior* 8, 1 (1995): 91–122.

question twice, for two different cases. In the first, Victoria knows the probability of Victor's going to the opera; in the second, she does not.

Knowledge of Relevant Probabilities

Assume Victoria knows that the answer to the question "How likely is it that Victor will go to the opera?" is 80 percent (and hence the probability of Victor's staying home alone is 20 percent). With these probabilities, she calculates the expected value to her of her going to the opera and of her staying home alone: 2.0 and 1.4, respectively.[39] So, insofar as she is rational, Victoria will go to the opera. Some will rightly object that people rarely explicitly reason their way through a calculation of expected value. The worry is a general – and old – one, as a 1918 critique of social science illustrates: "In the social sciences we are suffering from a curious mental derangement ... the orthodox doctrines of economics, politics and law rest upon a tacit assumption that man's behavior is dominated by rational calculation ... [even though] this is an assumption contrary to fact."[40] The objection does not apply here because our description of Victoria as explicitly calculating is just an expositional device. It is convenient to describe her, in the idealized world of mathematical precision we are imagining, as explicitly reasoning. That is harmless because, in the unidealized reality, Victoria does something similar. Perhaps without consciously realizing it, she takes her rough estimates of probability and combines them with a nonquantitative understanding of how much she values the various options to make the best compromise she can between how much she values the options and the likelihood of realizing what she values by the actions open to her.

The point to emphasize here is that Victoria reasons her way to a more general conclusion: to go to the opera only if she believes the probability of Victor's going is 76 percent or greater. She arrives at that conclusion by asking "When do going to the opera and staying home have the *same* expected value?" The answer is when the probability of Victor's going to the opera is 76 percent, which can be derived using high school algebra.[41] Below 76 percent, staying home has the better expected value, so Victoria will only go to the opera if she believes the probability of Victor's going is at least 76 percent.

Assume Victoria happens to believe the probability of Victor's going to the opera is 80 percent; then, she will go too. That does not mean she and Victor will

39 Going to the opera has two outcomes: meeting Victor, and not meeting Victor. Its expected value is the sum of the expected values of those two options: $(0.8 \times 5) + (0.2 \times -10) = 2.0$. Staying home likewise has two options: staying home when Victor does, and staying home when he does not, so the expected value of staying home is $(0.2 \times 3) + (0.8 \times 1) = 1.4$.

40 Wesley Clair Mitchell, "Bentham's Felicific Calculus," *Political Science Quarterly* 33(2)(1918): 161.

41 For any probability p, the expected value of the utility of going to the opera is $(p * 5) + ((1 - p) * -10)$, and the expected value of the utility of staying home is $((1 - p) * 3) + (p * 1)$, so Victoria solves this equation to find the value of p: $(p * 5) + ((1 - p) * -10) = ((1 - p) * 3) + (p * 1)$. The value of p is $13/17 \approx 0.76$.

coordinate their actions by either both going or both staying home. That depends on how *Victor* carries out his version of the above calculations. Suppose Victor, who has a slightly different utility function, determines that for him going to the opera and staying home have the same expected value when the probability of Victoria's going to the opera is 81 percent. If he believes the probability of Victoria's going to the opera is in fact 85 percent, then he will go to the opera and Victoria and Victor will meet, but if Victor were to believe the probability of Victoria's going was lower, say 80 percent, Victoria would find herself at the opera alone.

Lack of Knowledge of Relevant Probabilities

Now let us turn to the case in which Victoria answers the question "What is the probability that Victor will go to the opera?" with "I have no idea." Imagine that she and Victor are new acquaintances and have little knowledge of each other's personal characteristics. She knows that there is some chance that Victor will go to the opera and some chance that he will decide to do something else, but she does not know, or even is able to make an educated guess about, what those probabilities are. We are often in Victoria's situation; interactions with strangers are a constant feature of people's lives. Many have emphasized the point. Recall the observation from security expert Bruce Schneier:

> Just today, a stranger came to my door claiming he was here to unclog a bathroom drain. I let him into my house without verifying his identity, and not only did he repair the drain, he also took off his shoes so he wouldn't track mud on my floors. When he was done, I gave him a piece of paper that asked my bank to give him some money. He accepted it without a second glance.[42]

How does Victoria decide what to do when she cannot assign any specific probability to whether Victor will go to the opera or stay home?

It may seem that Victoria's uncertainty makes the expected value calculations we used earlier irrelevant. But not quite. She knows a crucial fact: she should only go to the opera if the probability of Victor's going is above 76 percent. The usefulness of this bit of knowledge depends on what Victoria knows about the distribution of opera-attending probabilities across people like Victor. If she assumes a normal distribution centered about a 50–50 chance, she will assume that the probability of Victor's going to the opera is only 50 percent. On the other hand, she may know that the distribution is not normal, but, for example, is skewed significantly toward going to the opera, and she will act accordingly.

Even on our assumption of an idealized world of mathematically precise reasoning, coordination turns out to be problematic. Additional difficulties appear when we drop the idealization. In the best-case scenario in the unidealized reality, Victor and Victoria approximate what they do in the idealized world. They take their rough

42 Bruce Schneier, *Liars and Outliers: Enabling the Trust That Society Needs to Thrive* (John Wiley and Sons, 2012), 1.

estimates of probability and combine them with a (typically nonquantitative) understanding of how much they value the various options to make the best compromise they can between how much they value the options and the likelihood of realizing what they value by the actions open to them. That is what they will do in the best case. Things need not go so smoothly. People tend to be rather poor at estimating probabilities, and may have no clue about the answer to questions such as "What is the probability of opera attendance for people like Victor in situations like this?"[43] In addition, it may be difficult for people to figure out how much they value the various options. Think of asking "What do you most want?" of yourself, or your friends, children, or spouse. It can be difficult to pin down the answer. The relative values we assign to options for action can be indeterminate and resist taking determinate shape. In addition, in our idealized version of Victoria and Victor, we represented them as reasoning explicitly about what do to. People only occasionally engage in detailed explicit reasoning about what to do – and, when they do, they often do so badly.[44]

When we dispense with common knowledge, we end up in a world where coordination is problematic. The point holds for the particular case of coordination under informational norms. In that case, we lose the coordination that creates the web of privacy in public and, along with it, diverse opportunities for self-realization.

Information Exchanges in Social Role Interactions

We can model many social role interactions involving the exchange of information as Assurance Games. The family holiday dinner illustrates the idea. To see it as an Assurance Game, we need to explain what counts as cooperating and defecting. To cooperate is to conform to conditions on information flow as a means to realizing the group-action goal of a harmonious dinner. To defect is to not conform. We attribute to the family members the following preferences in the following order:

1. Cooperate when enough others also do so. To see why this takes first place, consider that proper performance of the role of a family member requires that one thinks one ought to cooperate (i.e., conform to strictures on information flow in order to realize the group-action goal of a harmonious dinner), and that one dominantly prefers to do so. Notice that the dominant preference is necessary, because surely many family members *also* like to gossip.
2. Defect when enough others defect. This comes after the first choice and ahead of cooperating when others defect because, when enough others defect, there is no point in conforming to strictures on information flow to realize the group-action goal of a harmonious dinner. Unilateral action cannot realize that goal. Furthermore, we assume that there is something that family members get by

43 Daniel Kahneman, *Thinking, Fast and Slow* (Farrar, Straus and Giroux, 2013), 419–31.

44 See, for example, Kahneman, *Thinking, Fast and Slow*.

defecting, such as the pleasure of gossiping, that is more valuable to them than cooperating when others defect.

3. Defect when enough others cooperate. This ranks third because defecting in this case means not doing what family members think they ought to do, and dominantly prefer to do.
4. Cooperate when enough others defect. The rationale for this ranking parallels the rationale for ranking defect/defect in second place: namely, there is no point in conforming to strictures on information flow in order to realize the group-action goal of a harmonious dinner. The difference is that instead of defecting along with the rest, the family member pointlessly cooperates.

Consider George, a family member. Will he cooperate by conforming to the strictures, or will he defect by not doing so? That depends on how he values the options. For the moment, return to the idealized view we took of Victoria. Assume George is able to assign precise numerical values to rank how he values the options open to him, and assume he is able to reason accurately about expected values. For simplicity, suppose the values George assigns to these options mirror Victoria's in the opera example: cooperate/cooperate = 5; defect/defect = 3; defect/cooperate = 1; cooperate/defect = –10. George reaches a general conclusion similar to Victoria's: He should conform to the strictures on information flow as long as the probability of enough others doing so is 76 percent or greater. Can George know this?

Knowledge of Relevant Probabilities

He could know it from observation. George is in his sixties, and he knows from having attended a large number of family holiday dinners that the probability that enough will conform is 76 percent or higher. The consequences are the same as in the Victor/Victoria example. Even in the idealized world of mathematical precision and accurate reasoning, coordination may be difficult when different family members arrive at different answers to "At which probability do conforming and not conforming to the strictures on information flow have the same expected value for me?" This problem is compounded by the poor probability estimates and poor reasoning characteristic of the real world.

Lack of Knowledge of Relevant Probabilities

The "lack of knowledge of probabilities" cases add the additional problem of estimating probability distributions. To illustrate these cases, we return to investigative journalists. For the Assurance Game model of investigative journalists, to cooperate is to participate in the tradition of investigative journalism to realize the group-action goal of preserving journalism as a political watchdog. To defect is to not participate to realize that goal. We attribute to investigative journalists the following preferences in the following order. We omit the rationales for the ranking since they are essentially the same as in the family holiday dinner:

1. Cooperate when enough others also do.
2. Defect when enough others defect.
3. Defect when enough others cooperate.
4. Cooperate when enough others defect.

Assume Jacob values the options just as George and Victoria do: cooperate/cooperate = 5; defect/defect = 3; defect/cooperate = 1; cooperate/defect = – 10. Jacob reaches the conclusion that he should cooperate as long as the probability of enough others doing so is 76 percent or greater.

What Jacob does depends on what he knows about the distribution of cooperation (i.e., participating in the tradition of investigative journalism in order to realize the group-action goal of preserving journalism as a political watchdog) across the population of journalists. Compare George, who can repeatedly observe the family at holiday gatherings. Jacob will know some journalists, but directly observing the whole group is out of the question. He might be able to rely on authoritative reports about their behavior. One report, for example, notes that "When courts and public authorities ask journalists to hand over material or information that may reveal a source of information, most reporters will instinctively demur."[45] However, the report continues that "occasions arise when journalists come to a different ethical conclusion and their conscience compels them to co-operate with the authorities, as some did by giving evidence at the International Criminal Tribunal for the former Yugoslavia in The Hague."[46] There will be considerable variation in what others are likely to do since that depends on how they value the options, and that will vary considerably. Thus, it will be difficult for Jacob to arrive at a reasonable estimate of the probability distribution of cooperation across the population of journalists. This is true even in the fictional world of mathematical precision and accurate reasoning. The problem becomes even more severe in the real world, in which people are often poor at estimating probabilities.

NOT OUR WORLD

Jacob's difficulties are not our difficulties. As noted earlier, common-knowledge-mediated social role interactions with strangers are a constant feature of our lives. Dispense with common knowledge and we end up in a world where coordination is problematic. People – people one knows and complete strangers – are not transparent in the way common knowledge makes them. We argue in Chapters 6 through 8 that surveillance threatens to undermine common knowledge and drive us toward a world of reduced privacy in public, and we propose taking control of the process and directing it in ways that create and preserve privacy in public. Some may object

[45] Stephen J. A. Ward, "Why Hyping Transparency Distorts Journalism Ethics," *Mediashift* (blog), November 4, 2013, http://mediashift.org/2013/11/why-hyping-transparency-distorts-journalism-ethics/.

[46] Ward.

that there is a far simpler approach to ensuring adequate privacy in public: namely Notice and Choice, the dominant regulatory approach to ensuring adequate privacy. This does not rely on coordination norms and so does not need to defend those norms in the face of surveillance. We criticize and reject Notice and Choice in the next chapter.

APPENDIX: INFORMATIONAL PRIVACY AS A COMMON POOL RESOURCE

As noted in the main body of the chapter, Ostrom and her followers demonstrate the descriptive and explanatory power of coordination norms in contexts concerned with framing public policy. Their work investigates common pool resources. In this Appendix, we connect our discussion of informational norms with that body of work by showing that norm-created informational privacy is a common pool resource. A resource is a common pool resource (CPR) if it is nonexcludable and subtractive (also called rivalrous). A resource is nonexcludable if it is sufficiently difficult to keep others out of it. It is subtractive if one person's use leaves less for others. Fishing grounds are a standard example. It is difficult to keep people out, and catching fish leaves fewer fish for others. Fishing grounds are an example of a *natural resource* CPR. Nature creates the resource which people may (or may not) manage by coordinating their behavior in ways that preserve it. We briefly discus natural resource CPRs and then turn to norm-created informational privacy.

NATURAL RESOURCE COMMON POOL RESOURCES

We focus on two features of natural resource CPRs: the threat, and its solution. The threat is that the combination of nonexcludability and subtractiveness will lead to overuse that depletes the resource and thereby threatens people's long-term use of it. This is the well-known Tragedy of the Commons.[47] The solution is for users to conform to a coordination norm requiring limited use.

We begin with the threat. We continue with the example of fisheries. The combination of nonexcludability and subtractiveness leads to resource-depleting overfishing if the following conditions are fulfilled. *First, preference maximization*: each fisher will act in ways the fisher thinks will best satisfy his or her preferences. *Second, a self-interested preference order*: each fisher has the following preferences in the following order: (1) maximize one's own catch when most limit theirs; (2) limit one's own catch when most limit theirs; (3) maximize one's own catch when most maximize theirs;[48] (4) limit one's own catch when most maximize theirs. A person meeting these conditions will reason as follows: "One of two things will happen: most will maximize their catch, or most will not. If most do not maximize, then I should maximize. If most maximize their catch, then I should too. Either way I should maximize my catch." When everyone reasons this way, everyone maximizes his or her catch and the fishing stock collapses.

The result is a Tragedy of the Commons. The Tragedy is not inevitable. It requires preference maximization and the self-interested preference order. We grant preference maximization for the sake of argument and focus on the

47 The Tragedy of the Commons was first described in Garrett Hardin, "The Tragedy of the Commons," *Science* 162 (1968): 1243–48; Hardin's historical claims and public policy conclusions have drawn sharp criticism. See Ostrom, *Governing the Commons*.

48 The order of the preferences in (2) and (3) does not matter for our purposes.

requirement of self-interested preferences. People need not have such preferences. They can – and in many cases do – have resource-preserving ones instead.[49] Indeed, a "large number of field studies have found that local groups of resource users, sometimes by themselves and sometimes with the assistance of external actors, have managed to create viable institutional arrangements for coping with common-pool resource problems."[50]

Those cases avoid the Tragedy through conformity to a coordination norm. The Alanya, Turkey inshore fishery that we discussed in the main body of this chapter is a good example. Recall that the result was that fishers conformed to the rule: fish only in one's assigned area. That regularity was a coordination norm. Conformity to the norm ensured that resource-preserving preferences took precedence over self-interested ones.

Similar remarks hold for informational privacy – with one crucial difference. In the case of natural resources, coordination norms preserve an already existing resource; in the case of informational privacy, coordination norms *create* the resource.

To see informational privacy as a CPR, we begin with the fact that a common pool resource involves a *resource*. In the case of natural CPRs, the relevant resource is typically clear: fish in fisheries, water in irrigation systems, and so on. But what is the resource in the case of informational privacy? In general, a resource is a supply that people can use to meet certain needs. To see what the resource is in the case of norm-created informational privacy, we first identify the relevant needs, and then explain what the resource is by explaining how informational norms create a supply that people use to meet those needs.

NEED, SUPPLY, AND USE

The needs are the various goals informational privacy serves. The supply consists in the informational privacy created by group control over the flow of information created by conformity to informational norms. People *use* the resource to meet the needs. So, what is the relevant use? There are two: norm-conforming and non-norm-conforming.

The norm-conforming use consists in group members coordinating under the norm to ensure a selective flow of information both during and after their interaction. Like conformity under the Alanya fishing norm, this use draws on the resource, but unlike conformity to the Alanya norm, it does not subtract an item from the resource – quite the opposite: it creates and maintains the resource. Conformity creates one more instance of the regularity in behavior that is the norm, and thereby helps maintain the expectation that people will conform to the norm. The continued existence of the norm depends on the continued existence of that expectation.

49 Ostrom, *Governing the Commons*, 39. "At the most general level, the problem facing CPR appropriators is one of organizing: how to change the situation from one in which appropriators act independently to one in which they adopt coordinated strategies to obtain higher joint benefits or reduce their joint harm."

50 Ostrom, *Understanding Institutional Diversity*, 221.

Non-norm-conforming uses divide into two: uses by *parties to the norm*, and uses by those *not parties to the norm*. We begin with uses by parties. Imagine that, on a visit to his professor's office, freshman Roger confesses his constant, debilitating anxiety in class. The professor can violate the student/professor norm by identifying Roger by name and making fun of his plight while at lunch with her colleagues. Turning to non-parties, consider OpenTable, the online restaurant reservation service. OpenTable is not a party to the informational coordination norm governing interactions between restaurants and their customers. That would require a jointly desired goal around which OpenTable and consumers coordinate to ensure a selective flow of information. This is very unlikely. OpenTable exploits the norm-governed transactions to extract information about restaurant customers. It allows "sommeliers and maitre d's [to] use the system to easily catalog diners' habits and quirks, resulting in a vast database of customer information."[51] Businesses routinely reduce norm-created informational privacy in this way. Even though they are not parties to the relevant norms, they monitor a wide variety of norm-governed interactions to siphon off massive amounts of information.[52]

SUBTRACTIVENESS

Norm-created informational privacy is subtractive if one person's use leaves less for others. Norm-conforming uses do not meet this condition. Quite the opposite: they create and maintain informational privacy. The subtractive uses are the non-conforming ones. Subtractive uses are non-conforming in two ways.

First, non-norm-conforming uses prevent the creation of particular instances of informational privacy. Consider parties to the norm first. When the professor violates the student/professor norm by revealing Roger's anxiety, the norm-created control over the flow information on which Roger mistakenly relied does not in fact exist. The same is true for surveillance by non-parties. Business data collection reduces the parties' control over the information they exchange. OpenTable's extraction of information, for example, reduces informational privacy by reducing the norm-created control customers would otherwise have over the information they exchange with restaurants.

[51] Carla Spartos, "Is Your Restaurant Spying on You?," *New York Post*, December 22, 2010, http://nypost.com/2010/12/22/is-your-restaurant-spying-on-you/. Other data aggregation and analysis services for restaurants abound. See Stephanie Miles, "6 Tools Restaurants Can Use for Better Guest Intelligence," *StreetFight*, July 22, 2103, http://streetfightmag.com/2013/07/22/6-tools-restaurants-can-use-for-better-guest-intelligence/.

[52] The literature is vast. See, for example, David Lyon, *Surveillance after Snowden* (Polity, 2015), and Julia Angwin, *Dragnet Nation: A Quest for Privacy, Security, and Freedom in a World of Relentless Surveillance* (2014). We review various aspects of the literature in Robert H Sloan and Richard Warner, "The Self, the Stasi, and the NSA: Privacy, Knowledge, and Complicity in the Surveillance State," *Minnesota Journal of Law, Science, and Technology* 17 (2016): 347–408, and Richard Warner and Robert H Sloan, "I'll See: How Surveillance Undermines Privacy by Eroding Trust," *Santa Clara Computer and High Technology Law Journal* 32, 2 (2016): 221–67.

Second, non-norm-conforming uses undermine the norm itself. A coordination norm exists only if people conform to behavioral regularity because they expect enough others to also conform. Non-conforming uses do not support and can undermine that expectation. First consider non-conforming uses by parties to the norm. The professor's violation of the student/professor norm at lunch may have little or no undermining effect, but if enough instructors violate the norm, conformity to the norm will cease, and that means the norm itself will cease to exist. Non-conforming uses by non-parties can have a similar effect. Suppose the professor, for many years a party to the student/professor norm, faces rapidly increasing university monitoring of students and instructors using student information systems such as Jenzabar.[53] In response, she decides that a significant number of people will cease conforming to the norm and henceforth withhold or share information as they see fit. As a result, her preferences alter. She now prefers to withhold or share information in whatever ways she sees fit, and not in ways required by the norm. If enough people react this way, the decisions aggregate in a way that destroys the norm. Informational coordination norms exist only as long as enough people conform to them.

NONEXCLUDABILITY

Norm-created informational privacy consists of the possibilities for selective information flow created by conformity to informational norms. It is nonexcludable if it is difficult to prevent people from making use of those possibilities. That is indeed difficult. You can exploit norm-created information flows as long as you know the relevant norm, and that knowledge is often easy to obtain. The family holiday dinner norm may be known only to the family members, but other norms, such as the restaurant norm, are generally known, and others, like the student/professor norm, are easily learned through observation and inquiry.

CONCLUSION

The point of connecting Ostrom's work to our discussion of informational norms is to further the goal of maintaining and creating informational norms. Realizing that goal is particularly important at present. As Neil Richards and Johnathan King note, "we are now at a critical moment; big data uses today will be sticky and will settle both default norms and public notions of what is 'no big deal' regarding big data predictions for years to come."[54]

[53] "Jenzabar," http://jenzabar.com/. On the effect on students and teachers, see, for example, Emmeline Taylor, *Surveillance Schools: Security, Discipline and Control in Contemporary Education* (Palgrave Pivot, 2013), and Andrew Hope, "Seductions of Risk: Social Control, and Resistance to School Surveillance," in *Schools under Surveillance: Cultures of Control in Public Education*, ed. Torin Monahan and Rudolfo D. Torres (Rutgers University Press, 2010), 230–46.

[54] Neil M. Richards and Johnathan H. King, "Big Data Ethics," *Wake Forest L. Rev.* 49 (2014): 393.

5

Notice and Choice: The Allure and the Illusion

Privacy in public is a form of informational privacy. Informational privacy consists in the ability to control what others do with information. At a minimum, having sufficient control requires that you can give free and informed consent to how others process your information. How do you ensure free and informed consent across a sufficient range of cases? Our answer is that informational norms ensure that. That is not, however, the dominant legislative and regulatory answer, which is *Notice and Choice*.[1] The Notice is a presentation of the terms governing the use of information. The Choice is an action signifying acceptance or rejection of the terms. The European Union's General Data Protection Regulation adopts a Notice and Choice approach,[2] as does the Federal Trade Commission in the United States. Another noteworthy example is California's Consumer Protection Privacy Act.[3]

The allure of Notice and Choice is that it appears, with one elegant stroke, to solve two fundamental problems about informational privacy. First, advocates of Notice and Choice claim that as long as the Notice is sufficiently informative, and the choice is sufficiently free, Notice and Choice ensures that each individual gives, or withholds, free and informed consent. Second, advocates claim that the combined effect of individuals' giving or withholding consent creates a society-wide selective flow of information that creates an acceptable tradeoff between privacy and the processing of information. In contrast to the norm-based approach we propose, Notice and Choice appears to solve these problems without recourse to social norms. That appeals to those who see social norms as too contested and uncertain to serve as a basis for legal regulation. We do not find this to be a serious concern.

1 See Fred H. Cate, "The Limits of Notice and Choice," *IEEE Security & Privacy* 8, 2 (2010): 59–62.

2 See "Art. 7 GDPR – Conditions for Consent," *General Data Protection Regulation (GDPR)* (blog), https://gdpr-info.eu/art-7-gdpr/, and "Chapter 3 – Rights of the Data Subject," *General Data Protection Regulation (GDPR)* (blog), https://gdpr-info.eu/chapter-3/. The GDPR imposes additional requirements beyond the minimal requirements of Notice and Choice. See, for example, Gabriela Zahfir-Fortuna, "10 Reasons Why the GDPR Is the Opposite of a 'Notice and Consent' Type of Law," *Future of Privacy Forum*, September 13, 2019, https://fpf.org/2019/09/13/10-reasons-why-the-gdpr-is-the-opposite-of-a-notice-and-consent-type-of-law/. It still requires, and relies heavily on, Notice and Choice.

3 See "California Consumer Privacy Act of 2018," California Civil Code § 1798.100–1798.198 (2018).

The legal system successfully appeals to norms in many areas.[4] More worrisome is the fact that, as we argue in Chapters 6 through 8, norms are collapsing in some cases and do not exist in others. Free and informed consent cannot be based on norms that do not exist. Should we turn to Notice and Choice in such cases at least?

We do not think so. Despite its appeal, Notice and Choice fails to ensure free and informed consent. Our argument begins with the norm-based alternative. We explain how informational norms can ensure free and informed consent to information processing. We critique Notice and Choice against that background. While we will argue that it fails for a variety of reasons, the fundamental problem is that it envisions people giving or withholding consent without knowing what others are choosing and without any mechanism of coordinating with them. Informational norms are the collective action alternative. The failure of Notice and Choice confirms the importance of that alternative.

FREE AND INFORMED CONSENT THROUGH INFORMATIONAL NORMS

Let us return to the example from Chapter 3 of Victoria entering a wine store to buy wine sometime in the mid-twentieth century. Her transaction is governed by an informational norm which makes it common knowledge between Victoria and the store that each will conform to certain conditions on the exchange of information as a means to realizing the group-action goal of meeting customers' wine shopping needs as long as (enough) others also conform. The norm implements a tradeoff between informational privacy and information processing by creating a selective flow of information that makes some – but only some – information available to the wine store, and that also limits what the wine store may do with the information it does obtain. Norm-implemented tradeoffs may be acceptable or unacceptable, as we discuss in detail in Chapter 8, where we explain acceptability in terms of being consistent with one's values. We assume, for our purposes in this chapter, that the parties to the norm know that the tradeoff is acceptable. We show that it follows that Victoria's consent is informed and free.

Informed Consent

What information does Victoria need for her consent to be informed? She realizes the store processes information about her, so one thing she wants to know is whether the tradeoff between informational privacy and information processing is acceptable. She knows that it is acceptable since she knows that the store conforms to an informational norm (the customer/retailer norm discussed in Chapter 3), and she knows that the norm implements an acceptable tradeoff. Victoria's informational-

[4] See, for example, Orin S. Kerr, "Norms of Computer Trespass," *Columbia Law Review* 116 (2016): 1143–82.

norm-mediated knowledge that the tradeoff is acceptable is a special case of the general fact that one can know that the outcome of a process is acceptable without knowing the details of the process. One can, for example, know that both the process and the outcome of a confidential vote were acceptable without knowing the details of the process or the voting (who voted what way and why). All that is required is that one share procedural and substantive standards of acceptability with the voters, and that one knows that the voters adhered to those standards. In complex systems of social and political organization, that is often the most one knows about decisions that affect one's life.

One may object that norm-mediated-knowledge of acceptability does not provide one with any detailed information on what data the store collects, how it analyzes and uses it, and to whom it distributes it. Doesn't one need to know that to count as informed? There are three reasons why such information is not required. For concreteness, we return to Victoria in the wine store to explain these reasons. First, it is unnecessary. The point of supplying the information would be to allow Victoria to determine whether there was an acceptable tradeoff between informational privacy and information processing, but she *already* knows that there is. Second, spending the time and effort needed to evaluate the information would conflict with Victoria's other goals. She allots a relatively small amount of time to purchasing wine before she returns to pursuing her other goals. Devoting time to evaluating details about information processing would be inconsistent with her plan of an efficient wine purchase. Third, at least some of the information is likely to be incomprehensible to her. Like most consumers, she lacks the expertise to understand and evaluate technical presentations about the store's information-processing practices.

Free Consent

When Victoria visits the wine store, she conforms to an informational norm that requires her to exchange certain information with the store. Does she consent freely to that exchange? We first explain the relevant sense of free consent. Free consent "requires [1] a knowing understanding of what one is doing [2] in a context in which it is actually possible for one to do otherwise, and [3] an affirmative action in doing something, rather than a merely passive acquiescence in accepting something."[5] Examples illustrate the idea. We begin with the requirement that it be possible to do otherwise.

Possible to do otherwise. We explain the sense in which it must be possible to do otherwise, with recourse to examples. As you walk along the street, a strong wind blows you uncontrollably into another person. Since you could not do otherwise,

5 Margaret Jane Radin, "Humans, Computers, and Binding Commitment," *Indiana Law Journal* 75 (1999): 1126.

you do not bump into the other person freely. For another example, imagine Noah suffers from an elevator phobia. Thinking he can control his phobia, he got into an elevator to ride to the twentieth floor, but when the door opens for others to get out at the eleventh floor, his phobia overcomes him and he bolts out. He does not exit the elevator freely. On the contrary, he cannot help himself.

Knowing understanding. The contract law case of *Henningsen* v. *Bloomfield Motors*[6] illustrates a lack of knowing understanding. A couple bought a new car. After 468 miles, the steering broke and Mrs. Henningsen was injured as a result. When the Henningsens sued, the seller pointed out that contract the Henningsens signed contained a clause waiving any liability for the seller for injuries as a result of defects in the car. The court rejected the seller's claim partly on the ground that the Henningsens did not enter the contract in an appropriately free manner. The seller presented the Henningsens with a "take it or leave it" standard form contract which contained the waiver of liability on the back in small print. The Henningsens were unaware of the clause, did not read it, and, even if they had, they would not have understood the legalese in which it was written. No one called their attention to it or explained it to them. The lack of that information, in the eyes of the court, means that their decision to enter the contract was not meaningfully free. The lack of a knowing understanding of what they were doing significantly limited their ability to guide their actions in light of their plans, projects, and values.

Passive acquiescence. A classic example of passive acquiescence is the thief who puts a gun to your head and demands, "Your money or your life!" When you hand over your money, you could do otherwise. You could keep your money and be shot. You also have a knowing understanding of what you are doing. You are handing over the money to avoid being shot. But if anything is a case of passive acquiescence, handing over the money is.

When Victoria visits the wine store, does she freely consent to the exchange of information? She can do otherwise. She is not, let us suppose, under the control of any external or internal force that compels her to buy wine. She also has a knowing understanding of what she is doing. She knows she is purchasing wine and, in the process, exchanging information in ways that implement an acceptable tradeoff between privacy and information processing. The only problem is that her exchange of information in conformity to the norm may look like passive acquiescence.

There is no thief with a gun to her head. In the store, Victoria nonetheless faces a highly constrained choice: exchange information in conformity to the norm or try to avoid that exchange. Avoiding the exchange is unattractive. Victoria allots a relatively small amount of time to purchasing wine, and she does not want to come away empty handed before she returns to pursuing her other goals. She wants her transaction to be as pleasant and efficient as possible. That is also one reason why, even if we move ahead in time to the early 1990s when discount cards first

6 *Henningsen* v. *Bloomfield Motors*, 32 NJ 358 (Supreme Court of New Jersey 1960).

became popular, Victoria probably would not limit data collection by refraining from using the store discount card. If she does not produce the card, the checkout clerk will ask her "You have one of our cards, don't you?" She doesn't like to lie and she does want the discount, so she will hand over the card after having pointlessly tried to avoid doing so. Convenience also explains why she pays with a credit card even though it leaves an electronic trail.

Victoria rejects the unattractive option of trying to avoid the information exchange and conforms to the norm. Does her compliance with constraints make her choice a case of passive acquiescence? Some think so. The law professor Todd Rakoff, for example, contends (writing in 1983) that "The consumer's experience of modern commercial life is one not of freedom in the full sense posited by traditional contract law, but rather one of submission to organizational domination, leavened by the ability to choose the organization by which he will be dominated."[7] Even in 1983, and thus well before the Internet was anything more than a small, noncommercial research effort, the domination that concerns Rakoff consists in consumers' submission to transaction terms that, practically speaking, they cannot change.

It does not, however, follow that Victoria's exchange of information is an instance of passive acquiescence. The reason is that even highly constrained choices can in some cases still be free. We explain the possibility and then turn to the question of whether that possibility is realized in practice. To illustrate the possibility, imagine your dream vacation is to go to the Cayman Islands. Your budget makes the trip impossible unless you opt for an "all-inclusive" vacation package offering airfare, hotel, and food at a price you can afford. When you sit down to eat the food, your choice is highly constrained (your options being going hungry or spending money you cannot afford). However, eating the food is also consistent with your values. Indeed, you chose the all-inclusive package in order to take a vacation you value highly. Contrast the gun to the head example. The thief's interference is not consistent with the pursuit of your plans and projects. It is a profound and wholly unjustified interference with them and with what you value. This difference explains

7 Todd Rakoff, "Contracts of Adhesion: An Essay in Reconstruction," *Harvard Law Review* 96 (1983): 1230. In a similar vein, see David Slawson, "Mass Contracts: Lawful Fraud in California," *Southern California Law Review* 48 (1974): 1–55. Courts routinely note that consumers lack power in commercial transactions. The court in *Henningsen*, for example, remarks that

> The status of the automobile industry is unique. Manufacturers are few in number and strong in bargaining position. In the matter of warranties on the sale of their products, the Automotive Manufacturers Association has enabled them to present a united front [by all using the same contract with the same waiver of liability]. From the standpoint of the purchaser, there can be no arms' length negotiating on the subject. Because his capacity for bargaining is so grossly unequal, the inexorable conclusion which follows is that he is not permitted to bargain at all. He must take or leave the automobile on the warranty terms dictated by the maker. He cannot turn to a competitor for better security.

Henningsen v. *Bloomfield Motors*, 32 NJ 358, 403 (1960).

why you eat the food freely – doing so is a justified component of a freely chosen overall plan. This is a common pattern. You may, for example, have no practical option other than driving your children to day care. You have to work, there is no one to care for them at home, and so on. But driving them to day care is part of the pursuit of the freely adopted project of raising your children and as such it is not passive acquiescence but an affirmative action. In general, a constrained choice can be free even when one surrenders control to others provided it is part of a broader plan one is freely pursuing.

Victoria's wine store visit is similar. The norm-governed transaction gives her what she wants and needs – a time-saving way to pursue the plans and projects to which she is committed. She knows the store will process some range of personal information, and she wants an acceptable (consistent with her values) tradeoff between informational privacy and benefits of information processing. The norm-governed transaction gives a *ready-made* acceptable tradeoff so that she can carry out her transaction with a minimum of effort and attention to privacy tradeoffs. Thus, as in the day-care and Cayman Islands examples, her constrained choice is the choice that fits in with her other freely pursued plans and projects and is in this way an affirmative action in the pursuit of those plans.

For Victoria's wine store visit, we imagined a mid-twentieth-century consumer transaction in which information processing is consistent with her values. It is that consistency with her values that makes her constrained choice still a free one. Turn the clock ahead to the 2000s. Is pervasive surveillance consistent with consumers' values? The law professors Paul Schwartz and Daniel Solove think not. They contend that

> the "choice" presented [by businesses to consumers] is more of a Hobson's choice than a real one. Many companies present consumers with a take-it-or-leave-it choice that provides hardly any ability for consumers to bargain about their privacy preferences. If a consumer wants to buy a product, visit a website, subscribe to a magazine, use a service, and so on, the consumer can be forced either to surrender privacy or to go elsewhere. But when nearly all companies offer the same take-it-or-leave-it approach, consumers desiring to protect their privacy have nowhere to turn.[8]

We agree that consumers' choices are unfree if they have "nowhere to turn" – nowhere consistent with the value they place on privacy. We consider the clash between peoples' values and pervasive surveillance in Chapters 6 through 8. Our discussion so far provides sufficient background for the critique of Notice and Choice in this chapter.

8 Paul M. Schwartz and Daniel Solove, "Notice and Choice: Implications for Digital Marketing to Youth" (The Second NPLAN/BMSG Meeting on Digital Media and Marketing to Children, Berkeley, CA, 2009), 3, http://digitalads.org/documents/Schwartz_Solove_Notice_Choice_NPLAN_BMSG_memo .pdf.

THE FAILURE OF NOTICE AND CHOICE

Three questions make it clear that Notice and Choice fails as an approach to ensuring free and informed consent. Is consent informed? Is it free? Does Notice and Choice implement an acceptable tradeoff between privacy and information processing? Some may object that proponents of Notice and Choice rarely address the tradeoff problem.[9] However, as Paul Schwartz and Daniel Solove note, "The idea behind notice and choice can be summarized in this fashion: As long as a company provides notice of its privacy practices, and people have some kind of choice about whether to provide the data or not, then privacy is sufficiently protected."[10] Schwartz and Solove do not provide any gloss on what they regard as "sufficiently protected," but, on any view that recognizes the need to balance the value of privacy against the benefits of information processing, privacy is not protected in the right way if the overall tradeoff is unacceptable,[11] so we take proponents of Notice and Choice to be committed to the claim that the approach ensures an adequate tradeoff.

Is Consent Informed?

The Notice – the presentation of the terms governing the use of information – is the Notice and Choice mechanism for securing informed consent. Consent is informed for consumers in a transaction when they know that the tradeoff between informational privacy and information processing is acceptable. The question, then, is

9 For example, one of the Federal Trade Commission's earlier endorsements of Notice and Choice came in Federal Trade Commission, "Privacy Online: Fair Information Practices in the Electronic Marketplace," May 2000, www.ftc.gov/reports/privacy2000/privacy2000.pdf. Commissioner Swindle, in dissent, sharply criticized the report for its lack of attention to tradeoff questions:

> "The Privacy Report fails to pose and to answer basic questions that all regulators and lawmakers should consider before embarking on extensive regulation that could severely stifle the New Economy. Shockingly, there is absolutely no consideration of the costs and benefits of regulation; nor the effects on competition and consumer choice; nor the experience to date with government regulation of privacy; nor constitutional implications and concerns; nor how this vague and vast mandate will be enforced."

Orson Swindle, "Dissenting Statement of Commissioner Orson Swindle in Privacy Online: Fair Information Practices in the Electronic Marketplace a Report to Congress," May 2000, www.ftc.gov/reports/privacy2000/swindledissent.pdf. Today, the enthusiasm for the New Economy looks naïve, but the point about the lack of attention to tradeoff effects remains valid. See Fred Cate, "The Failure of Fair Information Practice Principles," in *Consumer Protection in the Age of the "Information Economy,"* ed. Jane Winn (Ashgate Publishing, 2006), 342–79.

10 Schwartz and Solove, "Notice and Choice," 1.

11 In his excellent book, *Privacy in Peril*, James Rule appears to endorse the claim that the combined effect of informed consent decisions yields an acceptable tradeoff. He recommends that in "the private sector [the following] precept should apply: no use of personal data for institutional surveillance without meaningful informed consent from the individual": James B. Rule, *Privacy in Peril: How We Are Sacrificing a Fundamental Right in Exchange for Security and Convenience* (Oxford University Press, 2007), 196. Rule notes that this precept would alter the existing tradeoff between privacy and a variety of competing concerns, and he endorses the change.

whether Notices convey sufficient information for consumers to know whether tradeoffs are acceptable. One objection to Notice and Choice is that a wide range of consumer contracting occurs in the complete absence of Notices. Victoria's wine store visit is a case in point. In other cases, such as the offline purchase of consumer goods, a Notice exists in the form of a contract for sale, but it is packaged with the good and consumers do not have the opportunity to see it until they purchase the good and open the package.[12] We will put these issues aside and focus on online transactions in which Notices consist of privacy policies and terms of use agreements accessible via hyperlinks.

There are three problems.

First, people do not read Notices.[13] Unread Notices cannot create actual knowledge that a tradeoff is acceptable. Some may object that contract law regards people as informed even if they do not read contracts. The doctrine of the duty to read deems a party to know the terms of the agreement even if he or she did not read it, as long as a party has an adequate opportunity to read and understand the agreement.[14] Why not handle the fact that people do not read Notices in the same way? Why not treat consumers as having the knowledge they would have if they read Notices? To answer, imagine Roger does not read Amazon's Conditions of Use. Under the duty-to-read approach, one treats the hypothetical knowledge he would have if he had read them as sufficient for being informed. The hypothetical knowledge cannot guide his choice on Amazon. To the extent that the point of informing people is to provide knowledge that actually guides choices, the duty-to-read-inspired approach is unacceptable.[15]

Second, even if people tried to read Notices, they are too long and too numerous to read: "[W]hen PayPal's privacy notice is added to its other terms of use, the total word count is 36,275 words, longer than *Hamlet*, which totaled 30,066 words."[16] The number of documents compounds the problem. A 2008 study that considered only

[12] As the court notes in the important case of ProCD v. Zeidenberg, 86 F.3d 1447 (United States Court of Appeals, 7th Circuit 1996).

[13] See, for example, J. Howard Beales III and Timothy J. Muris, "Choice or Consequences: Protecting Privacy in Commercial Information," *University of Chicago Law Review* 75 (2008): 109–35. With regard to standard form contracts generally, "[t]he fact that consumers do not read standard form contracts is so well accepted and documented as to be virtually enshrined as dogma within the contracts literature": Wayne Barnes, "Toward a Fairer Model of Consumer Assent to Standard Form Contracts: In Defense of Restatement Subsection 211(3)," *Washington Law Review* 82 (2007): 237.

[14] The rule is sometimes formulated this way: "One having the capacity to understand a written document who reads it, or, without reading it or having it read to him, signs it, is bound by his signature": Joseph Perillo, *Corbin on Contracts*, vol. 7 (Mathew Bender, 2020), 402–3. When one looks at the exceptions to the doctrine as stated, it is clear that the actual rule is that one is bound if one has *adequate opportunity* to read and understand.

[15] See Margaret Jane Radin, *Boilerplate: The Fine Print, Vanishing Rights, and the Rule of Law* (Princeton University Press, 2013), chapter 5. She argues that only actual knowledge can fulfill the "knowing understanding" requirement, and she concludes that visitors' consent is not free on the ground that nonreading visitors have only hypothetical knowledge of the terms in Notices.

[16] Christopher Wolf, "A Practicing Privacy Lawyer's Perspective on Use Analysis as a Way to Measure and Mitigate Harm," *Colorado Technology Law Journal* 12, 2 (2014): 357.

privacy policies (not terms of use or terms of sale) notes that "[w]e estimate that reading privacy policies carries costs in time of approximately 201 hours a year, worth about $3,534 annually per American Internet user. Nationally, if Americans were to read online privacy policies word-for-word, we estimate the value of time lost as about $781 billion annually."[17] In 2020, the number of documents a consumer encounters is far greater than it was in 2008. Some have suggested shorter, easier to read Notices.[18]

However, simplifying Notices is problematic when it ignores the complexity inherent in contemporary information processing. If you make Notices simple by ignoring that complexity, you very likely fail to provide adequate information, and the inadequate or inaccurate descriptions may expose a business that uses such Notices to unwanted legal liability.[19]

Third, Notices do not contain all the information one needs. If one is (independently of informational norms) to evaluate information-processing practices to determine if they are acceptable, one needs to know what information businesses collect, how they use it, and where they distribute it. However, as Helen Nissenbaum notes, the "technical and institutional story is so complicated that probably only a handful of deep experts would be able to piece together a full account."[20] Nissenbaum concludes that "the complexity makes it not only difficult to convey what practices are followed and what constraints respected, but practically impossible."[21]

Given current business practices, Notices cannot contain sufficient information. Businesses collect information for one or more specific purposes and then retain it for use in a variety of unpredictable future ways. They also collect information without any specific current purpose. The reason for both practices is the same. Businesses may not know at present what information will be relevant for future business activities, cybersecurity purposes, and research. Research provides one well-known example. Microsoft allowed Dr. Russ Altman to analyze Bing searches for search terms correlated with dangerously high blood sugar levels. This was a key step in Altman's confirming that the antidepressant Paxil together with the anticholesterol drug Pravachol could result in diabetic blood sugar levels. Microsoft did not of course collect the search information for the purpose of investigating drug interactions – rather, Altman saw a use for information collected for other purposes.

Such practices make it impossible for Notices to contain detailed information about future uses of collected data. You can't put in a Notice what you do not know.

17 Aleecia M. Macdonald and Lorrie Faith Cranor, "The Cost of Reading Privacy Policies," *I/S: A Journal of Law and Policy for the Information Society*, 2008, 565.

18 See, for example, M. Ryan Calo, "Against Notice Skepticism in Privacy (and Elsewhere)," *Notre Dame Law Review* 87 (2012): 1027–72.

19 Cate, "The Limits of Notice and Choice."

20 Helen Nissenbaum, "A Contextual Approach to Privacy Online," *Dedalus* Fall (2011): 35.

21 Nissenbaum, 36.

Proponents of Notice and Choice typically respond to this problem by arguing for restrictions on data collection and use that greatly reduce both complexity and long-term data retention. The Federal Trade Commission, for example, insists that "companies should limit data collection to that which is consistent with the context of a particular transaction or the consumer's relationship with the business, or as required or specifically authorized by law."[22] The Commission also demands that companies "implement reasonable restrictions on the retention of data and should dispose of it once the data has outlived the legitimate purpose for which it was collected."[23] However, we think minimizing data collection is unwise and unrealistic. The Paxil/Pravachol example illustrates why "specific purpose and deletion" is unwise: maintaining large collections of data can lead to important discoveries. It is unrealistic because, as noted in Chapter 2, "information – rather than information technology – is the fundamental building material of the modern enterprise."[24] Insisting on "specific purpose and deletion" is akin to standing on the tracks trying to stop the speeding train. Actually, it is more futile than that: it is standing on the tracks after the train has already passed by.

Is Consent Free?

Suppose Roger purchases a book from Amazon. Amazon's Privacy Notice and Conditions of Use constitute the Notice, and Roger's visit and purchase are the Choice. Does the Notice and Choice approach ensure that his consent is free? We consider each of the requirements for a free choice.

Possible to do otherwise. Roger is under no compulsion to use Amazon. He could buy books from Barnes and Noble, or not buy at all.

Knowing understanding. Like most consumers, Roger does not read the Notice. Unread Notices provide mere hypothetical knowledge about information processing practices, and hypothetical knowledge is insufficient for knowing understanding. That requires actual knowledge that allows one to determine the extent to which a choice furthers one's plans, projects, and values.

Passive acquiescence. Is Roger's Amazon transaction "an affirmative action in doing something, rather than a merely passive acquiescence in accepting something"?[25] The question arises for the reason we noted earlier. The take-it-or-leave-it choice businesses present to consumers is a highly constrained choice. We argued that a constrained choice may still be free if it furthers one's plans and projects in a way consistent with one's values. Notice and Choice, however, ignores that point. It

22 Federal Trade Commission, "Protecting Consumer Privacy in an Era of Rapid Change," March 2012, 27, www.ftc.gov/opa/2012/03/privacyframework.shtm.

23 Federal Trade Commission, 28.

24 James W. Cortada, *Information and the Modern Corporation* (The MIT Press, 2011), x.

25 Radin, "Humans, Computers, and Binding Commitment": 1126.

simply assumes that people have a relatively unconstrained choice in a sufficiently competitive market.[26]

Does Notice and Choice Find an Acceptable Tradeoff?

Notice and Choice's approach to tradeoff issues may be one of its most appealing features. To see why, consider that, as John Rawls emphasizes,

> reasoned and uncoerced agreement are not to be expected ... Our individual and associative points of view, intellectual affinities and affective attachments, are too diverse ... to allow of lasting and reasoned agreement ... [The appropriate view of social organization] takes deep and unresolvable differences on matters of fundamental significance as a permanent condition of human life.[27]

Part of the appeal of Notice and Choice is the ease with which it implements a tradeoff in the face of "deep and unresolvable differences on matters of fundamental significance." The overall pattern of giving or withholding consent draws a line between consented to and unconsented to uses of information. It is a complex line varying with the vagaries of consent, but it is a line nonetheless, and, as such, it defines a complex and varying tradeoff between the benefits of processing information and the need to protect informational privacy.

Merely to define a tradeoff is of course not necessarily to define an *acceptable* one. An acceptable tradeoff has to adequately balance the benefits and risks to society as a whole. Do the individual consent decisions of Notice and Choice sum to precisely, or at least approximately, that balance? It may seem obvious that they do. Grant for the sake of argument that each person gives free and informed consent to the tradeoffs that are acceptable to that person. Then, why should not the overall result of all such decisions be an acceptable tradeoff for society as a whole? If so, there is no need to seek political agreement on what counts as an acceptable tradeoff – a daunting task given the widespread disagreement on the issue.

However, this is a case of decision-making where it is unlikely that the sum of individuals' decisions on tradeoffs will implement an *acceptable* tradeoff for society as a whole. We offer two examples: one fictional, one real. For the fictional example, imagine students at a small liberal arts college want to present a petition to the administration demanding that the university divest its holdings in a corporation the students see as a major contributor to climate change. Every student wants the petition to be presented with almost all the names of the student

[26] Notice and Choice "imagines the creation of perfect market conditions where consumers are suddenly negotiating over a range of uses for personal information": Marc Rotenberg, "Fair Information Practices and the Architecture of Privacy (What Larry Doesn't Get)," *Stanford Technology Law Review* 2001 (2001): 32.

[27] John Rawls, "Kantian Constructivism in Moral Theory," *The Journal of Philosophy* 77, 9 (1980): 534.

body, but each prefers not to sign as long as enough others do so. When individually asked to sign, each refuses. Thus, the combination of individual choices yields a result no one wants. The problem is not a lack of free consent. The students freely decide not to sign. Is the problem a lack of informed consent? Yes and no. The students have relevant information. They understand the petition and the need for enough signatures. The problem is that they fail to consider a key fact: that when asked individually, each student will refuse to sign, with the result that the petition bears no signatures.[28]

The real-life example illustrating that problem is the story of railway transportation to and from Ithaca, New York, sixty years ago – a story that prompted the economist Alfred E. Kahn to write his famous article *The Tyranny of Small Decisions: Market Failures, Imperfections, and the Limits of Economics*.[29] The last passenger train left Ithaca, New York, in 1961.[30] Faced with the decision to travel by car, bus, air, or train, so many choose car, bus, or air that the train service was no longer profitable, and the railroad ceased to offer it. Unfortunately, the train was the only reliable form of transportation in snowy winter weather and in summer peak traffic conditions when roads were crowded and airfares expensive. The lack of train service was unacceptable to most of those affected. As Kahn observes:

> Suppose each person in the cities served were to ask himself how much he would have been willing to pledge regularly over some time period, say annually, by purchase of prepaid tickets, to keep rail passenger service available to his community. As long as the amount that he would have declared (to himself) would have exceeded what he actually paid on the period – and my own introspective experiment shows that it would – then to that extent the disappearance of the passenger service was an incident of market failure.[31]

As in the petition example, the combined individual choices yielded an unwanted result.

Compare informational privacy. Individuals' distinct one-by-one decisions under Notice and Choice are all too likely in aggregate to further decrease informational privacy in society – that is, a society-wide decrease in privacy whereby society-as -a-whole trades too much privacy for too little overall societal gain from additional

28 In economic terms, the "no signatures" result is a negative externality – a cost of a decision that falls on third parties (in this case the student body as a whole) but not directly on the individual decision makers. The example shows that when significant negative externalities are present, summing individual decisions can lead to unacceptable results. For a discussion of externalities, see, for example, Charles E. Lindblom, *The Market System: What It Is, How It Works, and What to Make of It* (Yale University Press, 2002), 146–66 (discussing externalities as "spillovers"). It would be interesting to investigate the connections between negative externalities and collective action problems, the Tragedy of the Commons, and the tyranny of small decisions, but we will leave this for another time.

29 Alfred E. Kahn, "The Tyranny of Small Decisions: Market Failures, Imperfections, and The Limits of Economics," *Kyklos* 19, 1 (1966): 23–47.

30 "Ithaca, New York," *Wikipedia*, https://en.wikipedia.org/wiki/Ithaca%2C_New_York.

31 Kahn, "The Tyranny of Small Decisions," 25.

information processing. To see why, consider that an acceptable tradeoff has to balance society-wide long-term effects. The information required to adequately balance the benefits and risks concerns complex society-wide consequences unfolding over a long period of time. That information is not available to people making decisions about entering transactions, so they could not take the information into account even if they tried.

THE NEED FOR COLLECTIVE CONTROL

Twenty years of criticism confirm the claim that Notice and Choice is "the worst of all worlds: privacy protection is not enhanced, individuals and businesses pay the cost of bureaucratic laws."[32] So why do regulators and many commentators cling to Notice and Choice? An apt analogy is the old joke about the drunk and the streetlight:

> A policeman sees a drunk man searching for something under a streetlight and asks what the drunk has lost. He says he lost his keys and they both look under the streetlight. After a few minutes the policeman asks if he is sure he lost them here, and the drunk replies, no, that he lost them in the park. The policeman asks why he is searching here, and the drunk replies, "This is where the light is."[33]

Policy makers search under the streetlight of Notice and Choice even though free and informed consent is not there – and even though they *know* it is not there. Why don't they look in the "park"?

32 Cate, "The Failure of Fair Information Practice Principles," 342. An early critique is Paul Schwartz, "Internet Privacy and the State," *Connecticut Law Review* 32 (2000): 815–59 (Notice and Choice as implemented is inconsistent with the requirements of free choice). Other works include Radin, *Boilerplate*; Comments of The Center for Digital Democracy and US PIRG, "In the Matter of a Preliminary FTC Staff Report on Protecting Consumer Privacy in an Era of Rapid Change: A Proposed Framework For Businesses and Policymakers," February 18, 2011, 33, www.ftc.gov/reports/protecting-consumer-privacy-era-rapid-change-recommendations-businesses-policymakers ("Informed consent in the digital marketing era requires ... a new commitment to candor and honesty ... [the online marketing industry] needs to clearly explain to the user how the data are collected and used"); Helen Nissenbaum, "A Contextual Approach to Privacy Online," *Dedalus* 140, 4 (2011): 36 (noting "the *transparency paradox*. Achieving transparency means conveying information-handling practices in ways that are relevant and meaningful to the choices individuals must make. If notice ... finely details every flow, condition, qualification, and exception, we know that it is unlikely to be understood, let alone read. But summarizing practices in the style of, say, nutrition labels is no more helpful because it drains away important details, ones that are likely to make a difference," and arguing for a much greater reliance on context); Cate, "The Failure of Fair Information Principles," p. 344 (arguing that consumers "confront ... full-on barriers to achieving meaningful understanding of the practice and uses to which they are expected to be able to consent"); Schwartz and Solove, "Notice and Choice" (arguing that Notice and Choice fails to ensure a free choice and fails to ensure an informed choice); Rule, *Privacy in Peril* (arguing that privacy advocates pay insufficient attention to how to balance privacy versus competing concerns).

33 Adapted from David H. Freedman, *Wrong: Why Experts Keep Failing Us* (Little, Brown and Company, 2010).

The problem is not that the "park" does not exist. The "park" consists of informational norms. Turning to informational norms replaces the Notice and Choice approach of controlling the flow of information through a sequence of individual choices with control through collective action. How, then, should we respond to the onslaught of surveillance which undermines the power of informational norms to control the flow of information? Since Notice and Choice is not an option, we argue for preserving and creating norms. Chapters 6 through 9 consider the onslaught of surveillance and the prospects for preserving and creating norms.

6

The Threat of Collapse, The Prospects of Resistance

Pervasive surveillance undermines self-realization. The warning comes from multiple quarters: from privacy advocates, technologists, psychologists, philosophers, sociologists, legal scholars, and novelists. Historical analogies reveal the seriousness of the threat. Suppose you want to resist. How do you do that? How do you combat something that works largely behind the scenes to invade privacy? We first clarify the threat by explaining how surveillance can undermine the common knowledge on which coordination under informational norms depends. We then answer the question of how to resist with four examples.

We focus on post-1980s surveillance. Surveillance was of course a concern well before the 1980s. The loss of informational privacy from credit reporting is one of Vance Packard's concerns in his 1964 book *The Naked Society*. He worries that a "quite different kind of electronic surveillance – and control – has become possible through the development of the giant memory machines. Each month more and more information about individual citizens is being stored away in some gigantic memory machine."[1] Further, 1973 was the date of the groundbreaking Health Education and Welfare report that expressed considerable concern about computerized surveillance and formulated the Fair Information Practices Principles as an antidote.[2] Commentators and policy makers expressed concern about surveillance, but the general public was more sanguine: "Even fear-baiting accounts of credit bureau espionage in several best-selling books – Hillel Black's *Buy Now, Pay Later* (1961), Myron Brenton's *The Privacy Invaders* (1964), and Vance Packard's *The Naked Society* (1964) – failed to raise concern. *Buy Now, Pay Later* included an entire chapter devoted to credit bureaus under the nefarious title 'Big Brothers' Big Brother."[3] Two

1 Vance Packard, *The Naked Society*, Revised (Ig Publishing, 2014), 68.

2 US Department of Health, Education, and Welfare, "Records, Computers, and the Rights of Citizens, Report of the Secretary's Advisory Committee on Automated Personal Data Systems," July 1973, http://aspe.hhs.gov/datacncl/1973privacy/tocprefacemembers.htm. The practices were later refined and expressed as Notice and Choice in "Personal Privacy in an Information Society; The Report of the Privacy Protection Study Commission," July 1977, https://epic.org/privacy/ppsc1977report/.

3 Josh Lauer, *Creditworthy: A History of Consumer Surveillance and Financial Identity in America* (Columbia University Press, 2017), 215.

important differences between recent years and the 1980s and earlier are the dramatic increase in surveillance power (as illustrated by the eventual rise of AI-driven surveillance) and the spread of concern about surveillance from commentators and policy makers to the general public. According to a recent Pew study, for example, 81 percent of US adults see the costs of surveillance as greater than its benefits.[4] Relying on such studies, we take it for granted that a significant number of people see surveillance as objectionable, at least to some extent and in some ways.[5]

THE THREAT OF COLLAPSE

Pervasive surveillance attacks coordination under informational norms at a vulnerable point: its reliance on common knowledge. Common knowledge consists in people knowing_1, knowing_2 they know_1, knowing_3 they know_2 they know_1, and so on. Pervasive surveillance attacks the very first "know_1" step. When the knowledge_1 foundation disappears, common knowledge collapses, and so does common-knowledge-facilitated coordination. All that remains are the impoverished possibilities discussed at the end of the preceding chapter. To see the precise point of attack, we restate the definition of a coordination norm filled out specifically for informational norms.

Recall from Chapter 4 that a behavioral regularity of exchanging information in a group is an *informational norm* when (and only when) it is common knowledge among the members of the group that, with regard to a group-action goal G:

1. As proper performance of the relevant role requires,
    a. each thinks he or she ought to conform to role-required conditions on the exchange of information as a means to realizing G as long as enough others also do so;

[4] Pew Research Center et al., "Americans and Privacy: Concerned, Confused and Feeling Lack of Control over Their Personal Information," November 15, 2019, www.pewresearch.org/internet/2019/11/15/americans-and-privacy-concerned-confused-and-feeling-lack-of-control-over-their-personal-information/.

[5] Another typical study found that 89% of consumers had either a "high concern" (53.7%) or a "medium concern" (35.5%) about "general privacy": Alessandro Acquisti and Jens Grossklags, "Privacy and Rationality in Individual Decision Making," *IEEE Security & Privacy* 3, 1 (February 2005): 26–33, https://doi.org/10.1109/MSP.2005.22. While a large number of studies show that consumers are concerned about losing control over personal information, "a number of … recent surveys, anecdotic evidence, and experiments … have … shown that individuals are actually less concerned about privacy than what they claim to be: many are willing to provide very personal information, in exchange for small rewards": Alessandro Acquisti, "Privacy and Security of Personal Information," in *Economics of Information Security*, ed. J. Camp and R. Lewis, Advances in Information Security (Springer US, 2004), 179–86, 182. Submitting to surveillance for small rewards is consistent with objecting to surveillance, as we explain in Chapter 7 when discussing acquiescence.

   b. at appropriate times, each dominantly prefers to conform to role-required conditions on the exchange of information as a means to realizing G;

2. as a result of (1), this past behavioral regularity exists: enough of the parties have exchanged information as a means to realizing G;

3. as a result of (2), enough of the parties continue in the future to exchange information as a means to realizing G.

We explain how surveillance undermines common knowledge in two steps. We first note that if parties to the norm object strongly enough to surveillance, they will think they *ought not to* exchange information in order to realize the relevant group-action goal. Then, we explain how "thinking one ought not to" leads to the collapse of common knowledge.

Reacting to Surveillance by "Thinking One Ought Not To"

Faced with pervasive surveillance, parties to an informational norm may react by thinking they *ought not to* exchange information in order to realize the relevant group-action goal. This falsifies the first requirement for the existence of an informational norm, which is that one thinks one ought to exchange information as a means to realizing the group-action goal. This is a key claim that underlies much of the discussion in this chapter and the next two. An analogy shows why it is true. Imagine that when Alice, Bob, and Carol discover they have tickets for the same concert, they plan to meet at the intermission. When they discuss how to realize the group-action goal of meeting, Carol says "Leave it to me. I will find you all." She does not tell them about the means she plans to use, which is to use a bullhorn to call out their names. She also plans to post a video of herself using the bullhorn on social media in the hope that it will go viral. Alice and Bob are furious when they hear their names broadcast at intermission. They indignantly inform Carol that they would have thought they ought *not* to meet if it meant blaring out their names. The next day, when they see the video, their reaction is the same. As they tell Carol, "The bullhorn alone was bad enough, but the video really crosses the line. If we had realized that was your plan, we would definitely have thought we ought not to meet by means of the bullhorn announcement." Alice and Bob object to two things: using the bullhorn as means to realize the group-action goal of meeting, and using it as a means to create a social media video. And they do not just object. They object *strongly enough* that they think they ought not to meet rather than be complicit in Carol's choice of means.

Like Carol's use of the bullhorn, businesses and governments use surveillance both as a means to realizing group-action goals and as a means to a variety of other ends. We discuss a number of examples in the next chapter. One of those examples – health insurance – suffices as an illustration here. Providing health insurance requires calculating probabilities of morbidity and mortality. Private insurance companies must do so to set premiums, and governments providing health care must do so to set health care budgets. Calculating the probabilities requires collecting and analyzing information about morbidity and mortality. The following informational norm governs this information processing: Insurers and insureds conform to role-specific conditions on the exchange of information as a means to realizing the group-action goal of setting budgets and premiums (as long as enough others also conform). If those who have or seek health insurance object strongly enough, they may, like Alice and Bob, think they ought *not* to exchange information to realize the group-action goal associated with the norm. And, as we discuss later in the chapter, people do object – and strongly. The reason is that twenty-first-century health insurers collect massive amounts of information: so much that some warn of a "future in which everything you do – the things you buy, the food you eat, the time you spend watching TV – may help determine how much you pay for health insurance."[6] Insurers describe their information gathering as a means to realizing the group-action goal of collecting information to set premiums to meet people's true health insurance needs and also to detect fraud. Commentators point out that insurers also use the information for other means as well – in particular, for maximizing profit, perhaps even at the expense of adequate healthcare.

But doesn't the health insurance example already show that we are wrong? After all, it can be a disaster not to have adequate health insurance in a system in which that is the primary way to pay for healthcare, and obtaining insurance means exchanging information, so surely most people will think they ought to do so. We don't disagree. Our point is that, if people object strongly enough to health insurance surveillance, they may not think they ought to exchange information as means *to realizing the group-action goal*. Compare Alice and Bob. When they hear Carol on the bullhorn, they might think that they should meet with Carol as quickly as possible, but *only* to prevent a second blaring out of their names, and, given the use of the bullhorn, they do *not* think ought to meet *to realize the group-action goal of meeting*. Similarly, parties to informational norms may think they ought to exchange information for various reasons even when they also think that they ought not to do so to realize the group-action goal. For instance, contemporary Americans may often think that they must exchange health data with their health insurer in order to preserve their coverage, even though they do not share any relevant group-action goal with their insurer. We will call such cases instances of *acquiescence* to surveillance. We discuss them primarily in the next chapter.

This chapter focuses on *resistance* to surveillance. Two conditions characterize resisters to exchanges of information under an informational norm. First, they think they ought *not* to exchange information as a means to realizing the relevant group-action goal. Second, they try to prevent surveillance. For clarity, we

6 Marshall Allen, "Health Insurers Are Vacuuming Up Details about You – And It Could Raise Your Rates," ProPublica, July 17, 2018, www.propublica.org/article/health-insurers-are-vacuuming-up-details-about-you-and-it-could-raise-your-rates.

TABLE 6.1 *Initial characterization of "before," resisting, acquiescing, and accepting*

	Ought thought	Reaction to Surveillance
c. 1950–1980 "before surveillance"	Ought to	Surveillance not a serious concern
Resisters	Ought not to	Try to prevent
Acquiescers	Ought not to	Do not try to prevent
Acceptors	Ought to	Accept

emphasize the contrast with acquiescers. As we will discuss in Chapter 7, acquiescers also think they ought *not* to exchange information as a means to realizing the relevant group-action goal, but they do not try to prevent surveillance even though they object to it. We also distinguish a third group, which we discuss in Chapter 8: acceptors. Acceptors think they *ought to* exchange information as a means to realizing the relevant group-action goal, and they do not object to surveillance. They accept it. Table 6.1 summarizes the possibilities. We include "circa 1950–1980 'before surveillance'" for comparison. We take it for granted, as discussed in Chapters 3 and 4, that, for the most part, people at that time thought they ought to conform to norm-imposed conditions on information flows, and, for the general public (as distinct from commentators and policy makers), surveillance was not a serious concern.

We emphasize that our categories are matters of degree. Resistance fades into acquiescence, which in turn fades into acceptance. In what follows, we refer simply to "resisters," "acquiescers," and "acceptors." The "matter of degree" qualification should always be understood.

The Collapse of Common Knowledge

To see how resistance collapses common knowledge, first notice that there are two ways to fail to know something. One is for what one thinks one knows to be false. Suppose, for example, Alice is talking to Bob about her recent job interview. She says "They asked some odd questions. One was, 'Who is the current world chess champion?' I was sure that I knew the answer, and I immediately said, 'Viswanathan Anand.' It turns out I didn't know. Carlsen is the current champion." The other way is to lack adequate reason for what you claim to know. Imagine Alice says, "Next, they asked me if 6 is a perfect number. It is, and that is what I answered." A surprised Bob responds, "A perfect number is a positive whole number equal to the sum of its positive divisors other than itself. How did you know that?" Alice answers, "I didn't. I had no idea. I just guessed."

Now consider a group of resisters. For simplicity, suppose it's a group of only two, Alice and Bob, who have resisted surveillance for the last two years, and who will continue to do so in the future. Consider an informational norm – like the customer/retailer norm where customers are subject to surveillance. Will Alice and Bob commonly know that they conform to the conditions (1)–(3) which define that norm? No, because, as we will now show, Alice and Bob cannot know *any* of the three conditions for the existence of an informational norm. They cannot know condition (1) because it is false. They do *not* think they ought to conform to the conditions on the exchange of information. They think they ought not to exchange information at all, and since they think that, it follows that it is also false that they dominantly prefer to exchange information. Alice and Bob cannot know condition (2) because they have *not* been regularly exchanging information to realize G. They haven't done so for two years. Alice and Bob may, however, know that condition (2) holds for others who are not resisters. Alice and Bob do not know condition (3) because they lack adequate reason to think it true. Parties who know they have exchanged information to realize G in the past reason that they will continue to do so in the future. But Alice and Bob know they have *not* exchanged information in the past to realize G. Thus, knowledge – and hence common knowledge – of all three conditions collapses.

Discoordination

When common knowledge disappears, discoordination replaces the cooperation that creates selective flows of information. Privacy in public declines as a result. We offer two examples: one hypothetical, one actual.

The hypothetical example is Mason's visit to the Italian trattoria. In Chapter 3, we described a mid-twentieth-century visit. Turn the clock ahead to today. Imagine that one week Mason dines at the trattoria on Monday and on Thursday. Between Monday and Thursday, he discovers that the restaurant compiles and analyzes dossiers about customers from information it obtains from OpenTable and other sources (such as the customers themselves). He objects to such information processing and reacts by thinking he ought *not* to exchange information with the restaurant as a means to realizing the group-action goal of meeting customers' needs. When he visits the restaurant on Thursday, it is no longer common knowledge between him and the restaurant that they will both exchange information in ways that realize the group-action goal of meeting customers' needs.

The restaurant may not realize this and may unsuccessfully attempt to coordinate information exchanges on the assumption that relevant common knowledge exists, and, of course, even if the restaurant does realize common knowledge no longer exists, it may still try to obtain information from Mason. However, since Mason is a resister, those attempts are unlikely to meet with success. He tries to prevent or evade surveillance. He makes his reservations by phone even though that is far less convenient than using OpenTable, and, when he calls, he does not use his normal cell phone. He uses a phone with a sim card from OneSimCard. The phone has a United States number, but dialing the number connects to a cell phone service in Estonia. He pays in cash to avoid creating a written record of the transaction. When the waiter says, "Good to see you again," he does not respond as he might in the mid-twentieth century with a few desultory pleasantries and a suggestion that the restaurant put the lamb shank back on the menu. Instead, he just says "Likewise" and conveys only the bare minimum information needed to order.

The restaurant example is hypothetical, and hypotheticals illustrate possibilities that may not be realized in practice. For that reason, we turn to an actual example of the loss of common knowledge: the initial communications between Edward Snowden and the journalist Glen Greenwald. For accuracy, we note that Snowden also contacted the documentary film maker Laura Poitras and the mainstream media journalist Barton Gellman. The communications with Poitras, Gellman, and Greenwald are interestingly different, but for our purposes, we focus on Greenwald. Snowden arrived in Hong Kong on May 20, 2013, with a trove of classified NSA documents. He had sent the documentary film maker Laura Poitras and the journalist Barton Gellman enough to convince them he was a genuine whistleblower. He needed to do the same with Greenwald, whom he had identified as a journalist willing to run risks to reveal government wrongdoing. "I liked him," Snowden remarks, "because he was skeptical and argumentative, the kind of man who'd fight with the devil, and when the devil wasn't around fight with himself."[7]

To see the undermining effect of surveillance, consider what would have happened without it. Greenwald would have presented himself to Snowden as an investigative journalist willing to run risks to expose government wrongdoing, *and* Snowden would have presented himself as a genuine whistleblower with authentic and accurate information by being "specific about what he had, or even who he was and where he worked."[8] Those role presentations would have made it common knowledge that Greenwald would reveal government wrongdoing while concealing Snowden's identity. Instead, Snowden reacted to the threat of government surveillance by thinking he ought not to exchange any sensitive information with Greenwald – not unless they could effectively prevent government surveillance. Snowden first contacted Glen Greenwald by email using the pseudonym Cincinnatus[9] and insisted that Greenwald use PGP encryption for further communication. Greenwald, in turn, thought he ought not to exchange information with

7 Snowden, *Permanent Record* (Macmillan, 2019), 250.

8 Glenn Greenwald, *No Place to Hide: Edward Snowden, the NSA, and the US Surveillance State* (Metropolitan Books, 2014), 10.

9 It was "a reference to Lucius Quinctius Cincinnatus, the Roman farmer who, in the fifth century BC, was appointed dictator of Rome to defend the city against attack. He is most remembered for what he did after vanquishing Rome's enemies: he immediately and voluntarily gave up political power and returned to farming life. Hailed as a 'model of civic virtue,' Cincinnatus has become a symbol of the use of political power in the public interest and the worth of limiting or even relinquishing individual power for the greater good." Greenwald, 7.

Snowden, and did not bother to respond. As Greenwald explains, "[we] found ourselves in a Catch-22. He was unwilling to tell me anything specific about what he had, or even who he was and where he worked, unless I installed encryption. But without the enticement of specifics, it was not a priority to respond to his request and take the time to install the program." He adds, "That is how close I came to blowing off one of the largest and most consequential national security leaks in US history."[10] Snowden and Greenwald did eventually create the common knowledge that Greenwald would protect his identity (at least for a while),[11] but that common knowledge arose from the role presentations *and* the measures they took to thwart surveillance. With those measures in place, Snowden's "ought not to exchange information" changed to an "ought to."

The example is not an isolated one. In the United States, government surveillance has increasingly targeted investigative journalists.[12] Such surveillance disrupts coordination between journalists and sources. As *New Yorker* reporter Jane Mayer observed, commenting on the Obama administration's aggressive stance against investigative journalists, "It's a huge impediment to reporting, and so chilling isn't quite strong enough, it's more like freezing the whole process into a standstill."[13] George Freeman, a former lawyer for *The New York Times*, notes that "reporters regularly worried to him that sources were growing more reluctant to share information."[14]

Some will rightly object that we cannot infer from the Greenwald/Snowden example that people *generally* will react to surveillance by thinking that they ought not to exchange information as required by informational norms (unless they can block surveillance). Investigative journalists are a special case (and Greenwald and Snowden a special case of that special case). Their profession makes them targets for government surveillance and exposes them to considerable risk. Compare people buying online. They are targets of private sector surveillance that processes information for business purposes, but they hardly face the threats of a journalist going to Hong Kong to participate in the publication of classified documents. Should we put aside as implausible the worry that surveillance will cause a wholesale disruption of coordination informational norms by systematically undermining common knowledge? That would be inadvisable. History attests that

10 Greenwald, 10.

11 Greenwald, chapter 2.

12 The Bush and Obama administrations' threats against and prosecutions of journalists were unprecedented, and that pattern continued under Trump. See Joel Simon, *The New Censorship: Inside the Global Battle for Media Freedom*, Reprint edition (Columbia University Press, 2019). See also "Leak Prosecutions under Trump Chill National Security Beat," *Committee to Protect Journalists* (blog), March 6, 2019, https://cpj.org/2019/03/leak-prosecutions-trump-national-security-beat/.

13 Molly Redden, "Is the 'Chilling Effect' Real?," *The New Republic*, May 15, 2013, www.newrepublic.com/article/113219/doj-seizure-ap-records-raises-question-chilling-effect-real.

14 Redden.

coordination under informational norms can collapse across the board.[15] The 1950–1990 East German Stasi is a case in point.[16] The Stasi is a convenient reference point that makes current surveillance practices stand out in sharp relief.

THE STASI AS A REFERENCE POINT

The "hidden, but for every citizen tangible omnipresence of the Stasi, damaged the very basic conditions for individual and societal creativity and development: Sense of one's self, Trust, Spontaneity."[17] The consequences we envision are less severe but still serious. The trust that surveillance undermines is the common knowledge on which coordination under informational norms depends. Undermining that undermines privacy in public, which in turn reduces opportunities for self-realization. The threat is indeed to "the very basic conditions for individual and societal creativity and development: Sense of one's self, Trust, Spontaneity." Four features characterized the Stasi's surveillance practices.

First, a massive capacity to know: The Stasi engaged in massive data collection and hence had the capacity to know a great deal about East German citizens: "What is remarkable about the Stasi is its penetration of the most ordinary, ostensibly non-threatening, areas of East Germany."[18] As a former Stasi agent put it, "There was nothing that we weren't interested in."[19] The Stasi "monitored 2,800 postal addresses; the agency steamed 90,000 letters a day."[20] It also used a large informant network: "[I]n 1989, there were precisely 91,015 full-time Stasi employees and 173,000 informants";[21] "This translates into roughly 1 in 50 East Germans working for the Stasi."[22]

Second, complicity: Informants "spied on friends, workmates, neighbours and family members. Husbands spied on wives."[23] Even if the people with whom you interacted were not Stasi informants, the 1 in 50 distribution of informants made it

15 See, for example, Orlando Figes, *Whisperers: Private Life in Stalin's Russia*, Reprint of 2007 edition (Penguin Books, 2008); Václav Havel and John Keane, *The Power of the Powerless: Citizens against the State in Central Eastern Europe* (Routledge, 1985); and Kai Strittmatter, *We Have Been Harmonized: Life in China's Surveillance State* (HarperLuxe, 2020).

16 Stasi is short for the German "Ministerium für Staatsicherheit"; in English, "Ministry for State Security."

17 Gary Bruce, *The Firm: The Inside Story of the Stasi* (Oxford University Press, 2012), 12.

18 Bruce, 11.

19 Bruce, 55.

20 Luke Harding, *The Snowden Files: The Inside Story of the World's Most Wanted Man* (Vintage, 2014), 254.

21 Bruce, *The Firm*, 10 (citing Friedrich-Ebert-Stiftung, "Im Visier der Geheimpolizei," 12). Bruce notes that "Piekert claims that monitoring in the GDR was not '100 percent blanket coverage, but it was extremely high,' and went on to say that if one considers the border controls, the Wall, and the Stasi, 'the GDR had a perverted approach to security'": Bruce, *The Firm*, 63.

22 Friedrich Ebert, "Im Visier der Geheimpolizei," 12. Available at http://library.fes.de/pdf-files/bueros/leipzig/05009toc.html.

23 Harding, *The Snowden Files*, 254.

likely that friends and acquaintances of your friends and acquaintances would be: "Relations between people were conditioned by the fact that one or the other of you could be one of them [the Stasi]. Everyone suspected everyone else and the mistrust this bred was the foundation of social existence."[24]

Third, pervasive repressive use: The Stasi translated its massive collection into pervasive repressive use of what it knew:

> At its heart, the Stasi was an organization that monitored society for those who … "thought differently." Stasi officers worked tirelessly to insure that a disruption to the socialist order – be it anti-state graffiti, the establishment of groups that did not conform to the SED's world-view, defections, or whatever form it might take – did not occur.[25]

As the novelist Anna Funder notes in her study of the Stasi, it "arrested, imprisoned and interrogated anyone it chose."[26] She adds that "[m]any of the punishments were simply for lack of belief, or even suspected lack of belief. Disloyalty was calibrated in the minutest of signs: the antenna turned to receive western television, the red flag not hung out on May Day."[27]

Fourth, curtailed self-realization: The massive capacity to know, complicity, and repressive use severely curtailed possibilities for self-realization. As Gary Bruce puts it in his study of the Stasi,

> One does not detect from East Germans' reflections on their past that they were gripped by a paralyzing fear, in the psychological sense of the word – although one interview subject did say she "was always afraid" – but rather a deep resignation that one was not the master of one's own destiny, that to run afoul of the Stasi, even unintentionally, was to sacrifice power over one's life and the life opportunities of family members.[28]

The contemporary United States outdoes the Stasi in terms of the amount it knows and, in a sense, even in the extent of complicity (and we believe the same is true of the UK and many European Union countries[29]). Everyone who communicates with others online participates in the transfer of information about those communications to businesses and governments. In that sense, complicity in surveillance greatly surpasses the Stasi's 1 in 50 informant ratio. Everyone online is an "informant." In this way, the United States has traveled down the road that leads to the Stasi. It differs – only, but critically – in being more restrained in its use of information to discourage and prevent behavior the government finds undesirable. This is less

24 Anna Funder, *Stasiland: Stories from behind the Berlin Wall* (Granta Books, 2011), 28.
25 Bruce, *The Firm*, 140.
26 Funder, *Stasiland*, 59.
27 Funder, 157.
28 Bruce, *The Firm*, 158.
29 See, for example, Kees Boersma et al., eds., *Histories of State Surveillance in Europe and Beyond* (Routledge, 2016).

reassuring than it may seem, however. There is a "tendency of surveillance systems to spread. It simply lies in the interests of both government and private surveillance operations to expand – to cover more people and more of the lives of the people they cover."[30]

The example of the Stasi makes a strong case for doing something *now* to ameliorate the effects of surveillance. Resistance is one option. But how do you resist? And, if you do, will your resistance help prevent the collapse of common knowledge? We begin with the first question.

MAKING SURVEILLANCE DIFFICULT

You can resist surveillance by making it difficult for people and organizations to acquire accurate information about you. The investigative journalist Julia Angwin did her best to resist surveillance for a year in this way, as she explains in her insightful book *Dragnet Nation: A Quest for Privacy, Security, and Freedom in a World of Relentless Surveillance*.[31] She shredded documents, used an RFID-shielded wallet, put tape over the camera on her laptop, used software to force secure https connections, connected to the Internet by Ethernet instead of wireless at home and carried a portable WI-FI hotspot when she traveled, used complex passwords generated at random, stopped searching on Google (using DuckDuckGo instead), installed privacy-protective software on her browser, created a false identity and got a credit card in that name, deleted her LinkedIn profile and quit Facebook, and used PGP to encrypt her emails.[32] She found her attempt to evade surveillance less than successful. "In the end," she writes,

> I felt that I had lost more than I gained in the opt-out process. I experienced a feeling of loss when I closed my accounts. I worried that I had shut off possible future job options. And I had reduced my "authenticity" – I was less verifiable in the personal data economy. And for all that loss, I had not even fully succeeded in opting out. My data were still on file with the worst actors – the ones who made it difficult for me to opt out. And even those who let me opt out didn't promise to delete my files, only to "suppress" them.[33]

She adds, "I didn't want to live in the world that I was building – a world of subterfuge and disinformation and covert actions. It was a world based on fear. It was a world devoid of trust. It was not a world that I wanted leave to my children."[34]

[30] James B. Rule, *Privacy in Peril: How We Are Sacrificing a Fundamental Right in Exchange for Security and Convenience* (Oxford University Press, 2007), 151.

[31] Julia Angwin, *Dragnet Nation: A Quest for Privacy, Security, and Freedom in a World of Relentless Surveillance* (Times Books, 2014).

[32] Angwin. Note that it is a felony to lie on a credit card application.

[33] Angwin, 166.

[34] Angwin, 212.

Angwin's efforts usefully illustrate the problems that can arise from attempts to resist surveillance. Avoiding surveillance does not, however, always require Angwin-like extreme measures. It can be as simple as getting lost in the crowd. Getting lost in the crowd helped Edward Snowden to elude US, Chinese, and perhaps other authorities in Hong Kong by shifting "between several homes ... [h]e was lost in a densely packed metropolis of seven million people."[35] Other traditional resistance strategies include secret meetings, talking in code, and encryption. However, if you want to resist surveillance across the board, Angwin's experience is a good illustration of what you would need to do.

Our question is whether, and to what extent, resistance will help preserve and restore the common knowledge that facilitates coordination under informational norms. There is one answer for the case in which the person or organization engaging in surveillance is also a party to the norm, and another for the case in which the surveilling entity is not a party to the norm.

CASES IN WHICH A PARTY TO THE INFORMATIONAL NORM CONDUCTS SURVEILLANCE

The restaurant norm is a convenient example. The norm is that customers and restaurants exchange information primarily in order to realize the group-action goal of meeting customers' restaurant needs. Proper performance requires exchanging information *with the restaurant*. Today, the restaurant, a party to the norm, typically has its customers under surveillance, partially via OpenTable, Tock, or another such service. Thus, customers cannot properly perform their role without providing information to the entity conducting the surveillance. The same point holds for any "party to the norm" cases where one party – typically a business, government, or other organization – engages in surveillance of the other parties.

How does one resist surveillance in such cases? One could try to continue sharing information with the entity conducting surveillance while preventing it from storing, analyzing, and distributing the information. But how many of us are capable of doing so? Few, if any. There is only one way to avoid surveillance: namely, not to share information. So, to return to the restaurant example, the question for a customer who wishes to avoid surveillance is "Given current levels of surveillance, should I continue to exchange information in order to realize the group-action goal of meeting customers' needs?" Two reactions to that question define resisters. First, they answer "no." They think they ought *not* to exchange information in order to realize the group-action goal of meeting customers' needs. Second, they attempt to prevent surveillance. This two-part characterization of resistance will be important later, in Chapter 7, where we

35 Harding, *The Snowden Files*, 215–16.

discuss acquiescence. Like resisters, those who acquiesce react to surveillance of activity governed by an informational norm by thinking they ought *not* to exchange information in order to realize the relevant group-action goal, but, unlike resisters, they do not try to evade surveillance. Our concern right now is with the two ways resisters have to avoid exchanging information. One is not to engage in the norm-governed activity – not go to restaurants, apply for jobs or health insurance, and so on. The other is to engage in the activity but refuse to exchange information as a properly performing party would and instead limit the information one exchanges as much as one can – like the reticent Mason in the trattoria.

To what extent will such resistance help preserve and restore the common knowledge that facilitates coordination under informational norms? At first sight, it looks like it does just the opposite. Resisters think they ought *not* to exchange information in order to realize the relevant group-action goal, and, as we noted earlier, common knowledge is not preserved when people think that. It would, however, be premature to conclude that resistance cannot preserve common knowledge. It could, if resistance were widespread enough. That is Angwin's vision. She hopes that "if enough people join me in refusing to consent to ubiquitous indiscriminate surveillance, we might also prompt a conversation that could unravel it."[36] If surveillance unraveled, the threat it poses to common knowledge would unravel along with it. Unfortunately, we think a mass transformative protest against surveillance is unlikely. Angwin's experience shows why: systematically escaping surveillance is extremely difficult and imposes costs that few will want to bear (recall Angwin's "I felt that I had lost more than I gained"). Moreover, resistance is not a viable option for those embedded in workplaces that have them under surveillance. Student Information Systems (SIS), such as Jenzabar[37] and Ellucian's Banner,[38] are good examples.[39]

Colleges, universities, and K–12 schools increasingly use such resources.[40] Jenzabar makes typical claims. It promises to "[t]urn complex data into strategic

36 Angwin, *Dragnet Nation*, 211.

37 "Jenzabar," http://jenzabar.com/.

38 "Ellucian Banner," Ellucian, www.ellucian.com/solutions/ellucian-banner.

39 SISs are typically used *in addition to* Learning Management Systems (LMS), such as Blackboard, Canvas, and Moodle, that will be familiar to most secondary and college students and professors.

40 For an overview, see Alan Rubel and Kyle M. L. Jones, "Student Privacy in Learning Analytics: An Information Ethics Perspective," *The Information Society* 32 (2016): 142–59, https://doi.org/10.1080/01972243.2016.1130502. K–12 schools use SIS, but they differ from the SIS used in higher learning:

> "A K-12 student information system (SIS) stores and tracks all student data that teachers and/or administrators need to manage their classroom or run their schools. Information such as grades and attendance records are tracked through these platforms. Many K-12 SISs give students access to the information that pertains to them. Parents also typically have access to a K-12 SIS, which is one component that differentiates these tools from a higher education SIS. Many K-12 student information systems have an SMS function that allows teachers and parents to communicate directly. This allows a teacher to keep that parent updated with their child's

insight with a portfolio of descriptive, diagnostic, and predictive analytics tools and capabilities."[41] It claims it allows a university to

> Identify, recruit, enroll, support, and retain your school's best-fit students through a single, end-to-end student information system. Jenzabar's web-based SIS integrates data from myriad sources to provide a 360-degree view of students, allowing higher education institutions to increase engagement, maximize retention, and remain focused on their mission: providing the best education experience to students.[42]

Surveillance is difficult for students to avoid when schools construct a "360-degree view" of them. The same is true for teachers. Some SIS systems track teachers' performance, and teachers participate in student surveillance by filing grade reports and (in some cases) narrative evaluations.

The surveillance violates the student/professor norm, which requires that university students, professors, and administrators limit the information they disclose in order to realize the group-action goal of impartial grading. Resistance is problematic, however. Not participating at all – the equivalent of a customer not going to a restaurant – is not an option for students who wish to complete their education and professors who wish to keep their jobs. Limiting the amount of information one provides is also not a viable option when one is required to provide the information.

SIS surveillance is just one instance of workplace surveillance, which has a long history. One early promotor was Winslow Taylor, who pioneered workplace surveillance in his influential 1911 book *The Principles of Scientific Management*. Taylor claimed "In the past man has been first; in the future the system must be first."[43] Computerization has led to a digital Taylorism. Christian Parenti offers a striking example:

> Winston [an intentionally Orwellian pseudonym] must log on to the computerized phone system at the Charles Schwab brokerage firm no later than seven minutes after eight lest a supervisor called a "team lead" harass her. Once her computer is up and running, a message appears announcing yesterday's "productivity scores" in the form of a list ranking, from best to worst, the performance of all thirty technicians at Schwab's tech-support call center. Arranged in clusters of low, see-over cubicles, the technicians work beneath a series of elevated LCD screens upon which are posted their names and minute-by-minute productivity scores.[44]

social and academic progress in the classroom. A K-12 SIS can typically integrate with a learning management system (LMS) and a classroom management tool."

See "Best K-12 Student Information Systems in 2020," G2, 12, www.g2.com/categories/k-12-student-information-systems (listing popular K–12 SISs).

41 "A Unified Cloud-Ready Higher Ed Platform – Jenzabar," Jenzabar, http://jenzabar.com/jenzabar-one.

42 "Cloud ERP and Student Information Systems for Higher Education," Jenzabar, http://jenzabar.com/products.

43 Frederick Taylor Winslow, *The Principles of Scientific Management* (Harper & Brothers, 1911), 6.

44 Christian Parenti, *The Soft Cage: Surveillance in America from Slavery to the War on Terror* (Basic Books, 2004), 131.

To summarize, when the party conducting surveillance is also a party to the norm, resistance can be difficult and impose significant costs, and is not a viable option for those embedded in workplaces that have them under surveillance. That makes it unlikely that enough will resist the "ubiquitous indiscriminate surveillance ... [to] prompt a conversation that could unravel it."[45] Resistance will not preserve common knowledge by ending the threat to it that surveillance poses.

CASES IN WHICH A NON-PARTY TO THE NORM CONDUCTS SURVEILLANCE

The investigative journalist norm is a good example of surveillance by an entity that is not a party to the norm. The norm is that journalists ensure a selective flow of information primarily to realize the group-action goal of revealing government wrongdoing while protecting the identity of their sources. Governments are not a party to the norm, but they do conduct surveillance of investigative journalists. Since the government is not a party to the norm, performance of the role of an investigative journalist does not require exchanging information with the entity conducting surveillance. That is the essential difference from the "surveilling entity also a party to the norm" cases. The difference means that a journalist can properly perform by creating the selective flow of information required by the norm while concealing the information from the government. The point holds for "surveilling entity not a party to the norm" cases generally: parties to the norm can properly perform by exchanging information with each other while concealing it from entities attempting to observe it.

Thus, there is a resistance option that does not exist in the "surveilling entity also a party to the norm" cases. You can resist by thinking you *ought to* create a selective flow of information to realize the relevant group-action goal while simultaneously preventing surveillance of that flow. Various options exist to prevent surveillance. They include secret meetings, microphone jammers, speaking in code, noisily running water while speaking softly, wearing masks to confuse facial recognition software, and encryption. Snowden and Greenwald illustrate the possibility. When Greenwald finally installed PGP encryption software, he and Snowden thought they ought to exchange information to realize the group-action goal of revealing government wrongdoing *and* protecting the identity of the source.

In Table 6.2, we refine the chart we gave in Table 6.1 in light of the new "ought thought/resistance" options. For completeness, the refinements include changes for acquiescence and acceptance as well. As we explain in Chapter 7, acquiescence is like resistance, except for acquiescing to some degree of surveillance. Acceptance, as we explain in Chapter 8, and as the name suggests, is accepting surveillance.

[45] Angwin, *Dragnet Nation*, 211.

TABLE 6.2 *Full characterization of "before," resistance, acquiescence, and acceptance*

	Entity conducting surveillance			
	Party to the norm		Not a party	
	Ought thought	Reaction to Surveillance	Ought thought	Reaction to Surveillance
c. 1950–1980 "before surveillance"	Ought to	Surveillance not a serious concern	Ought to	Surveillance not a serious concern
Resisters	Ought not to	Try to prevent	Ought to	Try to prevent
Acquiescers	Ought not to	Do not try to prevent	Ought to	Partially accept
Acceptors	Ought to	Accept	Ought not to	Accept

Investigative journalists are not an isolated example. Another illustration is government surveillance of privileged communications between lawyers and their clients. The attorney–client privilege gives clients the right to refuse to disclose and to prevent the disclosure of confidential communications between the client and the attorney.[46] The privilege is essential to ensuring a fair trial and hence to ensuring that one is presumed innocent until proven guilty. The informational norm is that lawyers and clients conform to conditions on their exchange as a means to realizing the group-action goal of maintaining the confidentiality of privileged communications. Government surveillance is inconsistent with that goal. Unfortunately, "Regulations enacted by the Bureau of Prisons after 9/11 opened the door to codifying the act of spying on lawyers – and in doing so violating the attorney–client privilege – when those lawyers represent controversial people and cases."[47] Those who resist the surveillance think they ought to conform to the norm-required conditions on information flow while preventing government surveillance. Attempts to conform to the norm while preventing surveillance were at the heart of Amnesty International's lawsuit against the National Security Agency, *Clapper* v. *Amnesty*.[48] On its website, Amnesty explains that it has "grown from seeking the release of political prisoners to upholding the whole spectrum of human rights … We speak out for anyone and everyone whose freedom and dignity are under threat."[49] Amnesty suspected that the NSA was intercepting their communications and thus in some cases compromising attorney–client privilege. It thought it ought

46 See "attorney–client privilege," *Black's Law Dictionary* (Bryan A. Garner, 10th ed. 2014).

47 Heidi Boghosian and Lewis Lapham, *Spying on Democracy: Government Surveillance, Corporate Power and Public Resistance* (City Lights Publishers, 2013), 164. They offer other examples as well.

48 568 U.S. 398 (2013). Technically, the issue was the constitutionality of Section 702 of the Foreign Intelligence Surveillance Act of 1978, 50 U.S.C. § 1881a (2006 ed., Supp. V).

49 "Who We Are," Amnesty International, www.amnesty.org/en/who-we-are/.

to conform to conditions on information flow that protect the confidentiality of client communications, and combatted government surveillance by filing the lawsuit.[50]

Our examples so far have been of government surveillance, but the widespread use of proxies in AI-driven surveillance means that "not a party to the norm" business surveillance is widespread. We begin our explanation with an analogy. Suppose, with professional ambitions for both, you play chess and sing opera.[51] Your opera coach hires your chess coach to keep and transmit detailed notes about your competitiveness. Your opera coach has you under surveillance – albeit indirectly through your chess coach. The indirect surveillance raises the question of whether you ought to continue exchanging information with your chess coach. If you decide you ought not, you could resist by limiting what you say, or by firing at least one of your coaches.

The use of proxies in AI-driven surveillance creates instances of indirect proxy surveillance, and that raises questions about whether those subject to the surveillance will resist. Recall the example of Sally's bankruptcy from Chapter 2. She declares bankruptcy after defaulting on a $50,000 credit card debt incurred by paying for lifesaving medical treatment for her eight-year-old daughter. We assumed that, postbankruptcy, Sally was a good credit risk, but that credit scoring systems predicted that she is a poor risk given her bankruptcy. Now add that her car insurance company, which uses her credit rating as a proxy for safe driving (as many insurance companies in fact do[52]), increases her premium.[53] Like the opera coach, the insurance company's surveillance is indirect. Retailers feed credit card usage information to credit agencies, which, for a fee, make it available to insurance companies. Such indirect surveillance is ubiquitous. Consider what Facebook says in its Privacy Policy: "We also receive information about your online and offline actions and purchases from third-party data providers who have the rights to provide us with your information."[54] Some of "your online and offline actions and purchases" will be governed by informational norms; others will be "no norm" cases. To

50 The Court decided against Amnesty partly on the ground that "it is speculative whether the Government will imminently target communications to which [Amnesty's staff] are parties." *Clapper* v. *Amnesty*, 411. The Supreme Court decided the case on February 26, 2013. Snowden's first revelations of NSA surveillance were published four months later, on June 6, 2013.

51 Vasily Smyslov, World Chess Champion from 1957 to 1958, was also a professional-standard opera singer.

52 "Special Report: Car Insurance Secrets: The Truth about Car Insurance," *Consumer Reports*, 2015, www.consumerreports.org/cro/car-insurance/auto-insurance-special-report/index.htm.

53 See, for example, Leslie Scism and Mark Maremont, "Insurers Test Data Profiles to Identify Risky Clients," *Wall Street Journal*, November 19, 2010, http://online.wsj.com/article/SB10001424052748704648604575620750998072986.html.

54 "Data Policy," Facebook, August 21, 2020, www.facebook.com/privacy/explanation. Google's Privacy Policy has a similar provision: "We may also collect information about you from trusted partners, including marketing partners who provide us with information about potential customers of our business services, and security partners who provide us with information to protect against abuse. We also receive information from advertisers to provide advertising and research services on their behalf":

the extent they are norm-governed, the transfer of information to Facebook is an instance of proxy surveillance. Facebook is far from an isolated example. Data aggregators make proxy surveillance common by aggregating information from diverse sources and then analyzing and distributing it.[55] The greater the use of AI-driven surveillance with its reliance on proxies, the greater the spread of proxy surveillance.

Are we overlooking a key point? Retailers (the points of initial data collection) and insurance companies operate under informational norms. Isn't that a significant difference from the coaches example? The insurance norm in particular allows auto insurers to collect information relevant to setting premiums, and that is what they do when collecting credit rating information.[56] That does not matter. The point is that the insurance company is not a party to the informational norm governing exchanges of information *between retailers and their customers*. In general, for there to be *a single* informational norm that governs the actions of consumers like Sally, retailers, *and* insurances companies, there would have to be a group-action goal they all share and which they coordinate their actions to realize. That is highly unlikely. Indirect "proxy surveillance" is highly controversial, as we discuss in Chapter 9, so it is unlikely parties share a group-action goal related to furthering proxy surveillance.[57]

"Privacy Policy," Google Privacy & Terms, September 30, 2020, https://policies.google.com/privacy?hl=en&fg=1#whycollect.

55 See, for example, "Factual | The Leader in Location Data," *Factual*, 2020, www.factual.com/. Despite its emphasis on location data, Factual also collects, analyzes, and distributes behavioral data. The discussion of behavioral advertising in Chapter 7 offers more examples.

56 On the arguable connection between safe driving and credit scores, see, for example, Linda L. Golden et al., "Empirical Evidence on the Use of Credit Scoring for Predicting Insurance Losses with Psycho-Social and Biochemical Explanations," *North American Actuarial Journal* 20, 3 (July 2, 2016): 233–51, https://doi.org/10.1080/10920277.2016.1209118.

57 Some may still object that there is an informational norm allowing car insurance companies access to third-party information. Insurance company access to driving records is a plausible example (similar remarks hold for credit checks). When you apply for car insurance, you consent to the insurance company having access to your driving record. See "How Do Auto Insurance Companies Check Driving Records?," *AutoInsurance.org*, www.autoinsurance.org/how-do-auto-insurance-companies-check-your-driving-record/. To begin with, we emphasize that your consent does not make the insurance company a party to the *customer/retailer norm*. The question is whether there is a different informational norm to which consumers, retailers, and insurance companies are all parties. That would require the existence of a group-action goal shared among the three groups where the parties coordinate to realize the use of retailer-collected credit card information to set premiums. If you did not *knowingly* consent, there is no reason to think this is true. If you did knowingly consent, it still does not follow that the requirement is fulfilled. That depends on *why* you consented. Did you consent because you thought new insurance might be unobtainable or your current insurance might be cancelled otherwise? Did you consent because you thought *your* premiums would be lower even though in general you object to such third-party surveillance? Your consenting need not signal sharing the relevant group-action goal.

In general, issues about whether one consented will not arise in most cases of proxy surveillance since one will not be aware that the surveillance is occurring.

Just as in the coaches' example, proxy surveillance raises the question of whether one ought to continue to exchange information. Consider Sally in a retail store. Conforming to the norm requires thinking she ought to conform to the conditions on the exchange of information as a means to realizing the group-action goal of meeting customers' retail needs. She realizes that information from her purchases will reach credit agencies and that insurers obtain information from them about her credit rating. Imagine she reacts by continuing to think she ought to conform to the conditions while trying to prevent indirect surveillance by, for example, using cash instead of credit cards. That is resistance.

Is Sally's "think ought to/prevent surveillance" reaction a common one to ubiquitous proxy surveillance? It may seem so. After all, people have a compelling reason to create the selective flows of information that facilitate self-realization. Unfortunately, the "think ought to/prevent surveillance" option is not always available in "not a party to the norm" proxy surveillance. It is available for Sally. She can stop using credit cards. It will, however, take seven (or more) years for negative information to be dropped from her credit report. In general, however, preventing proxy surveillance is extremely difficult. First, merely not using credit cards is becoming progressively more difficult in a world that has become increasingly reliant on online transactions (even before the COVID-19 pandemic). Second, defeating proxy surveillance online often requires strong cybersecurity measures, and people lack adequate knowledge of cybersecurity to defend themselves against surveillance.[58] The majority of United States adults "feel they have little or no control over how [businesses and governments] use their personal information."[59] Third, a sufficiently skilled and determined adversary will penetrate any defense a nonexpert can mount. The journalist Barton Gellman cannot prevent surveillance even though he takes every antisurveillance step he reasonably can. He notes that

> Richard Ledgett, who oversaw the NSA's media leaks task force and went on to become the agency's deputy director, told me matter-of-factly . . . to assume that my defenses were breached. "My take is, whatever you guys had was pretty immediately in the hands of any foreign intelligence service that wanted it," he said over lunch in suburban Maryland. "Whether it was Russians, Chinese, French, the Israelis, the Brits. Between you, Poitras, and Greenwald, pretty sure you guys can't stand up to a full-fledged nation-state attempt to exploit your IT. To include not just remote stuff, but hands on, sneak-into-your-house-at-night kind of stuff."[60]

58 See, for example, Aaron Smith, "What the Public Knows about Cybersecurity," *Pew Research Center: Internet, Science & Tech* (blog), March 22, 2017, www.pewresearch.org/internet/2017/03/22/what-the-public-knows-about-cybersecurity/, and "Consumers' Awareness, Behavior and Concerns around Cybersecurity," FirstData, 2019, www.firstdata.com/images/fd-facelift/images/FDC_Cybersecurity_and_Awareness_eBook.pdf.

59 Pew Research Center et al., "Americans and Privacy."

60 Barton Gellman, *Dark Mirror: Edward Snowden and the American Surveillance State* (Penguin Press, 2020), 214.

Where you cannot prevent surveillance, you have two alternatives in the "not a party to the norm" cases. The first is to avoid exchanging information altogether. For investigative journalists, that would mean opting for the unattractive alternative of ceasing to be investigative journalists – that is, ceasing to reveal government wrongdoing while protecting sources. For consumers, it would be choosing the wildly impractical option of, for example, avoiding retail purchases. The second option is acquiescence, which we turn to in the next chapter. It may at least be more appealing than avoiding exchanging information entirely. We conclude this chapter with a consideration of resistance where relevant information norms do not exist.

RESISTANCE WHERE RELEVANT NORMS DO NOT EXIST

Resisters react to surveillance of activities under an information norm with an "ought not to" thought in the "party to the norm" cases and an "ought to" thought in the "not a party to the norm" cases. In both, they attempt to prevent surveillance. Where applicable informational norms do not exist, one cannot think one ought not or ought to conform to norm-imposed requirements, but one can still resist by attempting to prevent surveillance. Resistance remains as problematic as it is where informational norms exist. People generally have a poor understanding of security issues, and, even if, like Gellman, one mounts a credible defense, a sufficiently skilled adversary can breach it. There is another downside to resistance in the "lack of norm" cases. Our basic policy recommendation is that we should maintain existing norms, and create them in the "lack of norm" cases. The rearguard action of preventing surveillance contributes little to the creation of informational norms.

The rapid evolution of digital devices and the Internet has created a wide range of novel relationships not governed by any relevant informational norms, so there is a pressing need to create needed informational norms. We address how to create norms in Chapters 8 and 9. We conclude this chapter by explaining in more detail why informational norms do not exist across a wide range of cases.

We begin with the example of Google. When you use Google's various services, it keeps track of the search terms you use, the videos you watch, the ads you click on, your location, device information, IP addresses, cookie data, emails, contacts, calendar entries, uploaded photos, your name, email address, birthday, gender, phone number and country.[61] Google's Terms of Service page notes that "We provide a broad range of

[61] "Online Data Privacy – Google Safety Center," Google Safety Center, https://safety.google/privacy/. Finding out what information Google collects takes some effort given its current presentation of its Privacy Policy. You need to go to https://myaccount.google.com/personal-info?utm_source=pp&hl=en_US&pli=1 to find the information in the laundry list in the text. You can decline to tell Google your gender and birthday at https://myaccount.google.com/personal-info?

services that are subject to these terms, including: apps and sites (like Search and Maps), platforms (like Google Play), integrated services (like Maps embedded in other companies' apps or sites), devices (like Google Home)."[62] It emphasizes that "Our services are designed to work together, making it easier for you to move from one activity to the next,"[63] and it explains that "We use the information we collect to customize our services for you, including providing recommendations, personalized content, and customized search results." The Privacy Policy clarifies that

> Depending on your settings, we may also show you personalized ads based on your interests ... We don't share information that personally identifies you with advertisers, such as your name or email, unless you ask us to. For example, if you see an ad for a nearby flower shop and select the "tap to call" button, we'll connect your call and may share your phone number with the flower shop.[64]

Is there an informational norm governing one's exchange of information with Google? That is highly unlikely. An informational norm exists only if it is common knowledge among the parties that they think they ought to create a specific type of selective flow of information as a means to realizing a group-action goal. The controversies surrounding Google's information processing practices show that there is no selective flow of information and group-action goal meeting that condition. One illustration of the controversies is a November 2020 lawsuit against Google. The complaint alleges that

> Defendant Google LLC ("Google") has a dirty little secret. It designed the Android operating system to collect vast amounts of information about users, which Google uses to generate billions in profit annually by selling targeted digital advertisements. There are privacy implications for an operating system specifically designed to surveil mobile device users in order to refine Google's targeted advertising business. But in the course of mobile surveillance, there is also an unlawful taking of Android users' property – namely, their cellular data. Google effectively forces these users to subsidize its surveillance by secretly programming Android devices to constantly transmit user information to Google in real time, thus appropriating the valuable

utm_source=pp&hl=en_US&pli=1. Of course, data analytics could reveal both, even if you do not disclose them, and Google may obtain the information from other sources. The Privacy Policy notes that "In some circumstances, Google also collects information about you from publicly accessible sources. For example, if your name appears in your local newspaper, Google's Search engine may index that article and display it to other people if they search for your name. We may also collect information about you from trusted partners, including marketing partners who provide us with information about potential customers of our business services, and security partners who provide us with information to protect against abuse. We also receive information from advertisers to provide advertising and research services on their behalf." See https://policies.google.com/privacy?hl=en-US#infocollect [details accurate as per webpage at October 21, 2020].

62 "Terms of Service," Google Privacy & Terms [March 31, 2020], https://policies.google.com/terms?hl=en&fg=1#toc-relationship.

63 "Terms of Service."

64 "Privacy Policy."

> cellular data users have purchased. Google does this, in large measure, for its own financial benefit, and without informing users or seeking their consent.[65]

We neither endorse nor reject the claims in the complaint. We offer them solely as an illustration of the controversies that surround Google.

Similar remarks hold for a wide range of cases. These are cases in which, as Shoshana Zuboff puts it, a business "claims human experience as free raw material for translation into behavioral data."[66] Zuboff continues: "Although some of these data are applied to product or service improvement, the rest are declared as a proprietary behavioral surplus, fed into advanced manufacturing processes known as 'machine intelligence,' and fabricated into prediction products that anticipate what you will do now, soon, and later."[67] As long as sufficient controversy surrounds the use of the "proprietary behavioral surplus," it is unlikely to be true that the business and its customers agree on a group-action goal that they achieve through restrictions on the flow of data. Plausible examples in addition to Google include (but are by no means limited to) Facebook, LinkedIn, Twitter, and Amazon.

RESISTANCE, ACQUIESCENCE, ACCEPTANCE

Resistance is problematic in both the "party to the norm" and the "not a party to the norm" cases. If you do not resist, what are your options? We consider acquiescence next, and acceptance in Chapter 8. We subsequently reject both options and argue for a third option in Chapter 9: transforming surveillance into an activity that respects privacy in public by constraining it through preserving and creating informational norms.

65 See *Taylor et al.* v. *Google LLC*, Case 5:20-cv-07956 (United States District Court, Northern District of California), Filed 11/12/20. For a summary, background, and a link to the complaint, see Thomas Claburn Francisco, "New Lawsuit: Why Do Android Phones Mysteriously Exchange 260MB a Month with Google via Cellular Data When They're Not Even in Use?," *The Register*, November 14, 2020, www.theregister.com/2020/11/14/google_android_data_allowance/. For a more extensive critique of Google's surveillance practices, see Yasha Levine, *Surveillance Valley: The Secret Military History of the Internet* (Icon Books Ltd, 2019).

66 Shoshana Zuboff, *The Age of Surveillance Capitalism: The Fight for a Human Future at the New Frontier of Power* (PublicAffairs, 2019), 8.

67 Zuboff, 8.

7

Acquiescence

What do ATMs, electronic tolls, logins to wireless networks, Bluetooth beacons, store discount cards, automatic ticketing machines, websites, and cell towers have in common? They are, in the words of the journalist and academic Christian Parenti, "registration kiosks … where we deposit personal information in exchange for services." Parenti sees the kiosks as "altars where we genuflect to authority, performing the quiet rituals of obedience by registering our locations in time and space."[1] But is "genuflect to authority" always the right description? It suggests obeisance – genuine deferential respect. There are other possibilities. Resistance is one. You could resist – even as you "genuflect." You could outwardly go through the motions as you inwardly bide your time on the lookout for opportunities for opposition. We devoted the preceding chapter to resistance. This chapter considers acquiescence. When acquiescers "genuflect," they are not biding their time, alert for opposition opportunities. They object, but they do not resist. Václav Havel – Czech writer, dissident, last President of Czechoslovakia, and first President of the Czech Republic – describes an illuminating example of acquiescence.

VÁCLAV HAVEL'S GREENGROCER

Havel's *The Power of the Powerless* examines attitudes and reactions of people living under totalitarian regimes. It includes the famous example of the greengrocer "who places in his window, among the onions and carrots, the slogan: 'Workers of the World, Unite!'"[2] The grocer does not display the sign out of the conviction that it would be good for workers to unite (even if he thinks it would be). The "poster was delivered … from the enterprise headquarters along with the onions and carrots. He put them all into the window simply because it has been done that

[1] Christian Parenti, *The Soft Cage: Surveillance in America from Slavery to the War on Terror* (Basic Books, 2004), 79.

[2] Václav Havel and John Keane, *The Power of the Powerless: Citizens against the State in Central Eastern Europe* (Routledge, 1985), 31.

way for years . . . If he were to refuse, there could be trouble."[3] The grocer has no illusions. He knows that the authorities have no interest in uniting the workers of the world, and he does not think he ought to put the sign in the window as means to realizing the group-action goal of uniting the workers. He thinks he ought to display the sign to avoid trouble. The grocer and those like him "live within a lie. They need not accept the lie. It is enough for them to have accepted their life with it and in it."[4]

Faced with the power of the state, the grocer acquiesced to the demands of life in Communist Czechoslovakia. Faced with the power of contemporary surveillance, how do people in twenty-first-century Western-style democracies acquiesce to surveillance of their informational norm-governed activities? That depends. As with resistance, there is one answer when the entity engaging in surveillance is also a party to the norm, and another when it is not.

ACQUIESCENCE IN "PARTY TO THE NORM" CASES

Acquiescence shares some features with resistance, and other features with Havel's greengrocer. Like resisters, acquiescers object strongly enough to surveillance that they think they ought not to exchange information *as a means to realize the relevant group-action goal.* However, they do not attempt to evade surveillance, and, indeed, they think they ought to exchange information, but *as a means to other goals.* Why do acquiescers think they ought to exchange information with the very party that has them under its persistent investigative gaze? The greengrocer points the way to the answer. He does not display the sign to support a movement to unite the workers of the world. He displays it to avoid trouble and get on with his life. Though the stakes are often lower for contemporary acquiescers than they were for citizens of Warsaw Pact states, acquiescers exchange information for the same reason.[5]

Table 7.1 shows the situation in terms of the chart introduced in the preceding chapter. Notice that the "ought not to" entry means "ought not to as a means to realize the relevant group-action goal."

We offer three examples of acquiescence when the entity conducting surveillance is a party to the norm. In each, acquiescers exchange information to get on with their lives.

[3] Havel and Keane, 27–28.

[4] Havel and Keane, 31.

[5] Providing an excellent example of acquiescence, one commentator notes that being "a new mom pushed her [wife Megan Smith, who was CTO of the United States under President Obama] from being a Never Amazoner to being a regular user of its home delivery services. 'I hate myself for this,' she said many times, like when the giant box of diapers arrived on our doorstep." Kara Swisher, "Opinion | Amazon Wants to Get Even Closer. Skintight," *The New York Times*, November 27, 2020, www.nytimes.com/2020/11/27/opinion/amazon-halo-surveillance.html.

TABLE 7.1 *Highlighting "party to the norm" acquiescence.*

	Entity conducting surveillance			
	Party to the norm		Not a party	
	Ought thought	Reaction to surveillance	Ought thought	Reaction to surveillance
c. 1950–1980 "before surveillance"	Ought to	Surveillance not a serious concern	Ought to	Surveillance not a serious concern
Resisters	Ought not to	Try to prevent	Ought to	Try to prevent
Acquiescers	**Ought not to**	**Do not try to prevent**	Ought to	Partially accept
Acceptors	Ought to	Accept	Ought not to	Accept

Restaurants

Restaurants increasingly have their customers under surveillance. The exhibitions at the National Restaurant Association's annual show reflect the trend. The exhibitions offer free food samples, celebrity chef demos, and paraphernalia – kitchen machinery, pots and pans, and the like. At the May 2019 show, however, you would have found none of that in Tech Pavilion, which was devoted primarily to resources for collecting and analyzing customer data.[6] Offerings ranged from means of collecting cell phone numbers (ostensibly to manage wait lists, but also for data analysis) to systems like Advanced Demand Forecasting offered by the hospitality management company Fourth:

> Advanced Demand Forecasting: Rather than simply cataloging historical data, Fourth's complete platform provides unrivaled advanced demand forecasting – using predictive algorithms and machine learning to factor in historical trends, weather and local events. By calculating a daily baseline forecast at 15-minute intervals by sales item, Fourth's demand forecasting capabilities enable customers to ensure they have the labor and the inventory to deliver a great guest experience – every time.[7]

Similarly, the restaurant reservation service OpenTable offers restaurants its GuestCenter Reporting Suite, which allows "sommeliers and maitre d's [to] use

[6] See David M. Perry, "The 'Internet of Restaurants' Is Coming for Your Info," *Pacific Standard*, July 25, 2017, https://psmag.com/economics/your-favorite-restaurants-are-surveilling-you (describing a similar setup in the 2017 show). The 2020 show was cancelled because of the pandemic. See also Whitney Filloon, "Why Restaurants Are Obsessively Collecting Customer Data," *Eater*, October 10, 2018, www.eater.com/2018/10/10/17957350/restaurants-data-mining-personal-information-privacy-loyalty-programs.

[7] "Fourth Launches End-to-End Restaurant and Hospitality HR, Benefits and Payroll Services in the US," *Fourth*, March 4, 2019, www.fourth.com/en-us/news/fourth-launches-end-end-restaurant-and-hospitality-hr-benefits-and-payroll-services-us.

the system to easily catalog diners' habits and quirks, resulting in a vast database of customer information."[8] Other data aggregation and analysis services for restaurants abound.[9]

Competitive pressures explain the embrace of data analytics. Even before the COVID-19 pandemic, restaurant profit margins were typically narrow, and competition could be intense. To increase net profit, restaurants need to increase sales volume, minimize costs, or sell more than just food and drink. Data analysis promises all three: greater volume from more effective marketing and more personalized customer service, reduced costs from better planning and management, and, possibly, an additional revenue source from the sale of data to third parties.[10]

Interactions between restaurants and customers illustrate a pattern that repeats in the other examples. The pattern has three parts:

(1) *Restaurants see surveillance as consistent with the norm.* The norm is that customers and restaurants exchange information as a means to realizing the group-action goal of meeting customers' restaurant needs. Restaurants present surveillance as a better way to meet that goal. They emphasize that data collection and analysis makes them better able to meet their customers' needs through better analysis of customer preferences[11] and through more efficient backend operations that allow them to devote more time to interacting with customers:[12] "For many restaurateurs, today's detailed dossiers are merely a modern spin on the old fashioned, high-touch service associated with legendary hosts such as Niccolini and Sirio Maccioni, who's been running Midtown's storied Le Cirque restaurant since 1974."[13] As one restaurateur put it,[14] "There's a fine line, but as long as you don't cross it, people just think you're good at your job." In a vision of the future, the National Restaurant Associations report *Restaurant Industry 2030* envisions restaurants that "interact in real time with ... apps, services and personal AI assistants ... that understand natural-language voice commands, complete tasks

[8] Carla Spartos, "Is Your Restaurant Spying on You?" *New York Post*, December 22, 2010, http://nypost.com/2010/12/22/is-your-restaurant-spying-on-you/.

[9] See Stephanie Miles, "6 Tools Restaurants Can Use for Better Guest Intelligence," *StreetFight*, July 22, 2013, http://streetfightmag.com/2013/07/22/6-tools-restaurants-can-use-for-better-guest-intelligence/.

[10] Restaurants turn to data analytics for the first two reasons, but typically not for the third. Restaurants tend to outsource data analysis to companies such as OpenTable, and those companies retain the contractual right to sell the data to third parties. "OpenTable GuestCenter Client Agreement," *OpenTable*, March 15, 2019, http://opentable.force.com/restaurantterms/resource/1552666401000/restaurant_terms_guest_center.

[11] CBS News, "How Data Analytics Is Becoming a 'Moneyball' for Restaurants," February 4, 2017, www.cbsnews.com/news/how-data-analytics-is-becoming-a-moneyball-for-restaurants/.

[12] "Fourth Launches End-to-End Restaurant and Hospitality HR, Benefits and Payroll Services in the US."

[13] Spartos, "Is Your Restaurant Spying on You?"

[14] Spartos.

for the user, and over time 'learn' their owners' preferences ... All will deeply integrate into consumers' everyday decision."[15]

(2) *Customers object.* We start with the general – i.e., not restaurant-specific – point that pervasive surveillance greatly reduces the control people have over what others do with data about them. More than twenty years of studies and surveys show that consumers want more control over their data than current business information-processing practices provide.[16] It is plausible that people take that attitude toward restaurant surveillance specifically. Two examples illustrate the point. When the Shiru Cafe coffee shop opened near Brown University, cashiers would not complete a sale without obtaining customers' "names, phone numbers, email addresses and majors, or in Brown's lingo, concentrations ... also dates of birth and professional interests."[17] Students took to Twitter to describe the practice as "depressing" and "dystopian."[18] Shiru Cafe's data collection practices were extreme, but even just Googling customers provokes strong objections. When the journalist Jason Heidemann "posted a note about the trend [of restaurants Googling customers] on ... a message board for Chicago foodies," the responses ranged from "That's just odd" to "I would like to know which restaurants research their clientele, so I make sure I never go there."[19]

(3) *Some customers acquiesce.* Some resist, some acquiesce, and some fully accept surveillance. There is no need to decide the percentage in each group. Our claim is simply that *some* acquiesce. We (the authors) do. We use OpenTable, for example, despite our concerns about surveillance. We do not do so because we think we ought

15 "Restaurant Industry 2030," National Restaurant Association, November 5, 2019, 30, https://restaurant.org/research/reports/Restaurant-Industry-2030.

16 See Alessandro Acquisti and Jens Grossklags, "Privacy and Rationality in Individual Decision Making," *IEEE Security & Privacy* 3, 1 (February 2005): 28, https://doi.org/10.1109/MSP.2005.22 A typical study found that 89% of consumers had either a "high concern" (53.7%) or a "medium concern" (35.5%) about "general privacy." Of course, finding that consumers are "concerned" does not mean that they are concerned about loss of control over their information, but why else would they be concerned? The worry is surely that others will do something unacceptable, so consumers must be concerned about some combination of the intertwined issues of trust and control. It would indeed be strange if this were not true. In general, control and trustworthiness are important considerations in determining whether to enter or continue a relationship; we may, for example, refuse to work with, go on a trip with, or associate with someone because they are too controlling or too untrustworthy. Studies of consumer attitudes toward direct marketing confirm this conclusion. One study found that when consumers are informed about current direct marketing information-processing practices, between 73% and 86% find such practices objectionable. Joseph Turow et al., "Americans Reject Tailored Advertising and Three Activities That Enable It," *SSRN*, 2009, http://ssrn.com/abstract=1478214.

17 Chaiel Schaffel, "No Cash Needed at This Cafe. Students Pay the Tab with Their Personal Data," *NPR.org*, September 29, 2018, www.npr.org/sections/thesalt/2018/09/29/643386327/no-cash-needed-at-this-cafe-students-pay-the-tab-with-their-personal-data.

18 Filloon, "Why Restaurants Are Obsessively Collecting Customer Data."

19 Jason A. Heidemann, "You've Been Googled – Bon Appetit!," *Crain's Chicago Business*, July 1, 2013, www.chicagobusiness.com/article/20130629/ISSUE03/306299997/#.

to as part of exchanging information *in order to realize the group-action goal of meeting customers' needs*. We object too strongly to surveillance for that to be true. However, despite our objections, we still think we ought to exchange information because it is convenient to do so, especially since both our favorite Italian restaurant and our favorite French restaurant to meet at are on OpenTable. We are reluctant to forego the convenience of online reservation platforms, such as OpenTable, and we have other uses for the time and effort it would take to investigate and evaluate restaurants' information-processing practices, so we "give up data about ourselves because we don't have the time, patience, or single-mindedness about privacy that would be required to live our daily lives in another way."[20] We expect many are like us given the popularity of online reservation services.

Employment

Employers obtain relevant information from job applicants and other sources to see if the applicant is a good fit for the job.[21] Technology has increased the availability of information. HireRight and Lexis/Nexis, for example, search county, state and federal criminal records, national criminal database records, international criminal records, civil court records, the national theft database, drug and alcohol databases, motor vehicle records, and ex-offender registries. Their services include verifying Social Security Numbers, employment, education, professional licenses, and professional credentials verification; they will provide professional reference checks and credit reports.[22] "Screening often goes far beyond the familiar checking of public criminal records. For $60 to $80 per applicant, ChoicePoint (now Lexis/Nexis) and its rivals assemble digital dossiers of educational degrees and credit histories as well as interviews with friends, past bosses, and colleagues."[23] Employers can discover additional information on their own by Googling applicants, visiting their social networking sites, or using sites like Intelius, Instantcheckmate, and Spokeo.[24] As per the three-part pattern:

(1) *Employers present surveillance as consistent with the norm.* The norm is that employers and job applicants exchange information as a means to realize the group-action goal of determining if the applicant is a good fit for the job. Businesses treat background checks as an improvement on the well-established practice of

20 Hal Abelson, Ken Ledeen, and Harry Lewis, *Blown to Bits: Your Life, Liberty, and Happiness after the Digital Explosion* (Addison-Wesley, 2008), 41–42.

21 See Oscar Gandy, "Legitimate Business Interest: No End in Sight – An Inquiry into the Status of Privacy in Cyberspace," *University of Chicago Legal Forum* 1996, 1 (1996): 100–21, https://chicagounbound.uchicago.edu/uclf/vol1996/iss1/4.

22 See "Background Screening," HireRight, n.d., www.hireright.com/Background-Checks.aspx?apsi=0. www.lexisnexis.com/backgroundchecks.

23 Chad Terhune, "The Trouble with Background Checks," *Bloomberg Business Week Magazine*, May 28, 2008, www.bloomberg.com/news/articles/2008-05-28/the-trouble-with-background-checks.

24 See www.intelius.com/, www.instantcheckmate.com/, and www.spokeo.com/, respectively.

determining how well an applicant will fit with the job. One defense of background checks argues that "background checks help employers make better hiring decisions. With screening, we can learn about the past behaviors and experiences of an individual in order to make informed predictions about how well an employee will perform inside our organization."[25] Similarly, the city of Bozeman, Montana, defended its practice of requiring social networking site passwords from applicants by insisting that

> Before we offer people employment in a public trust position, we have a responsibility to do a thorough background check ... Shame on us if there was information out there available about a person who applied for a job who was a child molester or had some sort of information out there on the Internet that kind of showed those propensities and we didn't look for it, we didn't ask, and we hired that person.[26]

There are many similar examples.

(2) *Job applicants object*. Pre-employment background checks in particular have caused a storm of protest.[27] The Bozeman city's defense of insisting on social networking passwords, for example, "wasn't good enough for many critics, who cited the move as an invasion of privacy. After the story was covered in the local news, residents sent hordes of letters and e-mails to city hall, eventually forcing officials to back down and discontinue the practice."[28]

There is an additional reason to object to job application surveillance: namely, to create a better distribution of employment than the one created by the current use of pre-employment background checks. A better distribution is called for because the current distribution strongly discriminates against "undesirable" applicants – applicants that impose a significant risk or cost to the employer. Imagine, for example, that Alice is a single mother whose three-year old child has a severe chronic illness requiring long-term expensive treatment. Alice will potentially increase an employer's health care costs and will have a greater than normal number of absences from work. She is, in this sense, an "undesirable" hire. This is inconsistent with (most) people's values. One reason, and the one most pertinent here, is that the practice works against the realization of multifaceted

25 Michael Gaul, "Where Do You Stand on Employment Background Checks?," *Proforma Screening Solutions*, August 17, 2010, www.proformascreening.com/blog/2010/08/17/employment-background-checks-stand/.

26 Declan McCullagh, "Want a Job? Hand over Your E-Mail Login," *CBS News*, June 18, 2009, www.cbsnews.com/news/want-a-job-hand-over-your-e-mail-login/.

27 See, for example, Eugene Frid, "Background Checks and Employment Discrimination: Distant Parallels between US and EU Privacy Regimes," *Hastings International and Comparative Law Review* 40 (2017): 159–76.

28 "37 Percent of Employers Screen Applicants on Facebook," *HuffPost*, April 20, 2012, www.huffpost.com/entry/employers-use-facebook-to-pre-screen-applicants_n_1441289.

selves by creating a very strong incentive to make sure that the shape your life takes is one employers find desirable, not one that reflects who you are.

(3) *Some acquiesce.* Job applicants acquiesce when they do not attempt to evade surveillance despite objecting strongly enough that they think that they ought not exchange information with employers in order to realize the group-action goal of determining fitness for employment. It is highly likely that some – perhaps most – acquiesce. Employer use of background checks is widespread, so not complying with employer background checks would mean not applying for employment in a significant range of cases.

Health Insurance

A ProPublica report notes that

> the health insurance industry has joined forces with data brokers to vacuum up personal details about hundreds of millions of Americans, including, odds are, many readers of this story. The companies are tracking your race, education level, TV habits, marital status, net worth. They're collecting what you post on social media, whether you're behind on your bills, what you order online. Then they feed this information into complicated computer algorithms that spit out predictions about how much your health care could cost them.[29]

The ProPublica report is unclear about the extent to which health insurance companies currently "vacuum up personal details" versus their plans to do so in the future. It is clear, however, that they currently use some credit information,[30] and commentators suggest that they may use social media posts in the future.[31] As per the three-part pattern:

(1) *Insurers present surveillance as consistent with the informational norm.* The health insurance norm is that insurers and insureds exchange information primarily in order to realize the group-action goal of determining the likelihood of morbidity and mortality. Insurers argue that their information-processing activities improve their ability to meet people's true health insurance needs. They contend that "they use the information to spot health issues in their clients – and flag them so they get services they need."[32] The health consulting company Avalere, for example, presents

29 Marshall Allen, "Health Insurers Are Vacuuming Up Details about You – And It Could Raise Your Rates," *ProPublica*, July 7, 2018, www.propublica.org/article/health-insurers-are-vacuuming-up-details-about-you-and-it-could-raise-your-rates.

30 Paul Sisolak, "How Does Your Credit Score Affect Your Insurance Rates?," *Easy Money by Policygenius*, May 1, 2017, www.policygenius.com/blog/how-does-your-credit-score-affect-your-insurance-rates/.

31 Mary Purcell, "Millennials: Can Your Social Media Posts Boost Your Insurance Premiums?," *Benzinga* (February 16, 2017), www.benzinga.com/general/education/17/02/9061232/millennials-can-your-social-media-posts-boost-your-insurance-premium.

32 Allen, "Health Insurers Are Vacuuming Up Details about You."

surveillance this way – in typical corporate-speak. The remarks concern health care delivery, but, as their report shows, Avalere regards the use of data by data-driven health insurers as an integral part of the delivery of care:[33]

> Health systems and plans increasingly seek novel methods of exchanging social-services data sources, patient-reported information, and various real-world data; integrating these data may support the development of more comprehensive care-management approaches that target the right interventions for the right patients at the right time. They are deploying new assessment methods to better screen for unmet social needs and establishing new care models that emphasize multidisciplinary care teams, community health workers, and partnerships with community-based organizations. Plans are also increasingly using primary-care engagement to better manage enrollees' health throughout the continuum of care, to close gaps in care, and to make their social interventions more effective.[34]

(2) *Customers object.* In a 2018 survey, 72 percent of the respondents thought insurance companies should not "be allowed to use big data to determine risk in a potential insurance policy."[35] This reaction is no surprise. As we noted earlier, it is clear that people object generally to a loss of informational privacy. In the case of health insurance, there is an additional distributive justice reason to object. In the United States, the distribution of health care is determined in large part by the distribution of private health insurance, and that distribution is a function of the information processing that drives the design of insurance options and the setting of premiums. The vast majority of those who have carefully reflected on the problem without bias or prejudice have concluded that the distribution is seriously flawed. One way to alter (and hopefully improve) the distribution is to constrain the collection and use of information on which it depends, as is the case for plans sold under the US Affordable Care Act.[36]

More generally, sharp criticism of the US health care system is common. Critics point out that we sell medical care like a commodity in a market, but, unlike properly functioning markets, prices are often unknowable or unpredictable. Reliable information about the quality of care is difficult or impossible to obtain. There is virtually no genuine competition among health care providers, and, even if there were, people are often locked in to providers in ways the limit their power to

33 "Avalere 2020 Healthcare Industry Outlook: See the Turns Ahead," *Avalere Health* (January 9, 2020), 7, 14–18, https://avalere.com/webinars/avalere-2020-healthcare-industry-outlook-see-the-turns-ahead.

34 "Avalere 2020 Healthcare Industry Outlook," 5.

35 "Insurance Companies Using Big Data to Decide on Consumers? Only 15% Are OK with This," *Lendedu*, September 25, 2019, https://lendedu.com/blog/insurance-companies-using-data-survey/#. The survey did not ask about health insurance specifically, but there is no reason to think the results would be different if it had.

36 "How Insurance Companies Set Health Premiums," *HealthCare.gov*, www.healthcare.gov/how-plans-set-your-premiums/.

choose.[37] These complaints do not focus specifically on information processing, but, as the Avalere report illustrates, health insurer information processing is an integral part of the market for health care.

(3) *Some acquiesce*. We assume that some object strongly enough to health insurance surveillance that they think that they ought not to exchange information in order to realize the group-action goal of assessing the probability of morbidity and mortality. It is likely that many of those do not attempt to evade surveillance, and hence acquiesce. One may occasionally succeed in concealing information about morbidity and mortality, but, on the whole, health insurance companies are likely to acquire such information despite attempts at concealment, and the likely sanction – denial of coverage – is a disaster in an economy in which one pays for health care through health insurance.

SHADOW CONFORMITY

Acquiescence in "party to the norm" cases has an important consequence. Recall that acquiescers do *not* try to prevent or avoid surveillance. Instead, acquiescers think they ought to conform to the strictures on information flow – that is, to being surveilled. They just do not think they ought to do so *as a means to realizing the group-action goal*. As a result, they create a shadow of genuine conformity to the norm by pursuing individual goals that create a selective flow of information – a compromised selective flow that includes feeding information to the surveilling entity. A variant on the holiday dinner illustrates the point.

Suppose wealthy Aunt Vivian hosts all the holiday dinners at her mansion. Her passion is studying family dynamics, and, to further her research, she has the family under surveillance, which all the family members know. The rooms contain microphones that feed comments and conversations to an artificial intelligence (AI) program that analyzes them and generates an interactive graphical display of the results. Aunt Vivian is a stickler for adherence to the strictures on information flow, and, during the family gathering, her AI program sends alerts to her phone when it detects any violation (including the use of surveillance evasion technologies, such as microphone jammers). She studies the graphical display for information that may lead her to alter the distribution of her wealth in her will. The rest of the family strongly objects to Vivian's surveillance and all think they ought not to conform to these strictures on information flow to realize the group-action goal of family harmony, but they acquiesce to the surveillance by attending the dinner and conforming to the strictures on information flow without any attempt to evade surveillance. They do so for a variety of reasons. Some think they ought to conform to the strictures on information flow as a means of preserving the best chance of

[37] Elisabeth Rosenthal, *An American Sickness: How Healthcare Became Big Business and How You Can Take It Back* (Penguin Books, 2018), 6.

getting a large share of Aunt Vivian's wealth. Some think they ought to because Aunt Jane or Uncle John would be terribly disappointed if they did not. Others think they ought to because they delight in fooling Vivian into thinking they approve of her surveillance practices. And others think they ought to for still other reasons. The result is that the following conditions hold. They are the conditions for the existence of an informational norm minus the reference to the group-action goal; in that way, they are a shadow of those conditions. Thus:

1. (a) They think they ought to conform to the strictures on information flow (except for allowing Vivian's surveillance), and (b) at appropriate times, they dominantly prefer to do so;
2. as a result of (1), this past behavioral regularity exists: they have conformed to the strictures (except for allowing Vivian's surveillance);
3. as a result of (2), the regularity continues to hold in the future.

The family members will observe each other observing that (1)–(3) hold, so it will be common knowledge among the family members that the conditions hold. The result is a compromised selective flow of information, and even that flow will cease when family members cease to have their diverse reasons for thinking they ought to conform to the strictures on information flow. The family members who think they ought to conform to preserve their chance at inheritance could learn that Vivian is leaving all her wealth to charity. Those who think they ought to conform to avoid disappointing Aunt Jane and Uncle John could discover that those two despise the strictures on information flow, and those who delight in fooling Vivian could discover that she is not deceived.

Similar remarks hold for acquiescence more generally. Appropriate versions of the three conditions we just discussed will hold, leading to a compromised selective flow of information. Moreover, those three conditions will be common knowledge. However, the flow of information will last only as long as the acquiescers continue to have their diverse reasons for thinking they ought to conform.

ACQUIESCENCE IN "NOT A PARTY TO THE NORM" CASES

In the "party to the norm" cases, acquiescers and resisters both think they ought not to conform to relevant strictures on information flow as a means to realizing the group-action goal. In the "not a party to the norm" cases, resisters and acquiescers also share the same "ought thought": they both think they *ought to* conform to relevant strictures on information flow to realize the relevant group-action goal. The difference is that acquiescers do not attempt to evade surveillance – at least, not entirely. Like the greengrocer who is willing to live with displaying the sign, they are willing to live with at least some degree of surveillance (see Table 7.2).

TABLE 7.2 *Highlighting "not a party to the norm" acquiescence*

	Entity conducting surveillance			
	Party to the norm		Not a party	
	Ought thought	Reaction to surveillance	Ought thought	Reaction to surveillance
c. 1950–1980 "before surveillance"	Ought to	Surveillance not a serious concern	Ought to	Surveillance not a serious concern
Resisters	Ought not to	Try to prevent	Ought to	Try to prevent
Acquiescers	Ought not to	Do not try to prevent	**Ought to**	**Partially accept**
Acceptors	Ought to	Accept	Ought not to	Accept

We begin with investigative journalists, then turn to proxy surveillance.

Investigative Journalists

Acquiescing journalists think they ought to ensure a selective flow of information primarily to realize the group-action goal of revealing government wrongdoing while protecting the identity of their sources. But they also, to at least some extent, tolerate surveillance without trying to avoid it. Why would journalists who think the first do the second? In order to publish in the mainstream media. Doing so ensures widespread readership and a patina of legitimacy and truthfulness. The issue is that "writers and editors for major publications and broadcast networks [engage in] a process of consultation with government, and of voluntary self-restraint, that is continual and intense."[38] Greenwald paints one picture of the process:

> written protective rules … govern how the establishment media report on official secrets. According to these rules, which allow the government to control disclosures and minimize, even neuter, their impact, editors first go to officials and advise them what they intend to publish. National security officials then tell the editors all the ways in which national security will supposedly be damaged by the disclosures. A protracted negotiation takes place over what will and will not be published. At best, substantial delay results. Often, patently newsworthy information is suppressed.[39]

38 Allan M. Siegel, "Secrets about Secrets: The Backstage Conversations between Press and Government," Working Paper Series (Joan Shorenstein Center on the Press, Politics and Public Policy, March 2007), 3, http://shorensteincenter.org/wp-content/uploads/2012/03/2007_02_siegal.pdf.

39 Glenn Greenwald, *No Place to Hide: Edward Snowden, the NSA, and the US Surveillance State* (Metropolitan Books, 2014), 55.

Barton Gellman offers another, more nuanced picture in *Dark Mirror: Edward Snowden and the American Surveillance State*.[40]

Twenty-first-century journalists face governments that have great power to monitor their communications, and they deal with major news organizations willing to engage in content-modifying negotiations – negotiations that may also involve disclosures of information from which the government can infer the source. Compare the publication of the Pentagon Papers in June 1971. Daniel Ellsberg began secretly copying the classified documents on October 1, 1969.[41] Without any evident concern about surveillance, Ellsberg discussed the papers with friends and colleagues, and from 1969 through 1971 he also talked with Senator J. William Fulbright, Chairman of the Senate Foreign Relations Committee, and Senator George McGovern.[42] He sought advice about what to do with the documents, and was not concerned that they would reveal to the Nixon administration that he was in possession of classified material. When it became clear in 1971 that neither Fulbright nor McGovern was likely to hold congressional hearings or take other actions that would make the information public, Ellsberg sought publication in *The New York Times*. After the *Times* published the first three installments in June 1971, Attorney General George Mitchell asked the newspaper to voluntarily cease publication. When the paper refused, a federal court enjoined further publication, leading to the landmark Supreme Court case *New York Times* v. *Sullivan*. Two days after the *Times* ceased publication following the injunction, *The Washington Post* published excerpts from the Pentagon Papers that Ellsberg had provided to it. Assistant Attorney General William Rehnquist asked the *Post* to voluntarily cease publication, and it refused.

In the twenty-first century, interactions between journalists and the government fit the following pattern:

(1) *The government presents that practice as consistent with the norm*. Governments argue that realizing the goal of investigative journalism as an effective political watchdog requires a tradeoff between the transparency created by journalistic disclosures and the secrecy necessary for adequate national security, and they contend that government surveillance of journalist plays an important role in implementing that tradeoff.[43]

(2) *Journalists object*. Objecting is built into being an investigative journalist. Faced with pervasive government surveillance, journalists must oppose it to conform to a norm that requires thinking one ought to ensure a selective flow of information

40 Barton Gellman, *Dark Mirror: Edward Snowden and the American Surveillance State* (Penguin Press, 2020), chapter 3.

41 Daniel Ellsberg, *Secrets: A Memoir of Vietnam and the Pentagon Papers*, Reissue edition (Penguin Books, 2003), 299.

42 Ellsberg, 326–410. The remarks which follow are taken from the same source.

43 Rahul Sagar, *Secrets and Leaks: The Dilemma of State Secrecy* (Princeton University Press, 2013).

primarily to realize the group-action goal of revealing government wrongdoing while protecting the identity of sources.

(3) *Some acquiesce.* On both Greenwald's and Gellman's accounts, the "unwritten protective rules" mean that media companies risk divulging information to the government in ways that are inconsistent with the journalistic norm of concealing the identity of confidential sources – either because the journalist outright discloses the source (presumably under legal compulsion), or because the government obtains enough information to infer the source's identity. Journalists working for mainstream media companies tend to acquiesce. They may think the concerns about national security justify acquiescing, or they may acquiesce for a variety of other reasons. The "protracted negotiation … over what will and will not be published" could be a slippery slope that leads journalists and media to accept ever greater government surveillance. After all, it is "the tendency of surveillance systems to spread. It simply lies in the interests of both government and private surveillance operations to expand – to cover more people and more of the lives of the people they cover."[44] The embrace of surveillance need not happen, however. Another possibility is that, as journalists, media, and the government negotiate, an informational norm emerges – a norm appropriately protective of journalists and their sources.

Proxy Surveillance

Recall the discussion of proxy variables in AI systems and proxy surveillance from Chapter 6. Proxy surveillance involves transferring information initially collected under an informational norm to an entity that is not a party to the norm. How do people react to proxy surveillance? Do they object to it? If so, do they resist or acquiesce? Acquiescence is a likely response given the difficulties in resisting proxy surveillance (as we noted in the preceding chapter). We offer three examples: credit reporting, behavioral advertising, and data aggregation and analysis services. All involve data from retail transactions, to one extent or another. That is hardly surprising since retail transactions serve as a conduit through which data flows to a variety of third parties, including credit rating agencies, behavioral advertisers, and data aggregators.

Credit Reporting

Retailers participate in credit reporting by serving as the conduit that feeds information to the reporting agencies.[45] Retail purchases reveal the pattern of what one buys, where, when, and at what price. Retailers may also have a variety of additional information about their customers, and that information may also be relevant to assessing

44 James B. Rule, *Privacy in Peril: How We Are Sacrificing a Fundamental Right in Exchange for Security and Convenience* (Oxford University Press, 2007), 151.

45 See Josh Lauer, *Creditworthy: A History of Consumer Surveillance and Financial Identity in America* (Columbia University Press, 2017).

creditworthiness. Indeed, by 1964 it was clear that "an applicant's monthly income and payment to income ratio – pieces of financial information with seemingly obvious relevance – were far less useful in predicting default than whether borrowers had a telephone, owned their home, or had a bank account (but, again, without knowing how much was in it)."[46] That is all the more true in the post-1980s period that is our focus as AI-driven surveillance draws data from virtually every aspect of one's life. How can retailer participation in credit reporting be consistent with the norm that requires that customers and retailers exchange information as a means to meeting the customer's retail needs? What conception of retail needs makes it permissible for retailers to serve as a data collection point for credit agencies? As per the three-part pattern:

(1) *Credit agencies present proxy surveillance as consistent with the norm.* During the first half of the twentieth century, credit rating agencies promoted a changed conception of consumer needs that presented credit reporting as a way to meet consumers' retail needs. Promulgating a "morality of creditworthiness,"[47] they "sought to inculcate norms of prompt payment and to shame consumers into honoring their promises . . . Americans were urged to 'treat their credit as a sacred trust' and to avoid the disgrace of 'Q.C.' (questionable credit)."[48]

Our reference to a *first half of the twentieth century* morality of creditworthiness campaign may seem inconsistent with our distinction between surveillance circa 1950–1980 and surveillance today. How does that fit with this chapter, which is about "surveillance after"? It fits because the distinction is between circa 1950–1980 *when surveillance was not a serious concern* and recent decades when surveillance became a matter of increasingly serious concern. As Lauer notes,

> Until the late 1960s, the American public was untroubled by credit reporting. Contrary to sensational press coverage of the time, credit surveillance was no dark conspiracy unmasked by Congress in 1968 [with the House hearings on credit reporting and the passage of the Consumer Credit Protection Act]. Americans had always known that their lives were held under a microscope when they applied for credit. They just did not care. Consumer groups had long fought for safer products, better labeling, and ethical advertising, but the one thing they did not demand was privacy.[49]

As we noted at the beginning of Chapter 6 (citing Lauer), the 1960s concern that commentators and Congress expressed about credit reporting did not extend to the general public, which remained largely unconcerned. Additionally, the "morality of creditworthiness" campaign continues to this day. In explaining why a credit rating is important, the lender Rocket HQ connects improving your credit score with making your "past faults" less significant:

46 Lauer, 206.
47 Lauer, 12–13.
48 Lauer, 13.
49 Lauer, 271.

> First and foremost, your credit score is a demonstration of how risky you are as a borrower. A poor credit score may demonstrate that you have a history of late payments, too much debt or not enough credit in the first place. Lenders won't be too pumped about loaning to someone who has a long history of being financially untrustworthy ... You should remember that your credit score doesn't just matter when it comes to getting the best rates and terms for loans and credit cards. There are a few other benefits to having a good credit score. For one, making a solid effort to improve your credit score will not be in vain. As your score improves, your past faults will become less and less significant in determining your overall score.[50]

The campaign to legitimize proxy surveillance also continued on the congressional front. The Fair Credit Reporting Act, passed in 1970, allows credit reporting agencies to sell information to a business "which it has reason to believe ... has a legitimate business need for the information in connection with a business transaction that is initiated by the consumer."[51] In 1989, Equifax explained to Congress that "[n]ew micro-targeting techniques help businesses understand more precisely who their customers are. We are trying to help them with our information services to improve their effectiveness."[52]

(2) *Customers object.* By the end of the twentieth century, concern about credit reporting had spread to the general public. Discussing a 1990 Equifax-commissioned nationwide survey of consumer attitudes about privacy and data sharing, Lauer notes that:

> The survey ... was headed by Alan F. Westin, the Columbia law professor who had embarrassed the credit reporting industry during earlier congressional hearings. Westin's participation lent legitimacy to the Equifax survey, but its findings were still unflattering. When it came to handling personal information, only 59 percent of Americans had a "high or moderate degree of trust" in credit bureaus. Government agencies, including the notoriously unpopular IRS, were trusted more than credit bureaus. On topics related to database marketing, the news was worse. Three-quarters of Americans said that the practice of prescreening was "not acceptable," and 69 percent said that the business of selling consumer lists – lists that included information "such as income level, residential area, and credit card use" – was a "bad thing."[53]

The impact of credit reporting on privacy figures prominently in Jeffery Rosen's 2004 book *The Naked Crowd*, in which he worries about "technologies [that] make it possible for more and more aspects of our lives to be observed by strangers ... [and] ensure that more and more aspects of our lives will be evaluated by

50 "Why Is a Credit Score Important?," Rocket HQ, www.rockethq.com/learn/credit/why-is-a-credit-score-important.

51 15 Unites States Code Annotated § 1861b(a)(3)(F).

52 Lauer, *Creditworthy*, 261. Citing US House, Fair Credit Reporting Act, 126.

53 Lauer, 261–62. Lauer is quoting The Equifax Report on Consumers in the Information Age (Atlanta: Equifax, 1991), 19, 69–70. He adds, "It is worth nothing that when the question about consumer lists was rephrased in pro-consumer language, the results were reversed – 67 percent responded that list selling was 'acceptable'" (72).

strangers."[54] In 2019, a bipartisan congressional group declared that the "commodification of consumers and their personal data is the core reason why our nation's consumer credit reporting system is broken."[55]

(3) *Some consumers acquiesce*. The lack of a credit score can affect your ability to rent an apartment, obtain a mortgage, get car insurance, and find employment, so it is understandable that many who object to credit agency surveillance will nonetheless acquiesce to it. The Federal Trade Commission, for example, observes that "We hear a lot about credit – credit reports, credit scores, credit freezes, credit monitoring. What does it all mean for you? Your credit matters because it affects your ability to get a loan, a job, housing, insurance, and more. It's important to understand what your credit is and how to protect it."[56]

Behavioral Advertising

Behavioral advertising is "the tracking of consumers' online activities in order to deliver tailored advertising."[57] It merges our digital footprints into pictures of surprising intrusiveness and accuracy. It is a twenty-first-century form of direct marketing. Since the 1970s, retailers have been a conduit of information to direct marketers, who sort buyers into groups according to their willingness to purchase various products and services. Direct marketing was not widely used prior to the 1970s because it was too difficult to differentiate among consumers. That changed in the 1970s when the government began selling census data on magnetic tapes. Marketing companies used the information to compile databases divided according to "age, income level, race, ethnicity, gender, and geographical location."[58] In the 1980s, they supplemented this data with information about opinions, lifestyles, likes and dislikes, hobbies, and so on:

> [Such was] the sophistication of [late-twentieth to early twenty-first-century] American direct marketing that companies hype highly targeted lists ... one can reasonably expect to purchase lists of women who are both public employees and wear sexy underwear; or business owners who espouse far-right political causes; or registered Republicans who are purchasers of pornography – or, for that matter, of

54 Jeffrey Rosen, *The Naked Crowd: Reclaiming Security and Freedom in an Anxious Age* (Random House Trade Paperbacks, 2005), 12.

55 Megan Leonhardt, "Democrats and Republicans in Congress Agree: The System That Determines Credit Scores Is 'Broken,'" *CNBC*, February 27, 2019, www.cnbc.com/2019/02/27/american-consumer-credit-rating-system-is-broken.html.

56 "Understanding Your Credit," Federal Trade Commission, January 15, 2020, www.consumer.ftc.gov/articles/understanding-your-credit.

57 Federal Trade Commission, "FTC Staff Report: Self-Regulatory Principles for Online Behavioral Advertising," February 2009, 3, www.ftc.gov/sites/default/files/documents/reports/federal-trade-commission-staff-report-self-regulatory-principles-online-behavioral-advertising/p085400behavadreport.pdf.

58 Daniel J. Solove, *The Digital Person: Technology and Privacy in the Information Age* (NYU Press, 2004), 19.

> pornography with S-M themes ... [and the] guest list information from a hotel frequented by lesbians[59]

Not to mention lists of female purchasers of wigs, online dating-service users, men who buy fashion underwear, impotent men, gamblers, hair-removal product purchasers, feminists, anti-gay activists, and advocates of school prayer.[60]

Behavioral advertising increases this already significant ability to see into people's lives.[61] We present a simplified model of the advertising ecosystem consisting of just five entities: profilers, advertising agencies, advertising networks or exchanges, websites that display the advertisements, and businesses that purchase the advertisements.[62] A single entity may perform more than one role, but we may ignore that complication for our purposes. Profilers create profiles that segment buyers into groups in order to predict their willingness to buy specific types of products and services.[63] The purpose of the profiles is to target advertising.[64] A business may create its own ads, or it may outsource that task.[65] Advertising exchanges and networks, such as Google's AdSense, deliver banner, text, rich media, and other types of advertisements to websites.[66] When a buyer visits a website, an advertising exchange combines the buyer's profile with information about their current website activity in order to target advertisements more precisely. The exchange creates an auction in which businesses bid for the opportunity to present their targeted advertisements (the whole process takes milliseconds). The goal is to tailor advertisements as closely as possible to the interests of the buyer receiving them. As per the three-part pattern:

59 Rule, *Privacy in Peril*, 104.

60 Rule, *Privacy in Peril*, 59.

61 Businesses engaged in one way or another in behavioral advertising include, among many others, Google, "Google Ads – Get More Customers with Online Advertising," Google, https://ads.google.com/home/; Facebook, "Advertising on Facebook," Facebook for Business, www.facebook.com/business/ads; Nielsen "Audience Segments," Nielsen, www.nielsen.com/us/en/solutions/capabilities/audience-segments; Neustar, "Marketing Solutions – Intelligence, Experience, and Analytics | Neustar," Neustar, n.d., www.home.neustar/marketing-solutions; OpenX "OpenX: Powering People-Based Marketing across the Open Web," OpenX, www.openx.com/; MediaMath "MediaMath: Future-Proofed DSP," MediaMath, www.mediamath.com; Pubmatic "Programmatic Digital Advertising Technology & Solutions," PubMatic, https://pubmatic.com/; and Oracle "Oracle CX Marketing," Oracle, www.oracle.com/marketingcloud/.

62 Models may distinguish several more entities and functions. See, for example, IAB Data Usage and Control Taskforce, "Data Usage & Control Primer: Best Practices & Definitions," May 2010, 6, www.iab.net/media/file/data-primer-final.pdf.

63 See Mark MacCarthy, *New Directions in Privacy: Disclosure, Unfairness and Externalities*, 6 I/S: *J.L. & Pol'y for Info. Soc'y* (2011): 462–64.

64 See Dustin D. Berger, "Balancing Consumer Privacy with Behavioral Targeting," *Santa Clara Computer and High Technology Law Journal* 27 (2011): 4. ("These profiles allow websites and ISPs to serve advertisements and other services that are targeted to their customers' interests").

65 For examples of advertising agencies, see Epsilon, *Strategy & Analytics*, www.epsilon.com/apac/products-and-services/marketing-services; Havas Media, *Our Group*, https://havasmedia.com/; Omnicom Group, *National Advertising Agencies*, www.omnicomgroup.com/.

66 "AdSense 101: What You Need to Know," Google, March 30, 2017, https://blog.google/products/adsense/adsense101-passionintoprofit/.

(1) *Behavioral advertisers present surveillance as consistent with the norm.* As with credit rating agencies, the question is how it serves consumers' retail needs for retailers to feed information to behavioral advertisers. The advertisers contend that the revenue from advertising keeps websites and apps free; provides content, services, offers, and ads that are better matched to consumers interests; reduces intrusive and annoying ads; helps businesses serve their customers better; plays an integral role in driving economic growth and encouraging competition among companies; and affords small businesses and startups the ability to create new content and services.[67]

(2) *Customers object.* The results of an influential 2009 survey "suggest that if Americans could vote on behavioral targeting today, they would shut it down."[68] A slightly later study reports somewhat more balanced results:

> Advertisers claim that consumers are clamoring for more interesting and relevant advertisements, while privacy advocates claim citizens' privacy rights are being trampled. We found support for both views: there are sizable groups of people with each of those views. In the middle, we found a large group of people who are disinterested in better ads since their goal is to ignore ads. They see no benefit to targeted advertising, so they do not see reason to share data with advertisers.[69]

(3) *Some consumers acquiesce.* Acquiescence requires two things. First, one must object strongly enough to surveillance that one thinks one ought not to exchange information with retailers in order to realize the group-action goal of meeting customers' needs. We assume some consumers object this strongly. Second, despite one's objections, one must not try to evade surveillance. In fact, most consumers do not. A consumer has two choices when dealing with retailers (online or off): allow the retailer to process information about them, or not deal with that retailer.[70] One reason the choices are restricted to those two is that a business's information processing does not vary to conform to the privacy preferences of individual buyers. Marketing objectives – not buyers' privacy preferences – drive the collection, analysis, and use of information. Efficient information processing requires standardized, automated routines that analyze the data. It is not an objection that some websites (Facebook is one) allow users to set privacy preferences to which the site will conform. Ninety percent of users never do so, so standardized processing remains unproblematic.[71] Faced with the choice

[67] "Understanding Online Advertising," NAI: Network Advertising Initiative, www.networkadvertising.org/understanding-online-advertising/.

[68] Joseph Turow et al., "Americans Reject Tailored Advertising and Three Activities That Enable It," 4.

[69] Aleecia M. McDonald and Lorrie Faith Cranor, "Americans' Attitudes about Internet Behavioral Advertising Practices," in *Proceedings of the 9th Annual ACM Workshop on Privacy in the Electronic Society*, 2010.

[70] For a fuller discussion, see Richard Warner and Robert H Sloan, "Behavioral Advertising: From One-Sided Chicken to Informational Norms," *Vanderbilt Entertainment and Technology Law Journal* 15 (2012): 49–83.

[71] For a fuller discussion, see Robert H. Sloan and Richard Warner, *Unauthorized Access: The Crisis in Online Privacy and Information Security* (Chapman Hall/CRC Press, 2013), chapter 12, appendix.

between using the site and submitting to its information-processing practices, or not using the site, most opt to use the site. Buyers' behavior – entering billions of transactions daily with sellers who give buyers no control over information processing – shows that buyers prefer permitting information processing to foregoing the use of a particular website.[72]

Data Aggregators

We will use the data aggregation and analysis service Factual as our example.[73] Factual claims it enables its customers to "make data-driven decisions by using high-quality location data and real-world behavior patterns to understand customer intent."[74] Factual presumably uses data from retail sales since it says it uses data from "any data resource or service that can be used to access data."[75] It remarks that these "resources may be thought of as raw data, what some have been referring to as the 'oil of the 21st century.'"[76] As per the three-part pattern:

(1) *Factual presents proxy surveillance as consistent with the norm.* Does it serve consumers' retail needs for retailers to feed information to data aggregators like Factual? Factual contends that it does because it helps businesses better understand their customers and meet their needs. It explains that "marketers today are expected to be data-driven experts, and location data is able to help them through every step of the process, from understanding their audiences and engaging customers, to measuring results and attributing success."[77]

(2) *Consumers object.* In the preceding chapter, we discussed concerns about fairness in AI-driven proxy surveillance, but proxy-surveillance concerns reach beyond concerns about AI. The worry is that a privacy harm "emerges from the fusion of small bits of seemingly innocuous data. When combined, the information becomes much more telling."[78]

(3) *Some consumers acquiesce.* As we note in the last chapter, defeating proxy surveillance online typically takes strong cybersecurity measures, and people lack

72 For a more detailed analysis, see Warner and Sloan, "Behavioral Advertising."

73 Factual merged with Foursquare in 2020. "Factual Insights," *Factual*, www.factual.com/products/insights/. The merged company is known as Foursquare.

74 Jordan Crook and Anthony Ha, "Foursquare Merges with Factual," *TechCrunch* (blog), April 6, 2020, https://social.techcrunch.com/2020/04/06/foursquare-merges-with-factual/.

75 Gil Elbasz, "The Data Stack: A Structured Approach," *Factual* (blog), July 24, 2012, www.factual.com/blog/how-the-data-stack-can-organize-your-data-science-program/. Elbasz was Factual's founder.

76 Elbasz.

77 Brian Czarny, "Factual's 2019 Location-Based Marketing Report," *Factual* (blog), June 12, 2019, www.factual.com/blog/factuals-2019-location-based-marketing-report/ (Brian Czarny is Factual's Chief of Marketing Operations).

78 Daniel J. Solove, *Nothing to Hide: The False Tradeoff between Privacy and Security* (Yale University Press, 2013), 27.

adequate knowledge of cybersecurity to adequately defend themselves.[79] Acquiescence, not resistance, is the most likely response.

ACQUIESCENCE WHERE RELEVANT INFORMATIONAL NORMS DO NOT EXIST

Acquiescers react to surveillance of activities under an informational norm with an "ought not" thought in the "party to the norm" cases and an "ought to" thought in the "not a party to the norm" cases. Where applicable informational norms do not exist, the "ought thought" drops out as irrelevant, and acquiescence consists in simply not trying to evade surveillance. We (the authors) acquiesce in this way to Google's surveillance. We use the search engine, Gmail, and Google Scholar, but make no attempt to evade surveillance.[80] As we argue in Chapter 8, informational norms are likely to eventually arise in such cases, but they will be norms that permit rather than limit surveillance.

HOW COMMON IS ACQUIESCENCE?

Think of people as spread out across a spectrum. One end is home to those who object in the strongest possible terms to surveillance. They think they "ought not" in the "party to the norm" cases and think they "ought to" in the "not a party to the norm" cases (provided they can prevent surveillance to at least some extent). The strength of the objections decreases as you move along the spectrum toward the other extreme. At that extreme, people do not object at all to surveillance. Acquiescers and resisters both occupy a region that starts at the "strongly as possible" end and extends some distance toward the middle. The two groups may be distributed a little differently within that region, with more resisters at the extreme "as strongly as possible" end. However, the key difference between the two groups is that only resisters try to prevent surveillance. Is acquiescence common? Do acquiescers outnumber resisters in the range from the "strongly as possible" end into the middle? Strictly speaking, we do not need to answer. It is sufficient for our purposes that some acquiesce, but, as we noted earlier, acquiescence is likely common in online proxy surveillance given the difficulties in avoiding it.

In the next chapter, we turn to the other the end of the spectrum: the end at which people do not object to surveillance.

79 Aaron Smith, "What the Public Knows about Cybersecurity," *Pew Research Center: Internet, Science & Tech* (blog), March 22, 2017, www.pewresearch.org/internet/2017/03/22/what-the-public-knows-about-cybersecurity/; FirstData, "Consumers' Awareness, Behavior and Concerns around Cybersecurity," *FirstData*, 2019, www.firstdata.com/images/fd-facelift/images/FDC_Cybersecurity_and_Awareness_eBook.pdf.

80 No effective attempt. We periodically delete cookies and use an ad blocker, but neither does much to prevent Google's data collection.

8

Accept or Take Control?

The sociologist Stephan Mau contends that the "evaluative structures embedded in [pervasive surveillance] are not something that remains external to the individual, but are instilled and consolidated by socialization, social expectations and legitimation efforts. They provide reasons, create incentives and assign relevance – in a word, they determine what is important in any given situation."[1] Is it true that surveillance embeds "evaluative structures ... [that] provide reasons, create incentives and assign relevance"? We argue that a process of acculturation will lead to that result – unless appropriate public policies intervene. Without intervention, the ultimate consequence will be informational norms that permit pervasive surveillance and hence do not allow for, much less create, adequate privacy in public. We examine the process of acculturation and then consider how to intervene.

A PROCESS OF ACCULTURATION

Acculturation is a "process of cultural and psychological change that takes place as a result of contact between two or more cultural groups and their individual members."[2] Pervasive surveillance involves contact between two cultures: the business/government culture of surveillance, and the consumer/citizen/personal life culture typified by interactions under informational norms. "All cultural groups in contact change; no group is immune from this culture-change process."[3] Recent history suggests that surveillance leads to "cultural and psychological change." As the sociologist David Lyon notes, when people "engage with the online world, . . . they not only improvise responses to the subtle ways that they are watched but also use those surveillance technologies for their own ends. Thus

[1] Steffen Mau, *The Metric Society: On the Quantification of the Social* (Polity Press, 2019), 169–70.

[2] John W. Berry, *Acculturation: A Personal Journey across Cultures* (Cambridge University Press, 2019), 15.

[3] Berry, 14.

are new surveillance cultures born."[4] Attempts to prevent the spread of surveillance have proven ineffective: "Ever-emerging technological possibilities … pose one challenge after another to the privacy-protecting protecting Davids, who mobilize thinly stretched resources against organizational Goliaths … even the most notable victories often appear as provisional non-defeats – subject to rude reversal down the road."[5] As the privacy-protecting Davids fight their rearguard action, familiarity and habituation appear to lead people to tolerate – or even embrace – surveillance.[6]

We do not claim that acculturation *inevitably* leads to surveillance-embracing norms. We do claim that it is likely that intervention is needed *now* to direct the process along lines that preserve enough privacy in public to ensure adequate opportunities for self-realization. We primarily rely on the work of others to support the likelihood claim, but we illustrate the point using ourselves (the authors) as an example. Our goal is to show how acquiescence can change to acceptance in the case of informational norms. We consider our own use of online resources. Similar remarks hold for offline activities. We divide our activities into five categories: convenience, communication, evaluation, access to information, and personalization.

Convenience. We use OpenTable because it is a convenient way to make reservations. We don't have to call restaurants during the hours they answer their phone, it is easy to see a range of reservations options, and changes and cancellations are straightforward. Convenience also explains why we go online to make travel reservations, do our banking, submit papers to conferences, and so on. In Chapter 7 we described our use of OpenTable as analogous to Havel's greengrocer putting out the "Workers of the World, Unite!" sign. We object – strongly, we claimed – to the surveillance, but do not try to evade it. Like the greengrocer, we live the lie to get on with our lives. Did we describe ourselves correctly in Chapter 7? After all, we participate daily in activities which we know put us under surveillance. Does that show that we do not really object – at least not as strongly as we claim? Do we really live with an unacknowledged embrace of

4 David Lyon, *The Culture of Surveillance: Watching as a Way of Life* (Polity Press, 2018), 4.

5 James B. Rule, *Privacy in Peril: How We Are Sacrificing a Fundamental Right in Exchange for Security and Convenience* (Oxford University Press, 2007), 144.

6 A large body of work studies the rise of and reactions to data collection and analysis, including Theodore Porter, *The Rise of Statistical Thinking, 1820–1900*, (Princeton University Press, 1986); David Lyon, *Electronic Eye: The Rise of Surveillance Society* (University of Minnesota Press, 1994); David Lyon, *Surveillance Society: Monitoring Everyday Life* (Open University Press, 2002); Sarah E. Igo, *The Averaged American: Surveys, Citizens, and the Making of a Mass Public* (Harvard University Press, 2007); Josh Lauer, *Creditworthy: A History of Consumer Surveillance and Financial Identity in America* (Columbia University Press, 2017); Jerry Muller, *The Tyranny of Metrics* (Princeton University Press, 2018); Dan Bouk, *How Our Days Became Numbered: Risk and the Rise of the Statistical Individual* (University of Chicago Press, 2018); Shoshana Zuboff, *The Age of Surveillance Capitalism: The Fight for a Human Future at the New Frontier of Power* (PublicAffairs, 2019).

surveillance? The question arises repeatedly as we review our online activities. The answer is unimportant (for this book, not to us individually). What matters is why the question arises. It arises because our engagement with surveillance illustrates a process of acculturation that has the potential to transform objections into acceptance.

Communication. Emails and texts dominate our communications. We both use LinkedIn, and one of us also uses Facebook to maintain geographically diverse contacts that would otherwise lapse.

Evaluation. We read, and occasionally post, reviews of restaurants and products. We should probably have written "*Even we* read and post." We are not nearly as active in this regard as many others are. Indeed, some contend that "forms of evaluation and rating are now second-nature in current modes of communication."[7]

Access to information. Our academic research needs make us avid users of Google, Google Scholar, Amazon, the Social Science Research Network (SSRN), arXiv, Academia, and ResearchGate. We spent a fair amount of our earlier academic lives in a world in which such online resources did not exist, and we have no desire to return to that world.

Personalization. Personalized service is both an often-cited benefit and a much-maligned feature of Internet surveillance. We share the concern that personalization can create filter bubbles which expose people only to views they agree with, but we appreciate receiving book and research article recommendations based on an analysis of our past activities.

In all these areas, there is a benefit we are reluctant to give up. When we engage in the above activities, we experience benefits. We appreciate the convenience, enjoy communicating, express our opinions in evaluations, gain access to information we want, and appreciate personalization. These benefits come at the price of pervasive surveillance that significantly reduces privacy in public through a progressive undermining of informational norms. However, we experience the benefits immediately, and incur the cost in a much more diffuse, delayed manner. We assume many are like us in this regard. Next, we show how these features – immediately experienced benefit, and delayed, often diffuse harm – can lead people to accept surveillance. The cases divide into the "party to the norm," "not a party to the norm," and "no norm" cases. Our chart, presented in Table 8.1, illustrates the first two.

The "no norm" situations comprise the third case for acceptance. People accept surveillance, and "ought thoughts" about conforming to norms are not an issue because there are no informational norms.

[7] Andreas Bernard, *The Triumph of Profiling: The Self in Digital Culture*, trans. Valentine A. Pakis (Polity Press, 2019), 129.

TABLE 8.1 *Surveillance chart, now highlighting acceptance*

	Entity Conducting Surveillance			
	Party to the norm		Not a party	
	Ought thought	Reaction to Surveillance	Ought thought	Reaction to Surveillance
c. 1950–1980 "before surveillance"	Ought to	Surveillance not a serious concern	Ought to	Surveillance not a serious concern
Resisters	Ought not to	Try to prevent	Ought to	Try to prevent
Acquiescers	Ought not to	Do not try to prevent	Ought to	Partially accept
Acceptors	**Ought to**	**Accept**	**Ought not to**	**Accept**

PARTY TO THE NORM

For an initial example, we return to the "Vivian version" of the holiday dinner. That gives us a tractable example that serves as a good lens through which to view more complicated examples. We put that lens to use when we turn from the holiday dinner to our (the authors') use of OpenTable. Recall that Vivian hosts all the holiday dinners at her mansion. To further her study of family dynamics, the rooms contain microphones that feed comments and conversations to an AI program which analyzes them and generates an interactive graphical display of the results. The family members acquiesce to the surveillance – that is, they object to the surveillance and react by thinking they ought not to conform to the conditions on information flow *as a means to realizing the group-action goal of harmony*, but they nonetheless conform to the conditions for a variety of other reasons and make no attempt to evade Vivian's surveillance.

How do you get from acquiescence to acceptance? The key difference between acceptance and acquiescence is that acceptors do not object to surveillance. The acquiescing family members do object to Vivian's surveillance, but behave (more or less) as they would without surveillance. They create a selective flow of information – among themselves, Vivian aside – as a means to harmony. How might their acquiescence develop into acceptance?

To answer, we add in the fact that many family members benefit from Vivian's surveillance. Imagine some family members make needed but unexpected business connections with strangers, and others in financial need find they are winners of contests they did not know they had entered. Vivian never takes credit, but family members are sure that the wealthy and well-connected Vivian is behind it all. The family members' objections to Vivian's surveillance are a counterweight to the benefits, but imagine those objections diminish over time as the family comes to believe Vivian's assurances that she will never reveal personally identifying information. As the ill will her surveillance initially caused evaporates, she resumes her role as the aunt of whom everyone is fond. When the divorced Vivian invites her first husband Vincent, who has returned from years away in Europe, to the family dinner, family members tell him, "Vivian has us all under surveillance, but no one complains about that anymore." Vincent nods knowingly.

Do the family members as we have just described them still think they ought not to abide by the strictures on information flow to realize the group-action goal of family harmony? They might, but the thought would just reflect some lingering concern about surveillance. There is no longer any internal debate about whether one should attend or stay home and avoid surveillance. Their "ought not" thought is a wheel that spins but turns nothing else. Moreover, it creates cognitive dissonance. They think – or profess to think – they *ought not* to conform to the conditions on information flow *as a means to realizing the group-action goal of family harmony*, but they also know that they do realize that goal by conforming to the conditions. The family members could persist in their "ought not" thought, but it would hardly be surprising if they began to think that they *ought to* conform to the strictures on information flow to realize the group-action goal of family harmony (even under Vivian's watchful eye).

We describe a process in which the change from "ought not" to "ought to" occurs as a part of a process leading to the creation of a new informational norm that embraces Vivian's surveillance. Creating that norm requires creating common knowledge of relevant instances of the three conditions in Chapter 4's definition of an informational norm. The process ensures that happens by ensuring that presentations in the social role of a family member serve as common knowledge generators. For convenience, we begin by restating the conditions for the existence of a common knowledge generator.

A New Norm

Common Knowledge Generators

Recall that a common knowledge generator is a situation meeting two conditions:

(G1) The situation results in all members of a group G knowing X.
(G2) The situation ensures that all members of G know that all members of G experience the situation and as a result come to know X.

For the family holiday dinner, we instantiate (G1) and (G2) as follows: The group is the family members, the situation consists of their presentations in the social roles of family members, and X is that the three conditions hold.

Condition (1) (Thinking One Ought, and Dominant Preference)

To imagine a scenario where these two conditions hold, suppose the family members discuss their changed attitude toward Vivian's surveillance. They note that they now understand proper performance of the role of a family member to require – even in the face of Vivian's surveillance – thinking that one ought to adhere to the strictures on information flow to realize the group-action goal of family harmony. They also note that proper performance requires dominantly preferring to realize that goal. One is not to be like the disaffected adolescent who thinks he ought to abide by the strictures, but prefers to violate them. Of course, the family members do not discuss proper performance using phrases such as "thinking one ought to realize a group-action goal" and "dominantly preferring to realize a group-action goal." But imagine they do use words to that effect. The discussions supplemented by observations of behavior make presenting oneself as a family member into a common knowledge generator. (G1) holds because the discussions and observations result in all family members knowing that they all think they ought to observe the strictures on information flow to realize the group-action goal of family harmony (as long as enough others do), and they dominantly prefer to do so. (G2) holds because the discussions and observations are like the banner over the stadium. They ensure that people $know_2$ that they $know_1$. Thus: (G2) Each family member $knows_2$ that the other family members $know_1$ that family members think they ought to observe the strictures, and that they dominantly prefer to do so.

Condition (2) (Enough Conform)

The family members dominantly prefer to conform to the strictures, and so (exceptional circumstances aside) will so conform at appropriate times. Each family member will observe the others conforming to the strictures, and the others also observe the others doing so. Those observations ensure that (G1) and (G2) are fulfilled for (2).

Condition (3) (Continued Conformity)

As the Polar Plunge example from Chapter 4 shows, common knowledge of past conformity does not entail common knowledge that conformity will continue into the future. It does so only when past conformity gives each family member adequate reason to expect conformity in the future. When that is true, they can reason their way to (G1) and (G2).

Family members reason their way to (G1) as follows:

> I think I ought to realize family harmony by conformity to the strictures on information flow as long as enough others also conform. Enough others have conformed in the past. Given what I know about the family, past conformity gives me adequate reason to expect conformity in the future. Given future conformity, I can count on being able to realize my commitment to family harmony by joining with others in creating a selective flow of information. Thus, I should continue to

think that I ought to observe the strictures on information flow as long as enough others also do so.[8]

Thus (G1): the family members each reason their way to the conclusion that they should continue to think that they ought to observe the strictures on information flow as long as enough others also do so. For (G2), each family member reasons as follows: "The premises on which my reasoning depends are all common knowledge.[9] So, the other family members will reason from those premises to the same conclusion." Thus (G2): Each family member realizes that the other family members will reason in the same way and hence realizes that the others will continue to conform.

The change from acquiescence to acceptance creates a norm. However, it is a different norm. Under the old presurveillance norm, the family members saw Vivian's surveillance as violating the strictures on information flow required by the norm. Under the new norm, they see Vivian's surveillance as permissible despite the fact that it siphons off information in ways that reveal to Vivian *everything* that is otherwise only selectively disclosed.

Our rationale for beginning with the holiday dinner was that it is a convenient illustration of a pattern that appears in more complicated examples. We now turn to those examples.

OpenTable

Restaurant customers use OpenTable (and its competitors, such as Tock and Resy) to make and manage reservations. In doing so, they indirectly exchange information with restaurants, which use information they receive from OpenTable to analyze customers' needs. For this reason, we treat restaurant customers' use of OpenTable as falling under the customer/restaurant norm that requires that customers and restaurants exchange information as a means to realizing the group-action goal of meeting customers' restaurant needs. Initially, OpenTable use appears to parallel the holiday dinner closely. The holiday dinner example begins with the family members as acquiescers engaged in mere shadow conformity to the norm. Many OpenTable users also acquiesce. They react to OpenTable's surveillance by thinking they ought not to exchange information to realize the group-action goal of meeting customers' needs, but they do not attempt to evade the surveillance. At

8 As we have noted, people rarely engage in such explicit reasoning. Our point is that family members could reason in the way described. They have the answer in hand even if they never have the need to produce it.

9 In particular, this is true of the premise "Given what I know about the family, past conformity gives me adequate reason to expect conformity in the future." (G1) holds: each family member's observations of the family lead that member to know$_1$ that past conformity is adequate reason to expect conformity in the future. (G2) holds: each family member knows$_2$ that family members' observations lead them to know$_1$ that past conformity is adequate reason to expect conformity in the future.

least, that is how we (the authors) described ourselves in Chapter 7, and we will continue with ourselves as the example. We assume, however, that many react similarly. The examples diverge when we turn to explaining how to restore the norm by ensuring the fulfillment of relevant instances of (G1) and (G2). In the family holiday dinner, a crucial part of our explanation imagined the family members discussing Vivian's surveillance and observing their reactions to it. We cannot appeal to discussions and observations among geographically distributed strangers sitting at computers using OpenTable. So how are (G1) and (G2) fulfilled?

We begin with acquiescence and explain how a process similar to the one in the Vivian dinner could change that "ought not" to an "ought to." A salient fact is that exchanging information with OpenTable secures diners the benefit of convenience. The benefit comes at the price of contributing to OpenTable's surveillance, but the harm – the incremental contribution to the eventual loss of self-realization – is not immediately palpable in the way the benefit is. We spend enough time thinking, writing, and teaching about such issues that the harm stays on our minds, but consider people like us but not professionally involved in thinking about norms, surveillance, and privacy. Imagine that over time awareness of the benefit stays in the foreground while concern about surveillance fades ever more into the background.

As the concern fades, do the OpenTable users – the authors and others with similar attitudes – still think they ought not to exchange information with OpenTable to realize the group-action goal of meeting customers' needs? They could, but the thought would again be a wheel that spins but generates no significant surveillance-evading action. Objections to surveillance will have become muted to the point where there is very little chance of their ever leading anyone to stop using OpenTable. What the "ought not" thought does is create cognitive dissonance. OpenTable users know (we may suppose[10]) that their exchange of information with OpenTable contributes to the group-action goal of meeting customers' restaurant needs (albeit under the persistent gaze of OpenTable's surveillance). They know that their actions help realize a goal that they think they ought not aim at. It need not happen, but, under these conditions, thinking one "ought not to" could easily change into thinking that, as a restaurant customer, one *ought to* exchange information with OpenTable to realize the group-action goal of meeting customers' needs (even subject to OpenTable's surveillance).

We present the change from "ought not" to "ought to" as a part of a process that leads to the creation of a new informational norm that embraces OpenTable's surveillance. The process yields that result by ensuring that presentations in the social role of restaurant customer serve as common knowledge generators of relevant instances of the three conditions from Chapter 4.

10 Many OpenTable users may be unaware of the business's surveillance practices. In that case, we intend our remarks to describe the reactions they would have after adequate, well-informed reflection.

Versions of (G1) and (G2)

(G1) The presentations in the role of restaurant customer result in customers knowing that the three conditions hold (under an interpretation that permits OpenTable surveillance).
(G2) The presentations in the role of restaurant customer result in customers knowing$_2$ that customers know$_1$ that the three conditions hold.

To see that these versions of (G1) and (G2) hold, we consider the conditions piecemeal, starting with the first.

Condition (1) (Thinking One Ought, and Dominant Preference)

We appeal to broadcast narratives to explain how (G1) and (G2) could come to hold. We envision a far more diffuse broadcast than the Super Bowl Groupon advertisement we discussed in Chapter 3. We envision a combination of traditional media articles, email newsletters, blog postings, online articles, and the like. Diffuse narratives can create common knowledge. Antilittering campaigns are one example, as discussed in Chapter 4. The mid-twentieth century US Civil Rights movement provides additional examples, as the political scientist Dennis Chong points out. He emphasizes that the public appearances, statements, and actions of Civil Right leaders and those around them created common knowledge that people thought they ought to join the protest to realize the group-action goal of an effective protest (as long as enough others did so too), and enough people dominantly preferred to join the protest.[11]

Similarly, a diffuse broadcast narrative could make it common knowledge that customers and restaurants will conform to new conditions on information flow as a means to meeting customers' restaurant needs – conditions allowing surveillance by reservations services and, depending on the exact path of acculturation, perhaps other forms of surveillance as well.

Condition (2) (Enough Conform)

Given that it is common knowledge that the restaurants and customers dominantly prefer to exchange information with restaurants to realize the group-action goal of meeting customers' needs (where OpenTable surveillance is now understood as an acceptable means), it will be common knowledge that, exceptional circumstances aside, restaurants and customers will exchange information with restaurants to meet the goal.

Condition (3) (Continued Conformity)

As in the family holiday dinner example, customers and restaurants reason their way to the relevant instances of (G1) and (G2).

[11] Dennis Chong, *Collective Action and the Civil Rights Movement* (University of Chicago Press, 1991).

The New Norm
Once that happens, the old norm is transformed into one that now permits surveillance impermissible under the original norm. Conformity to the norm no longer ensures adequate privacy in public but undermines it.

NOT A PARTY TO THE NORM

We begin with the investigative journalist example to illustrate how acquiescence can turn into acceptance. We then turn to proxy surveillance.

Investigative Journalists

As before, we explain acceptance by contrasting it with acquiescence. Journalists who acquiesce think they *ought to* conform to the conditions on information flow as a means to realizing the group-action goal of revealing government wrongdoing while protecting the identity of their source, but they partially accept surveillance, which is what distinguishes them from resisters. The "partially" is an essential qualification. Acquiescers cannot consistently *completely* allow surveillance and also think they *ought to* conform to the conditions on information flow that require protecting the identity of sources. Acceptors fully embrace surveillance and consequently think they *ought not* to conform to the conditions on information flow that require protecting the identity of sources. To be an acceptor is necessarily to abandon the role of an investigative journalist.

For investigative journalists, the path from acquiescence to acceptance is the slippery slope of protracted negotiations with the government which acquiescers engage in as the price of publishing in the mainstream media. We do not claim that it is inevitable that those negotiations lead eventually to acceptance. The government might make only limited, reasonable demands, and journalists might unwaveringly insist on surveillance limits. We claim only that it *could* lead to acceptance, and that it is best to intervene now to ensure that it does not. The comments of a German philologist who witnessed the rise of the Nazis are a reminder of how easy it can be to slide down the slope. We emphasize that we are *not* implying that the rise of pervasive surveillance is analogous to the rise of the Nazis. The following observations apply generally to assertions of governmental power:

> What happened was the gradual habituation of the people, little by little, to be governed by surprise, to receiving decisions deliberated in secret; to believe that the situation was so complicated that the government had to act on information which the people could not understand, or so dangerous that, even if people could understand it, it could not be released because of national security … This separation of government from the people, this widening of the gap, took place so gradually and insensibly, each step disguised (perhaps not even intentionally) as a temporary emergency measure or associated with true patriotic allegiance or with

> real social purposes. And all the crises and reforms (real reforms too) so occupied the people that they did not see the slow motion underneath, of the whole process of government growing remoter and remoter ... Each step was so small, so inconsequential, so well explained or, on occasion, "regretted." That, unless one were to detach from the whole process from the beginning, unless one understood what the whole thing was in principle, what all these "little measures" that no "patriotic German" could resist must some day lead to, one no more saw it developing from day to day than a farmer in his field sees the corn growing ... Believe me this is true. Each act, each occasion is worse than the last, but only a little worse. You wait for the next and the next. You wait for one shocking occasion, thinking that others, when such a shock comes, will join you in resisting somehow ... Suddenly it all comes down, all at once. You see what you are, what you have done, or, more accurately, what you haven't done (for that was all that was required of most of us: that we did nothing) ... You remember everything now, and your heart breaks. Too late. You are compromised beyond repair.[12]

Proxy Surveillance

Similar points hold for business "not a party to the norm" surveillance in the form of proxy surveillance. Might acquiescence to proxy surveillance turn into acceptance? A slippery slope is again the concern. It can still be true that each step is

> so small, so inconsequential, so well explained or, on occasion, "regretted." That, unless one were to detach from the whole process from the beginning, unless one understood what the whole thing was in principle, what all these "little measures" ... must some day lead to, one no more saw it developing from day to day than a farmer in his field sees the corn growing.

One noteworthy development in this regard is the *Internet of Things*. The Internet of Things (IoT) refers to "things" that are connected to and communicate via the Internet and also can either sense or alter things in the physical world, or both. The "things" can be anything, but the term typically indicates a focus on items that were unconnected until relatively recently – light fixtures, thermostats, kitchen appliances, wearables, medical devices, components of cars, baby monitors, cameras, and so on. For our purposes, it is sufficient to consider the "things" as being connected to the network and containing sensors, actuators or both, and sometimes also data storage and analysis (the same device may have one or more of these). Billions of sensors collect data and feed it to data storage and analysis components that typically are elsewhere on the Internet. Those components instruct actuators to take actions (control air conditioning and heating, turn on lights, and so on). As Bruce Schneier notes, systems

12 Milton Mayer, *They Thought They Were Free: The Germans, 1933–45*, 2nd Revised ed. (University of Chicago Press, 1966), 166–72.

> will interpret the data and figure out what to do. And the actuators will do things in our world. You can think of the sensors as the eyes and ears of the Internet, the actuators as the hands and feet of the Internet, and the stuff in the middle as the brain . . . We're building a world-sized robot, and we don't even realize it.[13]

Living inside the robot potentially subjects us to "not a party to the norm" surveillance to the extent that IoT surveillance collects data from activities under informational norms – norms to which the IoT entity conducting surveillance is not a party.

NO NORMS

In many cases in the new online world, no relevant informational norms have yet arisen. In the preceding chapter, we used ourselves (the authors) as an example of acquiescence – specifically, acquiescence to Google's surveillance. We mentioned in passing that this is a case where there is not, and never has been, any relevant informational norm. Certainly we object to Google's surveillance, but that does not affect our behavior. It could. We could actively campaign against Google by demanding that it provide better privacy protections. Or we could at least abandon the Google search engine for the privacy-protective (but somewhat less effective) search engine DuckDuckGo. But that is not what we do. We use Google (constantly, as it happens), and do not protest against its privacy practices except occasionally when teaching and in academic writing. Our attitude is again a wheel that spins but turns nothing.

Could a process of acculturation turn acquiescence into acceptance? In particular, into acceptance that gives rise to an information norm that permits surveillance? While such a process is far from inevitable, we note, along with Bicchieri, that a "vast psychological literature, supported by experimental data, shows that when individuals are faced with new tasks or an uncertain situation they will, whenever possible, look to behavioral regularities for guidance in making choices."[14] Informational norms may arise as people "look to behavioral regularities for guidance." To see how, consider Google's services. A diffusely broadcast narrative of proper performance for a user of Google's services could replace the idly spinning wheel of acquiescence with a conception of proper performance that requires (1) that one think one ought to allow Google's surveillance as a means to realizing the group-action goal of providing data for Google's information-processing purposes, and (2) that one dominantly prefer, at appropriate times, to allow the surveillance as a means to realizing that goal. That change could be the first step in generating an informational norm through a process similar to the one just described in the "norms exist" cases.

13 "The Internet of Things Will Be the World's Biggest Robot," *Schneier on Security*, February 2, 2016, www.schneier.com/blog/archives/2016/02/the_internet_of_1.html.

14 Cristina Bicchieri, *The Grammar of Society: The Nature and Dynamics of Social Norms* (Cambridge University Press, 2005), 216.

TIME TO TAKE CONTROL

So far, we have painted an unattractive picture of the present and the future. The present is a present of ineffective resistance, acquiescence to surveillance through shadow conformity, and interactions with businesses and governments unmediated by informational norms. The future sees the likely rise of surveillance-embracing norms. We should not let processes of resistance, acquiescence, and acceptance run without intervention. It is time to take control. As Bruce Schneier observed back in 2007, history "will record what we, here in the early decades of the information age, did to foster freedom, liberty, and democracy. Did we build information technologies that protected people's freedoms even during times when society tried to subvert them? Or did we build technologies that could easily be modified to watch and control?"[15] Schneir's 2013 answer to his own question was a resoundingly negative one:

> So, we're done. Welcome to a world where Google knows exactly what sort of porn you all like, and more about your interests than your spouse does. Welcome to a world where your cell phone company knows exactly where you are all the time. Welcome to the end of private conversations, because increasingly your conversations are conducted by e-mail, text, or social networking sites. And welcome to a world where all of this, and everything else that you do or is done on a computer, is saved, correlated, studied, passed around … Welcome to an Internet without privacy, and we've ended up here with hardly a fight.[16]

Are we really done? Our hope is "not yet." We can "foster freedom, liberty, and democracy" by maintaining and, where necessary, creating, a complex of informational norms sufficient to ensure adequate privacy in public.

To carry out that task successfully, one must resolve difficult tradeoff questions. Tradeoff questions arise because informational norms implement a selective flow of information. Each norm thereby makes a tradeoff between the benefits of information processing and the value of information privacy. Helen Nissenbaum makes the point with the metaphor of a river: "My definition of privacy is 'an appropriate flow of information' (or, 'data,' if you prefer). If you imagine a river, you can think about ways in which we can shape its flow. We can pause, dam, or divert it with different means and for different reasons."[17] Different ways of shaping the flow of data with informational norms yield different tradeoffs. What tradeoffs should we make?

[15] Bruce Schneier, "Risks of Data Reuse," *Crypto-Gram* (blog), July 15, 2007, www.schneier.com/crypto-gram-0707.html.

[16] Bruce Schneier, "The Internet Is a Surveillance State," *CNN*, March 16, 2013, www.cnn.com/2013/03/16/opinion/schneier-internet-surveillance/index.html.

[17] Interview with Nissenbaum in Scott Berinato, "Why Data Privacy Based on Consent Is Impossible," *Harvard Business Review*, September 24, 2018, https://hbr.org/2018/09/stop-thinking-about-consent-it-isnt-possible-and-it-isnt-right.

ACCEPTABLE TRADEOFFS

We answer in two steps. We first define the notion of a value-optimal norm, and then define an acceptable tradeoff as one implemented by a norm that adequately approximates being value-optimal.

Value-Optimal Norms

Value-optimality (or the lack thereof) is a feature of coordination norms generally, not just informational norms. The idea is that a norm is value-optimal when no alternative norm is a better fit with one's values. More precisely, a coordination norm is value-optimal when, in light of the values of all (or almost all) members of the group in which the norm obtains, the norm is at least as well justified as any alternative. A good way to illustrate the definition is with an example of a coordination norm that is not value-optimal.

As we mentioned in the game theory appendix to Chapter 3, professional ice hockey players were trapped in a coordination norm that required playing without a helmet until 1979, when the National Hockey League mandated the wearing of helmets. Before that, most players did not wear helmets despite the obvious risk of severe head injury. They were reluctant to wear helmets because non-helmet-wearing players would perceive them as lacking toughness, and because they would incur a small loss in playing effectiveness against non-helmet-wearing players from the helmet's restriction of peripheral vision. We assume that proper performance of the role of a pre-1979 professional hockey player required thinking one ought not to wear a helmet in order to realize the group-action goal of all players not wearing them, and dominantly preferring (at appropriate times) not to wear a helmet in order to realize that group-action goal.

Not wearing a helmet was a coordination norm. When, prior to 1979, they presented themselves to each other as professional hockey players, they made our standard three conditions for norms common knowledge among themselves.[18] That norm was not value-optimal. There was an alternative coordination norm that the players regarded as better justified: all players wear helmets. If someone had conducted a secret ballot, the vast majority of players would have voted for all players to wear helmets: "One player summed up the feelings of many: It is foolish not to wear a helmet. But I don't – because the other guys don't. I know that's silly, but most of the other players feel the same way."[19]

Some may object that value-optimal norms must be rare, because a norm is not value-optimal if there is *any* better justified alternative norm. Won't that almost

[18] See T. C. Schelling, "Hockey Helmets, Concealed Weapons, and Daylight Saving: A Study of Binary Choices with Externalities," *Journal of Conflict Resolution* 17, 3 (September 1973): 381.

[19] The remark is reported in Schelling, 381. This work appears to be the source of this well-known Hockey Helmet example.

always be the case? Won't there be at least some minor adjustments that would make the norm better? There is no need to argue the point. We propose value-optimality as an *ideal* that we approximate in practice. We want our norms to be *close enough* to being value-optimal.

Acceptability

So, how far away can a norm be from value-optimality and still be acceptable? *Fully* value-optimal norms implement clearly acceptable tradeoffs. There is no better-justified alternative norm, so the tradeoff is the best we can get. Best-we-can-get norm-implemented tradeoffs are clearly acceptable. However, norms that fall short of full value-optimality can still implement acceptable tradeoffs. Imagine that even in pre-COVID 2019 Mason had an intense aversion to overcrowding and felt very uncomfortable in elevators when people were closer to him than twelve inches. If he could have had things his way, the elevator norm would have been to maximize the distance from your nearest neighbor and always to maintain a minimum distance of twelve inches. People would not have entered elevators when it was not possible to maintain that distance. The 2019 elevator norm was not value-optimal for Mason. Indeed, given the strength of his aversion to overcrowding, the norm was at best a middling approximation to value-optimality for him. Mason nonetheless regarded the 2019 tradeoff as acceptable. He was confronted with a norm already in place that he could not change, and he wanted to use elevators when they arrived, even when he knew that it was likely that, as others entered, people would stand closer to him than twelve inches. The tradeoff was close enough to be acceptable to Mason.

In general, what counts as close enough to be acceptable? This is typically a judgment call, as is true for most questions about when something is close enough to optimal. Cases spread out across a range from "meeting the formal definition of value-optimal" to "clearly nowhere close to value-optimal." Unclear cases occur in the middle. We note in passing that one source of unclarity is that people may not always know what they consider value-optimal. As the philosopher John Gray notes,

> We are none of us defined by membership in a single community or form of moral life. We are . . . heirs of many distinct, sometimes conflicting, intellectual and moral traditions . . . The complexity and contradictions of our cultural inheritance give to our identities an aspect of complexity and even of plurality which is . . . essential to them . . . [T]he power to conceive of ourselves in different ways, to harbour dissonant projects and perspectives, to inform our thoughts and lives with divergent categories and concepts, is integral to our identity as reflective beings.[20]

For "heirs of many distinct, sometimes conflicting, intellectual and moral traditions," it can be challenging to determine what one values. It may be clear that one

[20] John Gray, *Post-Liberalism: Studies in Political Thought* (Routledge, 1993), 262–63.

values something from one perspective, and that one does not value it from another, and one may lack a unified perspective from which one can confidently declare "I value this."

In any event, tradeoffs at or close to the value-optimal end are clearly acceptable. At what point do they cease to be so, as one moves away from the value-optimal end? People answer that question differently. Some may object that people do not actually answer the question at all. Only theorists explicitly concerned with value-optimality and acceptability even formulate the question. We agree that people do not raise and answer the question. Our talk of people's views about the acceptability of tradeoffs is talk about what they would think if they considered the question under ideal conditions that include adequate information, adequate time for reflection, and an adequate, unbiased, and unimpaired capacity to reason. This is hardly unusual. People would, for example, be hard pressed to give any adequate general account of fairness, justice, or happiness. Those concepts nonetheless play an important role in people's thoughts and actions. Acceptability is the same. Back in Chapter 3, when Victoria was in the wine shop, she sought and obtained an acceptable privacy tradeoff (e.g., the store didn't ask her for information about her liver function nor publicize details of the party for which they advised her on wine choices), even though she would have been hard pressed to explicitly define *precisely* which tradeoffs qualified as acceptable for her.

We conclude our discussion of tradeoffs by noting that finding acceptable tradeoffs is not only a matter of imposing limits on surveillance. In some cases, one may want to ensure that adequate surveillance *can* occur. There are several examples where surveillance, far from threatening the self, is *essential* to adequate self-realization. Public health is a good example. Ensuring adequate public health promotes healthy individuals, and being healthy typically facilitates self-realization. Surveillance is an essential means to these ends. Public health officials record details of disease and treatment, often in ways that allow personal identification. Such information

> has provided the foundation for planning, intervention, and disease prevention and has been critical for epidemiological research into patterns of morbidity and mortality for a wide variety of diseases and conditions. Registries have been essential for tracking individuals and their conditions over time. Surveillance has also served to trigger the imposition of public health control measures, such as contact tracing, mandatory treatment, and quarantine.[21]

[21] Amy L. Fairchild et al., *Searching Eyes: Privacy, the State, and Disease Surveillance in America* (University of California Press, 2007), 204. For concern about the sharing of health information, see, for example, Lori Andrews, "Privacy Policies of Android Diabetes Apps and Sharing of Health Information," *JAMA: The Journal of the American Medical Association* 315 (2016): 1051–52, and Lori Andrews and Erin Shaugnessy Zuiker, "Ethical, Legal, and Social Issues in Genetic Testing for Complex Genetic Diseases," *Valparaiso University Law Review* 37 (2003): 793–829.

Commentators debate both the appropriate type and the acceptable extent of public health surveillance,[22] but few would deny that *some* appropriately constrained surveillance is justified to promote health. There are other cases where appropriately constrained surveillance arguably *facilitates* self-realization. Analysis of large data sets, for example, can reveal patterns that would otherwise go unnoticed, and this has already yielded a wide array of benefits. It is difficult to see why appropriately constrained surveillance would not promote self-realization.

How do we maintain and create norms in ways that address and resolve complex tradeoff questions? We propose a three-step process based on the conditions for the existence of an informational norm. We initially present it as a model for the *creation* of norms, but it applies equally to the preservation or restoration of existing norms. The task in all cases is to ensure that the three steps are fulfilled.

A NORM-CREATION MODEL

Our three-step process is a generalization of the norm-creation examples we discussed in previous chapters. Focusing initially on norm-creation has the advantage of directly connecting our discussion to Christina Biccheri's recent empirical study of the creation of norms, which revealed a pattern that occurs with remarkable frequency.[23] Bicchieri summarizes her observations as revealing a five-step pattern: *One*: change factual and normative beliefs. *Two*: create a collective decision to change. *Three*: introduce sanctions for noncompliance with the decision to change. *Four*: create empirical expectations. *Five*: create normative expectations.[24] Our model differs by explicitly referring to social roles and common knowledge, and by having only three steps.

Assume you want to create an informational norm in a group. The three-step process we give next does so. Each step creates common knowledge of one of the three conditions defining informational coordination norms. In summary, the three conditions are:

1. Conditionally thinking one ought to conform plus a dominant preference to conform.
2. Enough conform.
3. Continuing conformity.

For concreteness, consider Google's services. As we argued in Chapter 6, people's use of Google services is not governed by an informational norm. Our argument was that there is no set of conditions on information flow and no group-action goal

22 See Fairchild et al., *Searching Eyes*.

23 Cristina Bicchieri, *Norms in the Wild: How to Diagnose, Measure, and Change Social Norms* (Oxford University Press, 2016).

24 Bicchieri, 118. Her examples include creating norms against child marriage and norms requiring the creation and use of latrines.

meeting this condition: both users and Google think they ought to conform to the conditions as a means of realizing the goal. Ensuring that users and Google have such an "ought thought" is the key step in creating a norm. We propose doing so by creating a conception of proper performance and ensuring that adherence to it is common knowledge. In the case of Google' services, for example, proper performance of the role of a user or provider of the services would require, with regard to a certain set of conditions on information flow and a given group-action goal, (a) that one think one ought to conform to the conditions as a means to realizing the goal, and (b) that, at appropriate times, one dominantly prefers to conform to the conditions as a means to realizing the goal. Emphasis on the dominant preference is in order. Our discussion so far has focused on the "ought thought," so we note that it is also essential that people dominantly prefer to conform to the conditions. The dominant preference is what leads from the "ought thought" to enough conforming. Thus, we propose:

Step 1: Common Knowledge of Proper Performance of a Social Role

As noted earlier, broadcasting a narrative can create common knowledge that proper performance requires (a) that people think they ought to conform to role-specific conditions on the flow of information as a mean to realizing a given group-action goal, and (b) that, at appropriate times, people dominantly prefer to conform to the conditions as a means of realizing the goal.

Our reliance on narratives raises two questions. Who determines the content of the narratives? And who promulgates them? Our answer to both: legitimate social and political processes. Those processes specify both the conditions on information flow and the group-action goal. In doing so, those processes determine a tradeoff between informational privacy and information processing. To illustrate the point with Google services, the more the conditions limit how Google can collect and use information, the more they protect privacy. The choice of a group-action goal also plays a role. Is the group-action goal to make Google's searches as accurate, personalized, and complete as possible, or is the goal to make Google's searches as accurate, personalized, and complete as possible within specified limits (e.g., abiding by a right to be forgotten, or not attempting to identify the user making the query)? Or is it some other option?

Choosing conditions and group-action goals will be controversial, and our example of norm-creation in the next chapter gives a governmental agency a central norm-creation role. Some may object that assigning political processes such a role violates the fairly widely held philosophical view that the state should not justify what it does by appealing to conceptions of what is desirable when those conceptions are subject to reasonable disagreement.[25] We reject that view. One

[25] For a good introduction, see Steven Wall, "Perfectionism in Moral and Political Philosophy," in *The Stanford Encyclopedia of Philosophy*, ed. Edward N. Zalta, Summer 2019 (Metaphysics Research Lab, Stanford University, 2019), https://plato.stanford.edu/archives/sum2019/entries/perfectionism-moral/.

cannot decide how to trade privacy off against information processing without taking a controversial stand about what outcomes are desirable, and, as we illustrate in the next chapter, we think political processes have an essential role to play in deciding what tradeoffs to make. This is not to say that we see no problem here. Quite the opposite. Constant claims of "fake news" and concerns about the manipulation of social media highlight the need to find a way to distinguish between the legitimate and illegitimate use of narratives to shape public opinion.

We conclude our discussion of Step 1 by noting the parallels with Bicchieri. Our Step 1 incorporates her step one (change factual and normative beliefs) and her step two (create a collective decision to change). Broadcast narratives change factual and normative beliefs. The Groupon Super Bowl narrative, for example, aimed at convincing people of the factual claim that not using Groupon was tantamount to disdain for small business, and it also sought to instill the normative belief that one ought to use Groupon. Our Step 1 aims at creating a collective decision to change by creating common knowledge among members of a group both that they think they ought to conform to certain conditions on information flow as a means to realizing a group-action goal, and that they dominantly prefer, at appropriate times, to do so. To create such common knowledge is to create common knowledge of a collective decision to change.

Step 2: Common Knowledge that Enough Conform

Dominant preferences result in action (exceptions aside), so Step 1 ensures that at least *some* members of G will conform to the conditions on information flow as a means to realizing the group-action goal. Will enough do so – enough to actually realize the goal? That depends in part on how effective one was at Step 1 in getting group members to have the dominant preference at appropriate times. If enough have the preference, enough will conform. If not, at Step 2 one may need to introduce sanctions for noncompliance with the conditions on information flow, as Bicchieri urges in her step three.[26]

Again, we rely on broadcast narratives to create common knowledge that enough conform.

Step 3: Common Knowledge of Continued Conformity

As we explained when discussing the Polar Plunge example in Chapter 4, common knowledge of past conformity creates common knowledge of future conformity – as

[26] And one would have to ensure not just that the sanctions secured conformity to the conditions, but that they secured conformity *as a means to realizing the group-action goal*. The "ought thought" – thinking one ought to conform as means to realizing the goal – is what connects means and goal, so one would have to combine sanctions with continued efforts to spread the "ought thought" throughout the group.

long as past conformity gives people an adequate reason to expect conformity in the future. The task at Step 3 is to ensure that people have adequate reason to expect future conformity by enough people. Broadcast narratives can serve that purpose. The Nobel Prize–winning economist Robert Shiller illustrates the reason-giving power of narratives with "narratives from the second half of the twentieth century [which] describe free markets as 'efficient' and therefore impervious to improvement by government action. These narratives in turn led to a public reaction against regulation."[27]

Steps 3 creates both empirical expectations (Bicchieri's step four) and normative ones (Bicchieri's step five). Indeed, at Step 3 people do not just expect others to conform to conditions on information flow, it is common knowledge that they will do so. The common knowledge supports the thought that one ought to conform. We illustrated the point in Chapter 4 by imagining Alice thinking of the icy water that awaits on the morning of the Polar Plunge. She asks herself, "Am I going?" She answers, "Yes, I ought to participate as long as the rest do, and I know they will participate, so I ought to participate too."

One can use the same three-part process to maintain norms. The elevator norm is a good example even though it is not an informational norm. Our prepandemic observations suggested that many were entering elevators while absorbed in their phones and paying little attention to where they stood. As we noted earlier, if enough elevator users failed to maximize their distance from their nearest neighbor for long enough, it would no longer be common knowledge that users maximize that distance, and the norm would collapse. Suppose you wanted to reverse this process. What parts of the three-part norm-creation process would be relevant? That depends on why people are not maximizing their distance from their nearest neighbor. There are three possibilities.

Riders no longer have the relevant "ought thought." One possibility is that riders do not think they ought to be nearest-neighbor-distance-maximizers as a means to realizing the group-action goal of minimizing crowding while maximizing elevator use. Steps 1 through 3 would be required.

Riders think they "ought to" but not enough dominantly prefer to. Suppose riders think they ought to be nearest-neighbor-distance-maximizers, but suppose that not enough dominantly prefer to do so when they enter elevators. The problem is that they have a conflicting "ought thought." They think they ought to pay attention to their phones in elevators instead of paying attention to where they stand, and the phone "ought thought" is the one that yields a dominant preference. One could try to restore the dominant preference to be a nearest-neighbor-distance-maximizer by

[27] Robert J. Shiller, *Narrative Economics: How Stories Go Viral and Drive Major Economic Events* (Princeton University Press, 2020), xii. Shiller does not endorse the claim that markets are "efficient" and hence not improvable through regulation. Neither do we.

fining phone use, or, as in Step 1, promulgating a narrative that promotes that preference and creates common knowledge that people have it.

Uncertainty whether enough will continue to be nearest-neighbor-distance-maximizers. Assume it is common knowledge among a group of elevator riders that enough think they ought to be nearest-neighbor-distance-maximizers, and dominantly prefer to do so, and assume that the result is that enough have been nearest-neighbor-distance-maximizers in the past. But suppose that it is not common knowledge that enough will continue to be nearest-neighbor-distance-maximizers in the future. That can happen only if – somehow – past conformity does not give people an adequate reason to expect future conformity. If that does happen, the solution is the Step 3 solution of a broadcast narrative that gives people a reason to expect future conformity.

A TEST CASE

How would one implement this abstract model of norm-creation in practice? As a test case, in the next chapter we show how to create norms to regulate certain aspects of the use of AI.

9

Regulating Artificial Intelligence

We show how to create an informational norm that constrains the use of proxies in AI-driven surveillance. The norm creates privacy in public by implementing conditions on the flow of information that control the use of that information as proxy variables. There are a variety of possible conditions. The task is to choose one that implements an acceptable tradeoff between informational privacy and information processing. The norm we propose ensures that the use of proxies is fair and to that extent implements an acceptable tradeoff between informational privacy and information processing. There is, of course, more to finding such a tradeoff than just ensuring that the use of proxies is fair, and the process we describe creates a forum for addressing tradeoff issues in general. Our focus for the moment, however, is on fairness. The example of Sally from Chapter 2 illustrates the questions that arise. Sally's car insurance premiums increase as a result of her bankruptcy. The bankruptcy was a consequence of her paying for lifesaving medical treatment for her daughter. Is it fair that saving her daughter's life makes Sally pay more for car insurance?

Fair in what sense? There are different concepts of fairness.[1] We focus on one: fairness as equality of opportunity. As the economist John Roemer notes, a conception of "equality of opportunity ... prevalent today in Western democracies ... says that society should do what it can to 'level the playing field' among individuals who compete for positions."[2] Most people think there are some attributes for which society should level the playing field, although they often disagree about which ones they are.[3] One of the less controversial examples is access to education. There is widespread agreement that children should have equal access to educational opportunities, and that lower socioeconomic status tilts the playing

[1] Abigail Z. Jacobs and Hanna Wallach, "Measurement and Fairness," *ArXiv:1912.05511 [cs.CY]*, December 11, 2019, 15–19, http://arxiv.org/abs/1912.05511 (noting that there are different conceptions of fairness and analyzing the impact of the failure to distinguish them on the computer science literature on fairness).

[2] John E. Roemer, *Equality of Opportunity* (Harvard University Press, 2000), 1.

[3] See, for example, Erik Olin Wright and Michael Burawoy, *How to Be an Anticapitalist in the Twenty-First Century* (Verso, 2019), 10.

field against equal access.[4] Our point is that the "which attributes?" question arises in a sweeping, across-the-board way as contemporary proxy-driven AI makes what happens in one area of one's life reverberate through the rest in ways that can dramatically tilt the playing field.

THE PROXY PROBLEM

To understand proxy variables, it helps to consider predictive systems that do *not* use them. The systems from the Camelyon16 Challenge to design systems for the "automated detection of metastases in … whole-slide images of lymph node sections"[5] are good examples. For concreteness, we consider a system from Google researchers,[6] but, except for the technical details, our remarks apply to all the systems in the challenge. The Google team trained a neural net to recognize cancerous cells by providing the system with 270 sample images, each correctly labeled as cancerous or noncancerous. The images were at 40x magnification, and contained *gigapixels* – that is, billions of pixels.[7] Each one of those pixels was an input variable for the Google system. The essential point is that the image they make up is precisely what either a human pathologist or a computer system is asked to classify. Being able to observe them is the equivalent of the teacher being able to observe the mental activity of paying attention (in our Chapter 2 example of proxy variables). There is no need for any proxy variables – variables distinct from the pixels and the image they make up. The pixels are *all* the relevant data. Contrast predicting whether someone will repay a loan or how they will vote from information that is limited either by the access you have to their data (e.g., only their web browsing history and credit rating) or by law. Outside factors such as age, income, occupation, race, religion, sexual orientation, and so on can be very helpful in making predictions.[8] Factors that are both legal and easy to obtain (e.g., a person's age, address, or location while browsing the web) are among the sorts of factors that can become proxy variables in an AI system.[9]

4 Roemer, *Equality of Opportunity*, chapter 11.

5 "CAMELYON16: ISBI Challenge on Cancer Metastasis Detection in Lymph Node," *grand-challenge.org*, https://camelyon16.grand-challenge.org/.

6 Yun Liu et al., "Detecting Cancer Metastases on Gigapixel Pathology Images," *ArXiv:1703.02442v2 [cs.CV]*, March 3, 2017, https://arxiv.org/abs/1703.02442.

7 "CAMELYON16: ISBI Challenge on Cancer Metastasis Detection in Lymph Node."

8 For example, work reported in *The New York Times* showed that by asking only eight or fewer questions, Americans could be fairly accurately classified as Democrats or Republicans. However, the first and most important question, race, would be illegal to ask in most situations. Among white people, the second most important question was "How religious are you?" which might both be illegal to ask and difficult to get honest answers to even if it was allowed. Sahil Chinoy, "Quiz: Let Us Predict Whether You're a Democrat or a Republican," *The New York Times*, August 8, 2019, www.nytimes.com/interactive/2019/08/08/opinion/sunday/party-polarization-quiz.html.

9 Jacobs and Wallach, "Measurement and Fairness" (discussing the use of proxy variables).

The use of proxy variables in AI systems gained wide attention across many research communities with the publication of Catherine O'Neil's *Weapons of Math Destruction* in 2016.[10] She rails against the use of proxies as one of the evils of the AI era.[11] However, as we noted in Chapter 2, proxy variables are not new to the AI era. Applied statisticians and economists have used the *term* "proxy variable" since at least the early 1970s,[12] and the variables themselves were in use much earlier. Extensive use of proxies characterized the reporting on the creditworthiness of merchants, which arose in the 1840s in the United States.[13] These agencies

> sought to compile [for use as proxies for the repayment of debts] information about the personal life, habits, property, and financial reputation of all American merchants and entrepreneurs. This confidential information was recorded in massive ledger books and shared only with subscribers who inquired at the agency's office. During the late 1850s, some of these firms began to publish rating books that displayed the creditworthiness of each individual in cryptic alphanumeric codes. In essence, what early commercial reporting firms sought to do was to convert an individual's local reputation into an easily readable, centralized summary of creditworthiness for remote lenders.[14]

Consumer credit reporting followed and was well established by the end of the 1880s,[15] and by then life insurance companies were using the information in credit reports as proxies for morbidity and mortality.[16] The consequence was clear as the nineteenth century drew to a close: an individual's credit rating "could have a profound impact on his future potential in matters economic or social."[17]

The consequence became more pronounced in the twentieth century. A 1964 study examining credit ratings found that "an applicant's monthly income and payment to income ratio – pieces of financial information with seemingly obvious relevance – were far less useful in predicting default than whether borrowers had a telephone, owned their home, or had a bank account (but, again, without knowing how much was in it)."[18] Numerous studies replicated that result.

[10] Cathy O'Neil, *Weapons of Math Destruction: How Big Data Increases Inequality and Threatens Democracy* (Broadway Books, 2016).

[11] O'Neil, chapters 8 and 9 (giving the example of one's browsing history and one's geographic location while browsing the web being used as proxies for one's ability to repay one's loans, which in turn will determine whether one is shown ads for payday loans); O'Neil also gives the example we rely on heavily here (using one's credit rating as a proxy for one's likelihood to get into an auto accident) as an input into setting auto insurance rates.

[12] Michael R. Wickens, "A Note on the Use of Proxy Variables," *Econometrica* 40, no. 4 (1972): 759–61.

[13] Josh Lauer, *Creditworthy: A History of Consumer Surveillance and Financial Identity in America* (Columbia University Press, 2017).

[14] Lauer, 6.

[15] Lauer, 56.

[16] Dan Bouk, *How Our Days Became Numbered: Risk and the Rise of the Statistical Individual* (University of Chicago Press, 2018).

[17] Bouk, xvii.

[18] Lauer, *Creditworthy*, 206.

> Study after study listed ... variables ... such as length of time at one's current job and address, as the most predictive of good and bad loans. The leading determinants of creditworthiness, in other words, were only indirectly or loosely financial. Simply having a telephone in one's home, a mortgage, and a checking or savings account – evidence of community and institutional connectedness – were among the best predictors of "good" borrowers.[19]

"During the 1970s databases proliferated and became integral to the conduct of everyday life in the United States ... Banks, insurance companies, retailers, airlines, hotels, mail order firms, and other businesses had their own databases."[20] A 1977 presidential privacy commission reported that

> [w]e live, inescapably, in an "information society," and few of us have the option of avoiding relationships with record-keeping organizations. To do so is to forego not only credit but also insurance, employment, medical care, education, and all forms of government services to individuals. This being so, each individual has, or should have, a concern that the records organizations make and keep about him do not lead to unfair decisions about him.[21]

The use of proxies in the mid-to-late twentieth century pales in comparison to their contemporary use. The use is so constant and pervasive that what one does in any area of one's life can have predictive consequences that reverberate with dramatic effects throughout a wide range of other areas of one's life. Contemporary questions about the fairness of this pervasive use give a new urgency and importance to the (now well over a century old) concern that the use of proxy variables can unfairly tilt the playing field.

Consumer scoring systems are a good illustration of this. The World Privacy Forum introduced the term "consumer scores" in 2014, defining a consumer score as a score

> that describes an individual or sometimes a group of individuals (like a household), and predicts a consumer's behavior, habit, or predilection. Consumer scores use information about consumer characteristics, past behaviors, and other attributes in statistical models that produce a numeric score, a range of scores, or a yes/no. Consumer scores rate, rank, or segment consumers. Businesses and governments use scores to make decisions about individual consumers and groups of consumers. The consequences can range from innocuous to important. Businesses and others use consumer scores for everything from predicting fraud to predicting the health care costs of an individual to eligibility decisions to almost anything.[22]

19 Lauer, 206.

20 Lauer, 243.

21 The Privacy Protection Study Commission, "Personal Privacy in an Information Society," July 1977, http://epic.org/privacy/ppsc1977report/. Quoted in Lauer, *Creditworthy*, 243. For more details, see "Overview of the Privacy Act of 1974," United States Department of Justice, June 16, 2014, www.justice.gov/opcl/role-privacy-protection-study-commission.

22 Pam Dixon and Bob Gellman, "The Scoring of America: How Secret Consumer Scores Threaten Your Privacy and Your Future" (World Privacy Forum, April 2, 2014), 8, www.worldprivacyforum.org/2014/04/wpf-report-the-scoring-of-america-how-secret-consumer-scores-threaten-your-privacy-and-your-future/.

Consumer scoring systems draw data from diverse sources[23] and frequently use a large number of proxy variables:

> a single score is often created from the admixture of more than 600 to 1,000 to even 8,000 individual factors or data streams. These factors can include race, religion, age, gender, household income, zip code, presence of medical conditions, zip code + 4, transactional purchase information from retailers, and hundreds more data points about individual consumers.[24]

Numerical scoring is nothing new. It appeared in the 1940s[25] and became standard in the 1960s and 1970s.[26] What concerned the World Privacy Forum was the proliferation of scoring systems.

eBureau's eScore system is a particularly striking example.[27] It calculates a customer's value for a business – using *up to 50,000* proxies.[28] As O'Neil notes, "E-scores . . . analyze the individual through a veritable blizzard of proxies. In a few milliseconds, they carry out thousands of 'people like you' calculations. And if enough of these 'similar' people turn out to be deadbeats or, worse, criminals, that individual will be treated accordingly."[29] Here is how eBureau works:

> A client submits a data set containing names of tens of thousands of sales leads it has already bought, along with the names of leads who went on to become customers. eBureau then adds several thousand details – like age, income, occupation, property value, length of residence and retail history – from its databases to each customer profile. From those raw data points, the system extrapolates up to 50,000 additional variables per person. Then it scours all that data for the rare common factors among the existing customer base. The resulting algorithm scores prospective customers based on their resemblance to previous customers.[30]

23 Dixon and Gellman, 30–34.

24 Dixon and Gellman, 14.

25 Lauer, *Creditworthy*, 182–211.

26 Lauer, 199–210. Bouk, *How Our Days Became Numbered*, 152. ("By midcentury, nearly all companies had moved to some kind of numerical method.")

27 eBureau appears to be unique in having once offered details about its numbers of variables. Today that information is only available on the Wayback Machine Internet Archive. Internet Archive: Digital Library of Free & Borrowable Books, Movies, Music & Wayback Machine, https://archive.org/. TransUnion acquired eBureau in 2017, and TransUnion's webpages provide minimal information about how the eScore system works. "TransUnion Acquires EBureau," *TransUnion* (blog), October 10, 2017, www.transunion.com/blog/transunion-acquires-ebureau.

28 "EBureau," CDW, April 2009, https://webobjects.cdw.com/webobjects/media/pdf/Apple/Apple-eBureau.pdf. eBureau also describes the proxies as numbering 25,000. "EScores Data Sheet," eBureau, www.ebureau.com/sites/all/files/file/datasheets/ebureau_escore_datasheet.pdf. This URL now takes one to www.transunion.com/solution/customer-data-analytics. The eScores Data Sheet is available at https://web.archive.org/web/20160208005758/http://www.ebureau.com/sites/all/files/file/datasheets/ebureau_escore_datasheet.pdf.

29 O'Neil, *Weapons of Math Destruction*, 145.

30 Natasha Singer, "Secret E-Scores Chart Consumers' Buying Power," *The New York Times*, August 18, 2012, www.nytimes.com/2012/08/19/business/electronic-scores-rank-consumers-by-potential-value.html.

Systems using vast numbers of proxies serve as a striking image of the use of proxy variables,[31] but the growth in the use of proxies is not just a matter of how many proxies a particular system uses. It is primarily a matter of the tremendous increase in the number of systems that use them.

In what follows, we will focus exclusively on systems that (a) generate numerical scores, and (b) use them to allocate costs and benefits to individuals. The vast majority of systems satisfy (a). A systems' "predictions are almost always represented by a single number – a score."[32] Not all systems satisfy (b). RiskIQ, for example, offers a variety of scoring programs,[33] but they do not use them to assign costs and benefits to people. They use them to rate the effectiveness of network defenses against hackers to help "CISOs to understand the effectiveness and impact of their security programs, tools and people."[34] Thus, our regulatory proposal will not cover the whole range of AI systems, but it will cover an important subset.

We build our regulatory proposal using the notion of level playing field fairness

[31] *Very* large numbers of variables may not be typical. As the data scientist Steven Finlay notes:

> As a rough guide, once you have samples containing more than 2–300,000 records and about 1–2,000 variables model building starts to become unwieldy using a single PC/Server. This is not to say that you can't use bigger samples with a single high end PC, but when building predictive models the process benefits from a degree of agility. Before a final model is delivered, a good data scientist will build many different versions of the model, exploring different methods of model construction, changing the way the data is formatted, including some variables and excluding others, to get the very best model possible.

Steven Finlay, *Predictive Analytics, Data Mining and Big Data: Myths, Misconceptions and Methods* (Palgrave Macmillan, 2014), 82–83. Of course, 1,000–2,000 variables are still a lot, and Finlay was writing back in 2014. Variable use has grown since.

[32] Steven Finlay, *Predictive Analytics in 56 Minutes* (CreateSpace Independent Publishing Platform, 2015), 4.

[33] "RiskIQ," www.riskiq.com/.

[34] RiskIQ, "How the Risk Reporting Score Is Calculated," Vimeo, March 22, 2018, https://vimeo.com/261343566. A World Privacy Forum report identifies a number of scoring systems, which it sorts into twelve categories. As the inclusion of RiskIQ shows, not all the systems assign costs and benefits to individuals. The report's list is:

> *Financial and Risk Scores*: ChoiceScore, Median Equivalency Score, RiskIQ Score, Consumer Profitability Score, Job Security Score, Consumer Prominence Indicator Score, Discretionary Spending Index Score, Invitation to Apply Score, Charitable Donor Score, Household Segmentation Scoring Systems, Collection and Recovery, Churn Scores.
>
> *Fraud Scores*: FICO Falcon Fraud Manager, Other Fraud Scores.
>
> *Custom Scores*: special purpose scores such as the Pregnancy Predictor Score.
>
> *Regulated Credit and Financial Scores*: FICO Score, Vantage Score, Beacon Score, Small Business Intelliscore, Tenant Scores.
>
> *Identity and authentication Scores*: ID Analytics ID Score, Insurance Scores.
>
> *Health Scores*: Affordable Care Act Individual Health Risk Score, FICO Medication Adherence Score (MAS), Frailty Scores: General, CMS Frailty Adjustment Score, Hopkins Frailty Score, Other Health, Scores Personal Health Scores: WebMD, others, Resource Utilization Group Scores, SF-36 Form, Complexity Scores.
>
> *Smart Grid and Energy Scores*: Peer-to-Peer Energy People Meter Score (EPM).
>
> *Social Scoring*: Klout Score, Employment Success Score.
>
> *Tax Return Scores*: IRS Discriminant Function System (DIF) score, IRS Unreported Income DIF (UIDIF) score.

LEVEL PLAYING FIELD FAIRNESS

We do not offer our version of level playing field fairness as a comprehensive theory of social justice. We offer it as a plausible component of social justice in societies in which market economies allocate socioeconomic positions based on attributes such as talent and degree of effort. For our purposes, it is sufficient to characterize a market economy as "a system of society wide coordination of human activities not by central command but by mutual interactions in the form of transactions."[35] The transactions involve the transfer of positions of employment, ownership of productive assets, goods, and services. The items have prices expressed in monetary amounts which the parties to the transaction pay or receive. Market competition for those items plays a large role in determining the distribution of socioeconomic positions. Note that the "not by central command but by mutual interactions" requirement does not preclude government regulation of the conditions under which the "mutual interactions" occur. States may, and typically do, impose conditions on competition, including exempting certain activities entirely from market competition (health care and education are two standard examples, although notably in the United States' economy they are only partially shielded from competition). Our concern is with the effect of proxy-driven AI on competition.

Explanation and Motivation

To motivate and explain level playing field fairness, we begin by explaining some terminology. Let us say that a person is advantaged to the extent that they have attributes that improve their likelihood of material success in the market economies typical of Western democracies, and disadvantaged to the extent that they lack those attributes.[36] One levels the playing field with regard to a set of attributes to the extent that one structures society to reduce the advantage or disadvantage those attributes confer. The basic rationale Roemer gives for leveling the playing field is that people may enjoy advantages or suffer disadvantages as a result of circumstances beyond

Law Enforcement Scores, Including Police, Transportation, Safety, and Other: Automated Targeting System Score, Richard Berk Algorithm, Youth Delinquency Scores, Predictive Anti-Fraud Scores: US Postal Service Office of Inspector General.

Environmental Scores: EP Health Risk Score, AIQ Green.

Other Consumer Scores. Potential Scores, Brand Name Medicine Propensity Score, Rx Online Search Propensity, Casino Gaming Propensity.

Adapted from Dixon and Gellman, "The Scoring of America: How Secret Consumer Scores Threaten Your Privacy and Your Future," 4–45, 74, 79.

35 Charles E. Lindblom, *The Market System: What It Is, How It Works, and What to Make of It* (Yale University Press, 2002), 4.

36 A more sophisticated approach would sort attributes into different types and combinations with different likelihoods of success, but we need not do so here. See Roemer, *Equality of Opportunity*.

their control.[37] As we noted earlier, one relatively uncontroversial example is education.[38] People are advantaged by an adequate education, and whether a person acquires an adequate education is dependent on a number of factors beyond that person's control. There is relatively widespread agreement that compulsory and voluntary educational opportunities are appropriate ways to narrow the gap between the more educated and the less educated. Additional, more controversial, examples of attributes include access to health care, and the availability of unemployment insurance.[39]

For our ultimate regulatory purposes, two further points are in order. First, not all examples of leveling the playing field fit comfortably with the "beyond one's control" rationale. Bankruptcy is a case in point. There are multiple reasons to have the institution of bankruptcy, and leveling the playing field is one, but only one. The US Supreme Court acknowledged the "beyond one's control" rationale when it noted that bankruptcy "gives to the honest but unfortunate debtor … a new opportunity in life and a clear field for future effort, unhampered by the pressure and discouragement of preexisting debt."[40] However, despite the Court's characterization of bankrupt debtors as "honest but unfortunate," not all bankruptcies are the result of circumstances beyond the bankrupt's control. Sally arguably faces such circumstances when her daughter's life is at stake, but let's compare Sally to Alan. He also declares bankruptcy after defaulting on a $50,000 credit card debt. However, he incurred his credit card debt by spending well beyond his means on five-star hotels and expensive restaurants. His plan was to declare bankruptcy when the borrowed money ran out. He does so, and the court approves his petition. Another plausible "level playing field" rationale for bankruptcy, applicable in cases like Alan's, is the severity of the consequences. One may struggle to buy or rent a home or a car, start a business, pay for higher education, find employment, or buy insurance. The debtor gets "a new opportunity in life and a clear field for future effort, unhampered by the pressure and discouragement of preexisting debt"[41] because the burden of the preexisting debt is too much of a handicap. "Too much of a handicap" considerations lead some to suggest formulations that expand the reach of level playing field fairness well beyond the confines of what is beyond a person's control. For example, "In a just society, all persons would have broadly equal access to the material and social means necessary to live a flourishing life."[42] There is no need here to settle on an exact formulation. It is sufficient to note that most people think there are some attributes

37 Roemer, 19.

38 Roemer, 16 and chapters 9 and 11.

39 Roemer, chapters 8 and 10.

40 *Local Loan Co.* v. *Hunt*, 292 US 234 (United States Supreme Court 1934).

41 *Local Loan Co.* v. *Hunt*, 292 US at 244.

42 Wright and Burawoy, *How to Be an Anticapitalist in the Twenty-First Century*, 10.

with regard to which society should level the playing field.[43] Of course, people disagree about which attributes.[44]

The second point concerns the way in which people traditionally interpret level playing field views. As Roemer explains,

> Among the citizens of any advanced democracy, we find individuals who hold a spectrum of views with respect to what is required for equal opportunity, from the nondiscrimination view at one pole to pervasive social provision to correct for all manner of disadvantage at the other. Common to all these views, however, is the precept that the equal-opportunity principle, at some point, holds the individual accountable for the achievement of the advantage in question, whether that advantage be a level of educational achievement, health, employment status, income, or the economist's utility or welfare. Thus there is, in the notion of equality of opportunity, a "before" and an "after": before the competition starts, opportunities must be equalized, by social intervention if need be, but after it begins, individuals are on their own.[45]

Is it true that, provided opportunities are equalized, it should be that case that "individuals are on their own" after competition starts? The answer matters greatly to our eventual regulatory proposal. Our answer is *no*. Even if opportunity is equal before competition, the effects of competition itself can still unfairly tilt the playing field. Some may object that this is not possible if the market is sufficiently competitive and opportunity is equal before competition starts. As the political economist Charles Lindblom notes, "In our day, perhaps most people would not defend the rule [that individuals are on their own after competition starts] unless it were supplemented by other rules and procedures, such as those of the welfare state. Some people nevertheless defend the rule as itself sufficient without such supplements as pensions and unemployment compensation."[46] Lindblom continues that, although people offer several defenses of the rule that individuals are on their own, "all are flawed; and the flaws represent misunderstandings of the market system."[47] Relying on Lindblom's critique, we take it for granted that market mechanisms will not be sufficient to prevent all "after start" unfair tilts.[48]

43 Wright and Burawoy.

44 See Roemer, *Equality of Opportunity*, 3: "More specifically, different people have different conceptions about where the starting gate should be, or about the degrees to which individuals should be held accountable for the outcomes or advantage they eventually enjoy." Both disagreements are disagreements about which attributes are relevant to leveling the playing field.

45 Roemer, 2.

46 Lindblom, *The Market System*, 115–16. We substituted "the rule that individuals are on their own" for Lindblom's "the rule of quid pro quo." The idea that, once opportunities are equalized, individuals are on their own is a special case of what Lindblom means by "the rule of quid pro quo," and all of Lindblom's criticisms apply.

47 Lindblom, 116.

48 For Lindblom's criticisms, see Lindblom, chapter 8. See also Adam Pham and Clinton Castro, "The Moral Limits of the Market: The Case of Consumer Scoring Data," *Ethics and Information Technology* 21 (2019): 117–26 (critiquing consumer scoring systems). See also Alan Rubel, Clinton Castro, and Adam Pham, "Agency Laundering and Information Technologies," *Ethical*

We add that bankruptcy's goal of providing "a new opportunity in life and a clear field for future effort, unhampered by the pressure and discouragement of preexisting debt" is an instance of society recognizing a need to adjust equality of opportunity *after* the competition starts. More generally, the history of consumer surveillance since the nineteenth-century rise of credit reporting is in part a history of concern about unfairly tilted playing fields as consumer surveillance makes it increasingly likely that one area of one's life would impact other areas. The concern is clearly with "after start of competition" unfairness. The worry is that as your market activity unfolds, some combination of circumstances in one area will – unfairly – reverberate to your disadvantage throughout a wide range of other areas. There are plausible examples of such unfairness. One is the Sally bankruptcy example. Another is the often-used example of American Express's 2009 lowering of credit limits based on the stores in which the cardholder shopped. American Express determined that cardholders who shopped in certain stores were less likely to repay than cardholders who did not patronize those stores.[49] This disadvantaged certain cardholders (in our sense of reduced likelihood of market success). They not only had less borrowing power, but also likely had their credit rating lowered and their borrowing costs increased. Some may not find our examples convincing. Although people will disagree on particular examples, there is widespread agreement that proxy-driven AI systems can generate "after start" unfair tilts of the playing field.[50]

Two Conditions on AI Systems

Against the background of the discussion of level playing field fairness, we formulate two conditions on any adequate process for regulating proxy-driven AI systems. The first is that the process should identify "before start" attributes whose use in AI systems would unfairly tilt the playing field, and prohibit their use.[51] For example, suppose a society attempts to level the playing field in part by ensuring that everyone has equal access to educational opportunities. To this end, it uses remedial reading programs to ensure that all elementary school children have the same basic reading skills. It would be unfair for an AI system to assign a lower score (i.e., less likely to be hired) to applicants who participated in a remedial reading program.

Theory and Moral Practice 22 (2019): 1017–41, https://doi.org/10.1007/s10677-019-10030-w (for a moral critique of the use of AI systems).

49 As Cathy O'Neil notes: O'Neil, *Weapons of Math Destruction*, 156–57 (American Express left affected cardholders "careening into a nasty recession with less credit").

50 Lindblom, *The Market System*.

51 An exception is that regulators may sometimes want to require *recording* an attribute that may not be used as an input for prediction, such as race. "If we include race in the analysis, as the computer scientist Cynthia Dwork has noted, we can quantify racial injustice where we find it. Then we can publicize it, debate the ethics, and propose remedies"; O'Neil, *Weapons of Math Destruction*, 219, note #1.

The second condition on processes regulating AI concerns the regulation of "after start of competition" attributes. One cannot regulate "after start of competition" tilts in the way we suggested regulating "before start" tilts, where we simply prohibited the use of certain attributes. As discussed, using the attribute of bankruptcy in setting auto insurance rates may unfairly tilt the playing field in some cases. Compare a program that uses the attribute of bankruptcy plus a combination of others to distinguish between bankruptcies such as Sally's and bankruptcies such as Alan's and avoids assigning a higher premium to the Sally-like applicants on the basis of their bankruptcy. The second program arguably avoids unfairly tilting the playing field against the Sally-like applicants. After-start tilts are the result of the *particular way* the AI program uses variables to allocate costs and benefits. Some allocations tilt the playing field, some don't. Thus, the second condition is that the process should identify which uses of "after start" attributes unfairly tilt the playing field and prohibit those uses.

How is a regulator supposed to implement these two conditions? Faced with the computational and mathematical complexity of AI systems, how do you tell whether they unfairly tilt the playing field? To answer, we recast these requirements in a somewhat more mathematic mode by adapting ideas from the computer scientists Dwork et al.'s influential article *Fairness through Awareness*. Dwork et al. offer a mathematical formulation of a Roemer-like approach to fairness.[52]

A Reformulation

An example is helpful. We use a highly simplified model for setting auto insurance premiums. The model, shown in Table 9.1, uses the four variables represented in bold type headings (excluding the identifier "Name"). We include the "Bankruptcy" heading for simplicity. A more realistic model would replace it with a heading for "Credit History" or something similar. Assume the model treats the attributes given in the headings as proxy variables for something like how careful a driver is. These assumptions are for illustrative purposes only. We do not claim they are valid.

TABLE 9.1 *Very simple four-attribute model for setting auto insurance premiums.*

Name	Age	Income	Occupation	Bankruptcy
Sally	35	88,000	Software Engineer	Yes
Joe	40	65,000	Police Officer	No

[52] Cynthia Dwork et al., "Fairness through Awareness," in *3rd Innovations in Theoretical Computer Science Conference (ITCS)*, 2012, 214–26, https://doi.org/10.1145/2090236.2090255.

The system uses an algorithm that assigns a numerical score to any combination of the four variables. Assume the scores run from 1 to 100, with higher scores indicating higher premiums. Suppose Sally's score is 75 (given her bankruptcy) while Joe's is 10. Subtracting Joe's score from Sally's represents the system's proxy-based determination of the relevant difference, or distance, between them in regard to the assignment of premiums – in this case, 65. (It is convenient to have the distance always be a positive number, so when subtracting Sally from Joe take the absolute value to also get 65.) Indeed, the absolute value of the difference between scores establishes a distance $d(x, y)$ between x and y for any two individuals x and y. The same would be true for any system that uses numerical scores. We will call any such $d(x, y)$ a system's *distance metric* (borrowing from Dwork et al.[53] and the mathematics of metric spaces[54]).

We can reformulate the two conditions on regulating AI in terms of distance metrics. The first condition becomes the following requirement:

> *Requirement 1:* Every system must generate its distance metric in ways consistent with "before start" equal opportunity.

The second condition is to identify and prohibit those uses of "after start" attributes that unfairly tilt the playing field. We divide this into two requirements. To formulate the first, let $A(x)$ be the cost or benefit that the system allocates to x. Assume, for the moment, that one can measure the extent of the cost or benefit quantitatively – on a very broad understanding of what cost/benefit analysis can include. It can include "everything that matters to people's welfare, including such

53 Dwork et al., 216 ("To introduce our notion of fairness we assume the existence of a metric on individuals"). Dwork et al. assume that *each* AI system has a relevant distance metric. They note that "one of the most challenging aspects of our work is justifying the availability of a distance metric" (p. 223). We have avoided the complexities of that challenge by limiting our attention to systems that assign numerical scores and use them to allocate costs and benefits. Dwork also notes the availability of distance metrics in such systems ("The imposition of a metric already occurs in many classification processes"; p. 224). For the purposes of this book, where we consider only systems that generate numeric scores, we could have simply used the formulation $|\text{score}(x) - \text{score}(y)|$ and not introduced the general mathematical notion of an arbitrary metric. However, Dwork et al.'s results cover cases where there is no score, but a distance metric can still be obtained.

54 Wikipedia provides an informal explanation of distance metrics: "In mathematics, a metric space is a set together with a metric on the set. The metric is a function that defines a concept of distance between any two members of the set, which are usually called points. The metric satisfies a few simple properties. Informally:

- the distance from a point to itself is zero,
- the distance between two distinct points is positive,
- the distance from A to B is the same as the distance from B to A, and
- the distance from A to B (directly) is less than or equal to the distance from A to B via any third point C."

"Metric Space," *Wikipedia*, https://en.wikipedia.org/w/index.php?title=Metric_space&oldid=933173922.

qualitatively diverse goods as physical and mental health, freedom from pain, a sense of meaning, culture, clean air and water, animal welfare, safe food, pristine areas, and access to public buildings."[55] For illustrative purposes, in the case of credit rating systems, $A(x)$ could be a credit rating or, in the case of car insurance, a premium.

To give a more precise formulation, assume that, roughly speaking, for any two individuals, $A(x) - A(y) \leq d(x, y)$.[56] Two problems make this rough speaking: one trivial, one slightly less so. The trivial one is that $d(x, y)$ is always a nonnegative number while $A(x) - A(y)$ will be negative when $A(y) > A(x)$. The easy fix is to use the absolute value $|A(x) - A(y)|$. The slightly more difficult problem is that $|A(x) - A(y)|$ and $d(x, y)$ may measure on different scales. Suppose $|A(x) - A(y)|$ is a number from 1 into the 1,000s, while $d(x, y)$ will be a number from 1 to 100. The solution is easy: re-express the measures on a common scale.[57] We will write $|A(x) - A(y)| \leq d(x, y)$, assuming the choice of some suitable scaling method that makes the comparison meaningful. Thus, we propose

Requirement 2: For a system S, it must be the case that

$$|A(x) - A(y)| \leq d(x, y).$$

Requirement (2) is the simplification of a requirement of Dwork et al.[58] to the case when we have scores that generate the distance metric, and it says that differences in allocations must be no larger than differences between individuals. Fairness requires this. Otherwise, the allocations do not treat like cases alike. Suppose, for example, an auto insurance system finds little difference between Alice and Bob but assigns Bob a much higher premium than Alice. Requirement (2) prohibits such systems. Two further points are in order.

First, in formulating Requirement (2) we assumed that the allocations $A(x)$ were quantifiable. When framing policies that affect millions, meaningful quantification of costs and benefits is often both possible and desirable,[59] but there are, of course, "values that are difficult or impossible to quantify, including equity, human dignity, fairness, and distributive impacts."[60] The list could be much longer. One could add – to take just a few examples – friendship, beauty,

55 Cass R. Sunstein, *The Cost-Benefit Revolution* (MIT Press, 2018), 23.

56 The allocation might be probabilistic, so a more precise description would require that the *expected value of* $A(x) - A(y)$ be at most $d(x, y)$.

57 For an accessible overview of scaling see, "Feature Scaling," *Wikipedia*, https://en.wikipedia.org/w/index.php?title=Feature_scaling&oldid=932463965.

58 Dwork et al., "Fairness through Awareness," 216. Their Definition 2.1, which handles arbitrary distance metrics that do not require the existence of a score, is designed to implement the "fairness constraint, that similar individuals are treated similarly"; Dwork et al., 214. Our point is that that is not sufficient to ensure level playing field fairness.

59 For relevant considerations, see Sunstein, *The Cost-Benefit Revolution*.

60 "Executive Order 13563 – Improving Regulation and Regulatory Review," whitehouse.gov, January 18, 2011, https://obamawhitehouse.archives.gov/the-press-office/2011/01/18/executive-order-13563-improving-regulation-and-regulatory-review.

meaningful work, kindness, and "capacity shown, in some form or other, by humans in all cultures to live under rules and values and to shape their behaviour in some degree to social expectations, in ways that are not under surveillance and not directly controlled by threats and rewards."[61] So how does this apply when $A(x)$ is not quantifiable? Replace $|A(x) - A(y)|$ with a qualitative comparison of the allocations, and a qualitative comparison of how well the difference in allocations matches the difference the system encodes in $d(x, y)$. Comparisons of non-quantifiable values are routine in framing public policy. Executive Order 13563 – Improving Regulation and Regulatory Review, for example, requires regulators to "take into account benefits and costs, both quantitative and qualitative."[62]

The second point is that Requirement (2) is not sufficient to ensure that a system does not unfairly tilt the playing field, because it ignores the *direction* of differences. We give an example of a system that obeys Requirement (2) but is patently unfair. Start with a system S whose allocation function obeys Requirement (2) and *does* make fair assignments. Assume in particular S assigns higher auto insurance premiums to drivers in category C1 of careless drivers with a history of moving violations, and lower premiums to drivers in category C2 of safer drivers. For simplicity, assume everyone in C1 pays the same premium H, and everyone in C2 pays the same premium L. Now create a new system S' which is like S except S' assigns L to the careless drivers in C1 and H to the careful drivers in C2. It is *still* true that $|A(x) - A(y)| \leq d(x, y)$. However – grant for the moment – treating the careful drivers in category C2 as if they were the careless drivers in category C1 unfairly tilts the playing field against the drivers in C1. The problem is that Requirement (2) creates no guarantee about the *direction* of the allocations – which category gets more or less. To address this, we add a third requirement:

Requirement 3: S's allocation function $A(x)$ does not unfairly tilt the playing field.

This may seem disappointing. We set out to explain how a regulator could fit fairness requirements onto the computational and mathematical complexity of AI systems, but, at a crucial point, we still require a judgment of fairness. This is

61 Bernard Williams, *Truth and Truthfulness: An Essay in Genealogy* (Princeton University Press, 2004), 24.

62 "Executive Order 13563 – Improving Regulation and Regulatory Review." The law professor Cass Sunstein also acknowledges the point. "It is true that moral commitments often signal values that are not adequately captured by private willingness to pay"; Sunstein, *The Cost-Benefit Revolution*. Nonetheless, he argues that regulators should consider quantifying the cost of meeting or violating moral commitments – at least in a wide range of cases. His argument rests on examples of a vast increase in the cost of legislation to protect a moral concern of relatively small importance. We agree that the cost of the legislation argues against protecting the moral concern, but do not think one can extrapolate from such examples to the *general* conclusion that one should consider quantifying the cost of meeting or violating moral commitments. Compare Stuart Hampshire, *Innocence and Experience* (Harvard University Press, 1991) (offering a well-considered view of how to include qualitative considerations in debates about public policy).

unavoidable. One cannot reduce questions of fairness to a mathematical test.[63] What one can do is provide a workable framework in which regulators are to make that judgment. The three requirements we have given so far provide part of that framework.

The next issue is whether regulators will be able to learn enough about AI systems to enforce compliance with those requirements. Assessing compliance requires relevant information about a system's distance metric $d(x, y)$ and its allocation function $A(x)$. Will regulators have access to that information?

It may seem that regulators could obtain access to the score of any individual and compute $d(x, y)$ for any pair of individuals x and y. For the toy example with four variables we gave in Table 9.1, that *might* be a plausible approach. If each of the variables *Age*, *Income*, and *Occupation* can take on at most 100 distinct values, and *Bankruptcy* has only two possible values, then regulators might be able to assemble a table of distances for each possible pair of distinct (by variable value) individuals. Of course, that would be two million distinct *individuals*, and roughly two *quadrillion* pairs, so it might be hard to work with the table. However, it would be deeply infeasible to compute all the $d(x, y)$ pairs for all the distinct possible values of x and y for a model where each individual is described by fifty variables each having two possible values. That computation would take *many* millennia![64]

Thus, regulators will need to gain a qualitative understanding of how AI systems assign scores to individuals. Many real-world systems will use a thousand or more variables, many of which might be considered to be proxy variables. The question then becomes: which of those variables have a significant impact on scores, and in which cases? That can be difficult to answer. We distinguish two cases: deep learning, which has been very popular in recent years, and all others. The "all others" approach

> is characterized by practitioners investing the bulk of their efforts into engineering features. This feature engineering is the application of clever, and often elaborate, algorithms to raw data in order to preprocess the data into input variables that can be readily modeled by traditional statistical techniques. These techniques ... are seldom effective on unprocessed data, and so the engineering of input data has historically been a prime focus of machine learning professionals.[65]

63 Dwork et al., "Fairness through Awareness," 216, is interesting in this regard. As we have mentioned, they limit allocations to individuals in a way that generalizes our Requirement 2 from score-based systems to ones with arbitrary distance metrics, and then suggest that a business may want to optimize a goal of the business, subject to the constraint of that generalization of Requirement 2. This does *not* preclude our "substitute categories C1 and C2" example.

64 There are 2^{50} possible individuals generating about 2^{99} distinct pairs, or about 10^{29}. If one billion $d(x, y)$ values could be computed each second (i.e., 1 per nanosecond, which is unreasonably fast), then about 10^{20} seconds would be needed, which is over a billion centuries.

65 Jon Krohn, Grant Beyleveld, and Aglaé Bassens, *Deep Learning Illustrated: A Visual, Interactive Guide to Artificial Intelligence* (Addison-Wesley Professional, 2019), 44–45.

It can be presumed that the variables that come out of such feature engineering are important. Thus, in such cases, the important proxy variables (at least a significant number of them[66]) will be readily available – at least as long as the system's creators have adequately documented their process of creation.[67] However, if the system is unexplainable, just knowing what the important proxy variables are will not give regulators enough information about its distance metric $d(x, y)$ and its allocation function $A(x)$. Deep-learning approaches compound the problem since there is no indication from feature engineering which of the proxy variables are important. The "practitioner typically spends little to none of her time engineering features, instead spending it modeling data with various artificial neural network architectures that process the raw inputs into useful features automatically."[68] Moreover, deep learning is typically *not* explainable.

Mention of one more point is in order before we leave the third requirement. One could broaden it to allow the consideration of tradeoff questions generally, not just questions of fairness. We have not done so because it is sufficient for our purposes to illustrate a process confined to considering fairness and to note that one can generalize the model to address as broad a range of tradeoff questions as one likes.

We now turn to the fourth requirement, which addresses regulator access to information about predictive systems.[69]

Requirement 4: Users of an AI system have the burden to provide sufficient information about the system's distance metric and allocation function to make it r-transparent for

66 The variables that are a result of the feature engineering may not be the only important proxy variables.

67 On documentation, see Inioluwa Deborah Raji et al., "Closing the AI Accountability Gap: Defining an End-to-End Framework for Internal Algorithmic Auditing," in *Proceedings of the 2020 Conference on Fairness, Accountability, and Transparency*, FAT* '20, 2020, 33–44, https://doi.org/10.1145/3351095.3372873.

68 Krohn, Beyleveld, and Bassens, *Deep Learning Illustrated*, 45. There is recent work devoted to explaining the operation of deep-learning systems. See, for example, Pieter Jan Kindermans et al., "Learning How to Explain Neural Networks: PatternNet and PatternAttribution," 2018, https://openreview.net/forum?id=Hkn7CBaTW, and Chun-Hao Chang et al., "Explaining Image Classifiers by Counterfactual Generation," *ArXiv:1807.08024 [cs.CV]*, February 25, 2019, http://arxiv.org/abs/1807.08024.

69 It is common to assume that revealing an algorithm's source code will reveal to regulators what they need to know. See, for example, Danielle Citron and Frank Pasquale, "The Scored Society: Due Process for Automated Predictions," *Washington Law Review* 89 (2014): 1–33 (insisting on the need to know source code). Compare Joshua A. Kroll et al., "Accountable Algorithms," *University of Pennsylvania Law Review* 165 (2017): 642–56 (discussing the assumption that one needs to know the source code and pointing out its difficulties). This is false. As Kroll et al. note, "The source code of computer systems is illegible to nonexperts" (p. 638). If the code were legible at least to experts, then expert reports could make algorithms consumer-transparent. However, "even experts often struggle to understand what software code will do: inspecting source code is a very limited way of predicting how a computer program will behave"; Kroll et al., 663. Indeed, some approaches to predictive analytics, including some that are very popular, such as support vector machines and deep learning of neural nets, give predictive models that are quite difficult for humans to comprehend. See Finlay, *Predictive Analytics, Data Mining and Big Data*, 126.

purposes of assessing compliance with the requirements (1)–(3). Failure to do so makes the system presumptively unfair.

Placing the burden on users to provide the information on pain of a finding of unfairness eases the investigative burden on regulators since users have a strong motive to provide the necessary information.

Note that the requirement of r-transparency does not preclude the possibility of an r-transparent but unexplainable system. Explainability requires a human-understandable explanation of why *any given* decision was reached in terms of only the training data used, the kind of decision function, and the particular inputs for that decision. The definition of r-transparency does not explicitly require that. A system is r-transparent for a regulatory purpose when regulators have an adequate explanation for that purpose of why it yields the predictions it does. A system may be explainable but not r-transparent since regulatory purposes (fairness, for example) could require more than just an explanation of a particular decision in terms of the training data used, the kind of decision function, and the particular inputs for that decision. We also leave open the possibility that a system may lack explanability but be r-transparent. Consider a non-algorithmic analogy: university tenure decisions. After discussion, a committee votes for or and against tenure. Beyond a limited number of administrators, the confidential discussion and vote may never be revealed to the tenure candidate or others affected, who thus have no explanation of the deliberative path that led to the decision. However, they can still be confident that the vote was fair as long as they are confident that the committee accepted and adhered to procedures that reliably yield fair decisions. We leave open the same possibility for predictive systems, where users could run any number of simulations to argue that a system reliably yields the desired results.[70] We leave the burden on users to provide an acceptable way to test outcomes for the desired result.

A REGULATORY PROPOSAL

We propose four criteria that any adequate regulatory scheme should meet and then suggest that regulation by some entity like the Federal Trade Commission (FTC) is a plausible way to meet them. The "entity like" qualification is necessary because our proposal significantly expands the powers of the actual FTC. The actual FTC serves as a useful yardstick to measure the extent of the changes needed to address AI systems.

Four Criteria of Adequacy

An adequate regulatory scheme in this context is one sufficiently well equipped to evaluate AI systems in terms of requirements (1)–(4). We discuss next what powers

70 A testing process could involve A-B testing. Starting with general criteria which almost everybody meets, it could randomly select a small number to get a new treatment/cost/benefit, for the purposes of studying it.

and attributes an adequate regulatory body would need to have. The first two criteria concern the ability to acquire and understand sufficient information about a system's distance metric $d(x, y)$ and its allocation function $A(x)$.

Broad Investigative Powers

Businesses increasingly use ever more sophisticated AI systems in a rapidly changing technological and economic environment. Any regulatory approach that hopes to keep pace with the developments will have to be an agile one with broad investigative powers. There is a historical parallel with the creation of the Federal Trade Commission in 1914. The end of the nineteenth century saw reduced competition and price fixing as a result of business growth and consolidation along with various forms of cooperation and collusion.[71] Congress perceived the need for a quick-acting, flexible organization with broad investigative powers that could effectively regulate those developments.[72]

Access to Expertise

At the turn of the twentieth century, the complexities of regulating market competition argued for regulation guided by adequate expertise.[73] Today, in the 2020s, the rapidly increasing use of and increasing complexity of AI systems similarly argues for regulatory access to relevant technical and business expertise.

Market Freedom within the Constraint of Fairness

Our third requirement is that a system's allocation function $A(x)$ does not unfairly tilt the playing field. Determining the fairness of an AI system can involve assessing the effects of allocations of costs and benefits over large numbers of individuals. Those effects may be difficult to determine, and fairness judgments based on them can involve complex tradeoffs.[74] Among the factors a regulatory body should consider is market freedom. We take it for granted that, in a market economy, it is desirable, as Dwork et al. note, to "permit the entity that needs to classify individuals, which we call the vendor [of an AI system], as much freedom as possible ... [to allow it] to benefit from investment in data mining and market research in designing its classifier."[75] We understand Dwork et al.'s "as much freedom as possible" to mean

71 Chris Jay Hoofnagle, *Federal Trade Commission Privacy Law and Policy* (Cambridge University Press, 2016), 4.

72 Hoofnagle, 4–10.

73 Hoofnagle, 9.

74 Fairly allocating resources can be quite complicated even when the only question is how to distribute a certain well-defined benefit in a limited, specific context; see, for example, H. Peyton Young, *Equity in Theory and Practice* (Princeton University Press, 1995). Young's discussion of demobilization after World War II is a good illustration of a complex distribution question (23–27). For an example of a broader question of social justice, see, for example, Victor R. Fuchs, *Who Shall Live? Health, Economics and Social Choice*, Expanded edition (WSPC, 2011), and Sunstein, *The Cost-Benefit Revolution*.

75 Dwork et al., "Fairness through Awareness," 214.

as much freedom as possible consistent *with the demands of fairness* (which is Dwork et al.'s understanding as well[76]).

Reason-Giving

Our fourth requirement is that, on pain of a judgment of unfairness, users of an AI system must provide sufficient information about its distance metric and allocation function. The corresponding fourth criterion of adequacy is a constraint on how the regulatory body uses that information: namely, they should use it to articulate reasons why a system is fair or unfair. An agency could, of course, simply announce that a system is fair *without* giving any supporting reasons, but it comports better with the requirements of legitimate democratic governance to provide supporting reasons: "[D]ecision making based on reason (within the same tradition), not on preference or faith, is crucial for legitimacy."[77]

A ROLE FOR THE FEDERAL TRADE COMMISSION

We propose regulation by the FTC – or, more accurately, by an FTC-like agency – as a plausible way to meet the criteria of adequacy. The agency we envision is politically empowered and adequately funded with significantly expanded powers to make and enforce judgments of fairness. We begin with 15 US Code § 45(n), the FTC's standard for an unfair business practice. A system should not cause or be likely to cause "substantial injury to consumers which is not reasonably avoidable by consumers themselves and not outweighed by countervailing benefits to consumers or to competition."[78] Our proposal is to see the consequences of unfairly tilting the playing field as constituting a "substantial injury," at least when those costs are great enough. This proposal greatly expands the power of the FTC to make judgments of fairness. In the FTC's current practice "[s]ubstantial injuries to consumers usually … involve monetary harm, coercion into the purchase of unwanted goods or services, and health or safety risks."[79] Does our proposed expansion of what counts as a substantial injury grant the FTC too unconstrained a power to make judgments of fairness?[80] We leave that question unanswered. Our point is that AI systems raise pressing issues of level playing field fairness. Given, as we have assumed, that market mechanisms will not be sufficient to ensure fairness,

76 Dwork et al., 214 (claiming their approach provides an "absolute guarantee of fairness").

77 Steven Burton, "Reaffirming Legal Reasoning: The Challenge from the Left," *Journal of Legal Education* 36 (1986): 368.

78 "15 US Code § 45 – Unfair Methods of Competition Unlawful; Prevention by Commission," LII/ Legal Information Institute, www.law.cornell.edu/uscode/text/15/45.

79 Hoofnagle, *Federal Trade Commission Privacy Law and Policy*, 132.

80 For a discussion of pros and cons, see Hoofnagle, *Federal Trade Commission Privacy Law and Policy*. Hoofnagle says of the book, "this book makes it clear that effective policing of information wrongs requires deviation from nineteenth-century limits on cases" (p. xvii).

some more or less constrained regulatory process will need to make the necessary judgments of fairness.

Broad Investigative Powers

The FTC has extremely broad powers to initiate investigations into a company's practices: "The FTC's investigatory power . . . is akin to an inquisitorial body. On its own initiative, it can investigate a broad range of businesses without any indication of a predicate offense having occurred."[81]

Access to Expertise

The FTC has ready access to experts.[82]

Market Freedom within the Constraint of Fairness

Earlier we agreed with Dwork et al. that it is desirable to allow creators and users of AI systems as much freedom as possible consistent with the requirements of fairness "to benefit from investment in data mining and market research."[83] The FTC's fairness standard in 15 US Code § 45(n) gives considerable weight to creators' and users' interest in freedom by balancing substantial injury to consumers against the "countervailing benefits to consumers or to competition."

Reason-Giving

Administrative agencies are well suited to reason-giving. The administrative law expert Jerry Mashaw notes that

> The path of American administrative law has been the path of the progressive submission of power to reason. The promise of the administrative state was to bring competence to politics. It is the institutional embodiment of the enlightenment project to substitute reason for the dark forces of culture, tradition, and myth. Administrators must not only give reasons; they must give complete ones. We attempt to ensure that they are authentic by demanding that they be both transparent and contemporaneous. "Expertise" is no longer a protective shield to be worn like a sacred vestment. It is a competence to be demonstrated by cogent reason-giving.[84]

81 Hoofnagle, 102.

82 Hoofnagle, 30.

83 Dwork et al., "Fairness through Awareness."

84 Jerry L. Mashaw, *Reasoned Administration and Democratic Legitimacy: How Administrative Law Supports Democratic Government* (Cambridge University Press, 2018), 11 (citing Citizens to Preserve Overton Park, Inc. v. Volpe, 401 U.S. 402 [Supreme Court of the United States 1971]). We note that one may take a less sanguine view of agency reason-giving. As the law professor Chris Hoofnagle notes (about agency rule-making, which involves reason-giving), a "1979 assessment of agency rule-making found that the average one created a record of over 40,000 pages"; Hoofnagle, *Federal Trade Commission Privacy Law and Policy*, 102, quoting "Hybrid Rulemaking Procedures of the Federal Trade Commission," Administrative Conference of the United States, June 8, 1979, www.acus.gov/recommendation/hybrid-rulemaking-procedures-federal-trade-commission. Hoofnagle observes,

We grant that, if anything, rule-making about consumer surveillance used as an input for AI might be even slower and more contentious than other privacy rule-making. Our point, however, is simply that, as Mashaw notes, "competence to be demonstrated by cogent reason-giving" is a hallmark of agency decision-making, and that decision-making need not take the form of rule-making.

We conclude that regulation by the FTC (or an FTC-like agency) is a plausible way to ensure that AI systems meet the following four requirements. For a predictive system with a distance metric $d(x, y)$ and an allocation function $A(x)$:

Requirement 1: The system must generate $d(x, y)$ in ways consistent with "before start" equal opportunity.

Requirement 2: It must be true that $|A(x) - A(y)| \leq d(x, y)$.

Requirement 3: The allocation function $A(x)$ must not unfairly tilt the playing field.

Requirement 4: Users of the system have the burden to provide sufficient information about its distance metric and allocation function to make it r-transparent for purposes of assessing compliance with the requirements (1)–(3). Failure to do so makes the system presumptively unfair.

CREATING AN INFORMATIONAL NORM

The dominant theme in the history of consumer surveillance has been the acceptance of surveillance, or at least of the products and services surveillance makes possible.[85] Fairness and tradeoff concerns have been a counterpoint, and so far a largely ineffective one. Without effective regulation, the story is likely to continue in the same way. Indeed, our view is that the story is likely to continue in the same way unless we supplement regulation with a process that maintains and creates informational norms. We see no other way to ensure adequate privacy in public.

It is well beyond the scope of this book to show in general when and how to create informational norms governing the use of proxy variables, so we show how to do so for one particular case: setting auto insurance premiums. We choose that case for two reasons. The first is that the use of proxies in that case is ripe for regulation. As

that it "is popularly believed that if a general, online privacy rule-making were to be started, it simply would be stale by its implementation date" (p. 102).

85 See Lauer, *Creditworthy*, 215 (noting that the mid-1960s outrage soon died down). See also Bouk, *How Our Days Became Numbered*, 240 (remarking that "conflicts over traditional, predictive risk making spur the creation of new forms of risk making supposed to change fates, such that more risks get made from more people in new ways"). For insightful studies of consumers' acceptance of statistical analyses, see Sarah E. Igo, *The Averaged American: Surveys, Citizens, and the Making of a Mass Public* (Harvard University Press, 2007), and Jerry Muller, *The Tyranny of Metrics* (Princeton University Press, 2018). For studies focused on consumer acceptance in the twenty-first century, see Andreas Bernard, *The Triumph of Profiling: The Self in Digital Culture*, trans. Valentine A. Pakis (Polity Press, 2019), and Steffen Mau, *The Metric Society: On the Quantification of the Social* (Polity Press, 2019).

a 2015 *Consumer Reports* study of auto insurance notes, "behind the rate quotes is a pricing process that judges you less on driving habits and increasingly on socioeconomic factors. These include your credit history, whether you use department-store or bank credit cards, and even your TV provider."[86] Many condemn the use of proxies that at least appear dubiously related to predicting driving safety.[87] In addition, in some cases there is no pretense that the proxies predict driving safety. The second reason is that the systems set premiums by assigning scores to people who have or seek insurance. Thus, the FTC regulatory model we just outlined applies. Our norm-creation process assigns an essential role to FTC regulation. In this way, we show how regulation and norm-creation can go hand in hand.

We show how to create the following informational norm: Consumers and insurance companies conform to conditions on the fair use of proxies as a means to realizing the group-action goal of setting premiums. We assume a background of the FTC holding auto insurance companies liable for the unfair use of proxies. Those decisions help give a sufficiently clear meaning to fairness that the norm can function effectively. The norm-creation process in Chapter 8 has three steps. We consider each in turn.

Step 1: Common Knowledge of Proper Performance of a Social Role

The relevant conception of proper performance requires two things. First: insureds and insurance companies think they ought to conform to conditions on the fair use of proxies as a means to realizing the group-action goal of fairly setting premiums as long as (enough) others conform. Second: at appropriate times, insureds and insurers dominantly prefer to conform to the conditions as a means to realizing the group-action goal. Broadcast narratives can create common knowledge of such a conception of proper performance. Diverse sources can contribute to the narrative – examples include the *Consumer Reports* study and FTC decisions declaring specific practices unfair. As narratives change consumers' attitudes, insurance companies will embrace the proposed conception of proper performance for three reasons. One is to avoid FTC actions that hold them liable. Another is to avoid lost sales. Consumers will turn away from sellers who do not fairly set premiums – provided the market is sufficiently competitive (an assumption we by no means wish to minimize). The third reason is that the businesses may come to think that they ought to use information to set premiums fairly – for other than the two prudential reasons just given. Despite the economic models that portray businesses as purely profit-driven, business people are not immune to cultural factors that affect what they think they ought to do.

86 "Special Report: Car Insurance Secrets," *Consumer Reports*, July 30, 2015, www.consumerreports.org/cro/car-insurance/auto-insurance-special-report/index.htm.

87 See, for example, O'Neil, *Weapons of Math Destruction*.

Step 2: Common Knowledge That Enough Conform

Sufficient FTC enforcement can ensure that enough conform. There may also be a market motive for insurance companies to conform. Assume a sufficiently competitive market. Then, once enough people seeking insurance opt for companies making fair use of proxies, the profit-maximizing strategy will be to offer premiums based on the fair use of proxies. Broadcast narratives can make it common knowledge that enough conform. Once the norm is established it becomes a self-perpetuating regularity that may persist even without significant legal enforcement.

Step 3: Common Knowledge of Continued Conformity

Common knowledge that enough have conformed in the past yields common knowledge that enough will conform in the future – provided that past conformity gives people an adequate reason to expect future conformity. Broadcast narratives can ensure the existence of that reason, and, indeed, make its existence common knowledge.

Conclusion

We conclude by considering four objections to our proposal that public policy should maintain and create informational norms.

First: we have done too little. We have only sketched how to create one informational norm. We agree, of course, that we have left a vast amount undone. We have, however, offered a model of how to create informational norms, and one can adapt that model to a wide range of cases in which the task is to maintain or create norms.

Second: we have not, in any detail, shown how to ensure that informational norms implement acceptable tradeoffs. We have done so only in one case, and, even there, we only considered fairness. Our answer again is to appeal to the model we have provided, which incorporates social and political processes to decide tradeoff questions. We see no substitute for that. Those processes generate the detail about how to make tradeoffs.

Third: our proposal is not politically viable. Our answer is that it is viable given appropriate conditions. But is there a practical path to our proposal under *current* conditions? One may well point to the social and political struggles to address crises such as COVID-19 and climate change as evidence of dysfunctional political processes, but, for our proposal, that just means there is another *prior* problem to solve – the problem of ensuring a well-functioning democracy – and the need to solve that problem is hardly unique to our proposal.

Fourth: we are too backward looking. Why are we trying to project into the twenty-first century a system of informational norms that flourished in the twentieth century? Why not regard that complex of norms as a thing of the past? Something that will disappear just as the cultural and economic patterns Justus Möser wished to preserve in Osnabrück were swept away in the eighteenth century by the rise of international market economies. Our answer is twofold. First, we see no other way to preserve the complex web of privacy in public on which adequate self-realization depends. Second, as we argued in Chapter 8, a process of acculturation to surveillance will ensure that existing informational norms change and new ones arise. The question is not whether informational norms will exist. The question is the extent to which they will embrace surveillance. Our argument is that we should take control of the process *now* by intervening to maintain and create informational norms that ensure adequate informational privacy.

Index

acceptance
  absence of norms and, 171
  in not party to the norm cases, 163, 169–172
    Internet of Things and, 170–171
    in investigative journalist contexts, 169–170
  in party to the norm cases, 163–169
    common knowledge generators, 164–166
    conditions for, 165–166
    new norms for, 169
    OpenTable, 166–168
  of pervasive surveillance, 121, 138
  of tradeoffs, in Notice and Choice, 113–115
acculturation, 160–162
  access to information and, 162
  communication and, 162
  for convenience, 161–162
  evaluation and, 162
  personalization and, 162
acquiescence
  absence of norms and, 171
  Havel on, 139–140
  informational norms and, 159
  in not party to the norm cases
    acquiescence in, 149–159
    in investigative journalist contexts, 150–152
  in party to the norm cases, 140–148
    in employment contexts, 144–146
    in health insurance contexts, 146–148
    public concerns over, 143
    in restaurant contexts, 141–144
  passive, 106–108, 112–113
  pervasive surveillance and, 121, 138
  prevalence of, 159
  proxy surveillance and, 152–159
    in behavioral advertising, 155–158
    in credit reporting, 152–155
    with data aggregators, 158–159
  shadow conformity and, 148–149
    group-action goals, 148
  theoretical approach to, 139
AI. *See* artificial intelligence
Altman, Irwin, 60
Amazon, 138
Amnesty International, 132–133
Angwin, Julia, 127–128, 129
artificial intelligence (AI), surveillance and
  accuracy of, 26–28
    definition of, 26
    through direct mail advertising, 26–27
    low, 26–28, 30
    Strategic Subject List algorithm, 27–28
  algorithm source code, 196
  data preparation, 30–35
    choice of attributes, 35
    cleaning processes, 33–35
    collection of data, 30–31
    selection of data, 31–33
    structuring processes, 33–35
  decision-making and, 24–25
  decontextualization in, 28–30
    data collection and, 30–31
    of individual life histories, 28–29
    in predictive analytics, 28
  deep neural networks, 30
  definition of, 24
  fairness and, 187–197
    conditions for, 190–191
    explanation of, 187–190, 197
    market freedom and, 198–199, 200
    motivation for, 187–190
    reformulated models for, 191–197
    social justice through, 187
  Federal Trade Commission and, regulation by, 199–201
    access to expertise by, 200
    investigative powers of, 200

artificial intelligence (AI), surveillance and (cont.)
  feedback mechanisms, 40–41
    error correction in, 25–26, 40
  informational norms and, 201–203
  machine learning, 24
  norm-creation models and, 202–203
  outcome control with, 42
  pervasive surveillance through proxies, 133–134
  predictions
    broad-based, 25, 41–42
    decontextualization in, 28
    false, 26
    with proxy variables, 41–42
  predictive analytics, 24
    decontextualization in, 28
    error rates, 26
  regulation of, 32, 197–201
    access to expertise, 198
    investigative powers in, 198
    proxy variables, 182–186
  supervised learning, 32
    COMPAS algorithm, 32–33
    training algorithms for, 32
  theoretical approach to, 22–25
  as threat, 42
  tradeoffs and, 21
  transparency and, 35–40
    definition and scope of, 36
    for regulatory purposes, 37
Assurance Games, 91–95
  common knowledge and, 92–93
  communication in, 91
  game theory and, 92
  player preferences in, 91–92
  relevant probabilities in, knowledge of, 93–95

Barocas, Solon, 115
Baudrillard, Jean, 2
behavioral advertising, 155–158
behavioral surplus, 23
Berger, Peter, 15
Bicchieri, Christina, 59–60, 79, 176
Black, Hillel, 117
Brenton, Myron, 117
Bruce, Gary, 126
Bush, George W., 65–66, 67
Buy Now, Pay Later (Black), 117

capacity to know
  in social roles, common knowledge and, 47–49
  the Stasi and, 125
  surveillance and, 12
CCTV. *See* closed-circuit television
center theory, for the self, 4
Chong, Dennis, 59–60, 168
Chwe, Michael, 47, 52, 59–60
Cincinnatus, Lucius Quinctius, 123
Clapper v. *Amnesty*, 132–133
closed-circuit television (CCTV), 3
collective control, in Notice and Choice, 115–116
Comey, James, 66
common knowledge. *See also* social roles
  Assurance Games and, 92–93
  coordination problems and, 76–77
  generators
    conformity through, 51–53
    through instruction, 51–53
    through narratives, 52–53
    through observation, 53
    social role of, 47, 50–53
  in norm-creation models
    conformity and, 178
    of continued conformity, 178–180
    ought thoughts and, 179–180
    of proper performance, 177–178
  pervasive surveillance and, collapse of, 118–125
    development of, 121
    discoordination and, 122–125
    privacy in public and, declines in, 122
  transparency created from, 18
  trust and, 18
common pool resources, informational privacy as, 99–100
communication, in Assurance Games, 91
complicity, 125
conditional thinking, 57
conformity
  common knowledge and
    generators, 51–53
    social roles and, 58–59, 62, 64, 65, 67
  in norm-creation models, 178
    continued conformity, 178–180
  to selective information flows, 8–9
  shadow, 148–149
    group-action goals, 148
consent
  free, 105–108
    control to do otherwise compared to, 105–106, 112–113
    knowing understanding and, 106, 112–113
    passive acquiescence and, 106–108, 112–113
  informational norms and, 104–108
  informed, 109–112
    informational norms and, 104–105
    knowing understanding requirements for, 110
    privacy policy information and, reading of, 110–112

tradeoffs with, 110–112
Notice and Choice and, 104–108
consumer credit reporting, 183–185
eBureau eScore system, 185
Consumer Protection Privacy Act (California, US), 103
Convention (Lewis), 85
coordination. *See also* coordination problems
through informational norms, 9–12
knowledge and, 13–16
second-level, 14
coordination games, 71–75. *See also* Assurance Games
coordination problems and, 72–73, 75–76
dominant preference requirements, 76
Driving Games, 72–73
equilibria in, 74–75
Nash Equilibrium, 74
game theory and, 72
Hockey Helmet Games, 73
Rock–Paper–Scissors, 71–72
strategy profiles in, 74
with three or more players, 75
zero-sum games, 72
coordination norms, 82–89. *See also* informational norms; informational privacy
common knowledge generators and, 83–85
definition of, 10, 82–83
in environmental contexts, 88–89
in fishing cooperative contexts, 87–88
game theory and, 14–15
objections in, 11
ought thoughts in, 10–11
in social distance contexts, 85–87
during global pandemics, 86
coordination problems
common knowledge and, 76–77
coordination games and, 72–73, 75–76
dominant preference requirements, 76
social roles and, 44–45, 53–56
definition of, 54–55
development of, 55–56
dominant preferences, 54, 56
group-action goals, 54, 55
proper performance requirements, 55–56
The Cost-Benefit Revolution (Sunstein), 194
credit reporting
for consumers, 183–185
eBureau eScore system, 185
Equifax, 154
under Fair Credit Reporting Act, 154
proxy surveillance in, 152–155
Dark Mirror (Gellman), 151
data mining, 24
proxy surveillance through, 158–159
data preparation, artificial intelligence and, 30–35
choice of attributes, 35
cleaning processes, 33–35
collection of data, 30–31
selection of data, 31–33
structuring processes, 33–35
decision-making, artificial intelligence and, 24–25
decontextualization, in artificial intelligence, 28–30
data collection and, 30–31
of individual life histories, 28–29
in predictive analytics, 28
deep neural networks, 30
direct mail advertising, accuracy of, 26–27
discoordination, 122–125
dominant preferences
coordination games and, 76
coordination problems and, 76
social roles and
common knowledge and, 58, 64, 65, 67
coordination problems and, 54, 56
requirements for, 56
Dragnet Nation (Angwin), 127–128
Driving Games, 72–73
Dwork, Cynthia, 190, 192, 193, 195
Dyson, George, 5

eBureau eScore system, 185
Ellsberg, Daniel, 151
employment contexts
acquiescence in, 144–146
social roles in, 68–69
Equifax, 154
equilibria, in coordination games, 74–75
Nash Equilibrium, 74, 92
EU General Data Protection Regulation, 103
explainability, in artificial intelligence, 35–40
definition of, 36
fairness and, 37–38
with r-transparency, possibilities of, 41
explainable and r-transparent, 39–40
explainable but not r-transparent, 39
not explainable and not r-transparent, 38–39
not explainable but r-transparent, 39–40
in scoring systems, 39
for consumers, 38–39
exposed public self, 7
externalities. *See* negative externalities
eye contact, common knowledge through, 49–50

Facebook, 133–134, 138
Fair Credit Reporting Act, US (1970), 154
fairness
artificial intelligence and, surveillance with, 187–197
conditions for, 190–191
explanation of, 187–190, 197
market freedom and, 198–199, 200
motivation for, 187–190
reformulated models for, 191–197
social justice through, 187
explainability and, 37–38
proxy variables and, 41–42
theoretical approach to, 181–182
Federal Trade Commission, in US, 103, 109
artificial intelligence surveillance regulation by, 199–201
access to expertise by, 200
investigative powers for, 200
feedback mechanisms, in artificial intelligence, 40–41
error correction in, 25–26, 40
Finlay, Steven, 31–32, 186
Foucault, Michel, 2
free consent, 105–108
control to do otherwise compared to, 105–106, 112–113
knowing understanding and, 106, 112–113
passive acquiescence and, 106–108, 112–113
Freeman, George, 124
Fry, Hannah, 29–30
Fulbright, J. William, 151
Funder, Anna, 126

game theory
Assurance Games and, 92
coordination games and, 72
coordination norms and, 14–15
social roles and, common knowledge and, 47
games. *See* Assurance Games; coordination games
Gellman, Barton, 123–124, 135, 151
Goffmann, Erving, 60
Google, 136–138, 182
government business, surveillance in, 4–5
compliance issues, 4–5
Gray, John, 174
Greenwald, Glen, 123–124
Grosz, Barbara J., 29–30
group-action goals
pervasive surveillance, 120
shadow conformity and, 148
social roles and, 54, 55
group-created selective information flows, 8–9
privacy in public, 9

harmony, through selective flow of information, 8
Hartzog, Woodrow, 20
Havel, Václav, 139–140
health insurance contexts
acquiescence in, 146–148
social roles in, 69–70
Henningsen v. Bloomfield Motors, 106, 107
Hockey Helmet Games, 73
Hoofnagle, Chris, 200–201

information exchanges, in social role interactions, 43, 95–97
relevant probabilities for, knowledge of, 96–97
information flows
selective
conditions on, 8
conformity to, 8–9
expectations about, 8–9
group-created, 8–9
harmony through, 8
privacy in public, 9
in social roles, common knowledge and, 58–59
information privacy, tradeoff questions and, 172
informational norms, 11–12, 89–98
acquiescence and, 159
Assurance Games and, 91–95
common knowledge and, 92–93
communication in, 91
game theory and, 92
player preferences in, 91–92
relevant probabilities in, knowledge of, 93–95
consent and, 104–108
informed, 104–105
definition of, 89–90
information exchanges and, in social role interactions, 43, 95–97
relevant probabilities for, knowledge of, 96–97
lack of, 90–91
pervasive surveillance and, 118–119
conducted by non-parties, 131–136
conducted by parties to, 128–131
resistance with lack of, 136–138
types of, 90
informational privacy, 2, 99–102. *See also* Notice and Choice
as common pool resources, 99–100
needs and, 100–101
nonexcludability of, 99–100, 102
Notice and Choice compared to, 114–115
self-realization and, 6–8
subtractiveness of, 99–100, 101–102
non-conforming uses and, 101–102
supply and, 100–101

as threat, 99–100
tradeoffs and, 20
Tragedy of the Commons, 99–100
uses of, 100–101
non-conforming, 101–102
informed consent, 109–112
informational norms and, 104–105
knowing understanding requirements for, 110
privacy policy information and, reading of, 110–112
tradeoffs with, 110–112
intelligence. *See* artificial intelligence
Internet of Things (IoT), 170–171
intuition, 26
investigative journalist contexts
acceptance in, 169–170
acquiescence in, 150–152
in not party to the norm cases, 169–170
social roles in, 65–68
IoT. *See* Internet of Things
Islands of Privacy (Nippert-Eng), 68

James, William, 16
on the self, 3–4
journalism. *See* investigative journalist contexts

Kahn, Alfred E., 114
knowing understanding
free consent and, 106, 112–113
informed consent and, requirements for, 110
knowledge. *See also* common knowledge
coordination and, 13–16
second-level knowledge and, 14
requirements of, 13
self-realization and, 13–16
Kyle, Thomas, 15

learning
machine, 24
supervised, 32
COMPAS algorithm, 32–33
training algorithms for, 32
Ledgett, Richard, 135
Lewis, David, 59–60, 79, 85
Lichtblau, Eric, 65–66, 67
Lindblom, Charles, 189
LinkedIn, 138
loss of norms, 17–18
Luckmann, Thomas, 15
Lyons, David, 160–161

machine learning, 24. *See also* predictive analytics
MacTavish, Craig, 75
Mashaw, Jerry, 200–201
Mau, Stephan, 160
Mayer, Jane, 124
McAdams, Richard, 81
McGovern, George, 151
Misztal, Barbara, 18
Mitchell, George, 151
Möser, Justus, 78, 204

Nagel, Thomas, 6–7
The Naked Crowd (Rosen), 154–155
The Naked Society (Packard), 117
narratives, common knowledge generators through, 52–53
Nash, John, 74
Nash Equilibrium, 74, 92
needs, informational privacy and, 100–101
negative externalities, 114
neural networks. *See* deep neural networks
New York Times, 65–66, 151
New York Times v. Sullivan, 151
Nippert-Eng, Christena, 16–17, 60, 68
Nissenbaum, Helen, 9, 60, 89, 111, 115, 172
nonexcludability, of informational privacy, 99–100, 102
norm-creation models, 176–180
common knowledge in
conformity and, 178
of continued conformity, 178–180
ought thoughts and, 179–180
of proper performance, 177–178
norms. *See also* coordination norms; informational norms; not party to the norm cases; party to the norm cases
absence of, 171
creation of, 79–82
definition of, 80–81
informational, 11–12
loss of, 17–18
social, 82
social roles and, 79–82
generated regularities through, 80–81
not party to the norm cases
acceptance in, 163, 169–172
Internet of Things and, 170–171
in investigative journalist contexts, 169–170
for proxy surveillance, 170–171
acquiescence in, 149–159
in investigative journalist contexts, 150–152
Notice and Choice
collective control in, 115–116
consent and, as concept within, 104–108
definition of, 103
EU General Data Protection Regulation, 103
failures of, 109–115

Notice and Choice (cont.)
free consent and, 105–108
control to do otherwise compared to, 105–106, 112–113
knowing understanding and, 106, 112–113
passive acquiescence and, 106–108, 112–113
informational privacy compared to, 114–115
informed consent and, 109–112
informational norms and, 104–105
knowing understanding requirements for, 110
privacy policy information and, reading of, 110–112
tradeoffs with, 110–112
limitations of, 104
scope of, 103–104
tradeoffs and, 103–104, 109, 113–115
acceptability of, 113–115
with informed consent, 110–112
transparency and, 115
in US.
Consumer Protection Privacy Act, 103
Federal Trade Commission and, 103, 109

Obama, Barack, 67
observation, common knowledge generators through, 53
O'Neil, Catherine, 35, 183
OpenTable, 101, 122, 143–144, 161–162, 166–168
Ostrom, Elinor, 11, 59–60. *See also* informational norms
ought not thoughts, 119–121
ought thoughts, 10–11
in norm-creation models, 179–180
pervasive surveillance and, 121
in social roles, common knowledge and, 57, 63–64, 65, 67

Packard, Vance, 117
Parenti, Christian, 44, 130, 139
party to the norm cases
acceptance in, 163–169
common knowledge generators, 164–166
conditions for, 165–166
new norms for, 169
OpenTable, 166–168
acquiescence in, 140–148
in employment contexts, 144–146
in health insurance contexts, 146–148
public concerns over, 143
in restaurant contexts, 141–144
passive acquiescence, 106–108, 112–113
pervasive surveillance
acceptance of, 121, 138
acquiescence and, 121, 138
by artificial intelligence, through proxies, 133–134
collapse of common knowledge, 118–125
development of, 121
discoordination and, 122–125
privacy in public and, declines in, 122
by governments, 132–133
group-action goals, 120
informational norms and, 118–119
conducted by non-parties, 131–136
conducted by parties to, 128–131
resistance with lack of, 136–138
ought not thoughts, 119–121
ought to thoughts, 121
by proxies, 135
with artificial intelligence, 133–134
public fears over, 117–118
resistance to, 120–121, 127–128, 138
informational norms and, lack of, 136–138
in retail contexts, 134
the Stasi, 125–127
capacity to know, 125
complicity and, 125
repressive use by, 126
self-realization curtailed by, 126–127
Student Information Systems, 129–130
player preferences, in Assurance Games, 91–92
Poitras, Laura, 123–124
The Power of the Powerless (Havel), 139–140
predictions, through artificial intelligence
broad-based predictions, 25, 41–42
decontextualization in, 28
false predictions, 26
with proxy variables, 41–42
predictive analytics, 24
decontextualization in, 28
error rates, 26
The Principles of Scientific Management (Taylor), 130
privacy. *See also* privacy in public
claims to, 20
informational, 2
self-realization and, 6–8
tradeoffs and, 20
secrecy and, 68
surveillance and, 2
trust and, 19–20
Privacy as Trust (Waldman), 20–21
Privacy in Peril (Rule), 109
privacy in public, 9
pervasive surveillance and, 122
self-realization and, 12, 16–17
tradeoffs and, 21
The Privacy Invaders (Brenton), 117

Privacy's Blueprint (Hartzog), 20
private business, surveillance issues, 5–6
ProPublica, 146–147
proxies, pervasive surveillance by, 135
with artificial intelligence, 133–134
proxy surveillance
acceptance in, 170–171
acquiescence and, 152–159
in behavioral advertising, 155–158
in credit reporting, 152–155
with data aggregators, 158–159
proxy variables
artificial intelligence and
predictions through, 41–42
regulation of, 182–186
fairness and, 41–42
The Psychology of Common Knowledge (Kyle), 15
pure ego theory, 4

Rakoff, Todd, 107
Rawls, John, 113
reasoning, common knowledge through, 48–49
regulation, transparency for, 37
Rehnquist, William, 151
resistance, to pervasive surveillance, 120–121, 127–128, 138
informational norms and, lack of, 136–138
restaurant contexts
acquiescence in, 141–144
OpenTable, 101, 122, 143–144, 161–162, 166–168
social roles in, 60–63
retail sales contexts
pervasive surveillance in, 134
social roles in, 63–64
Risen, James, 65–66, 67
risk, with trust, 18
Rock–Paper–Scissors, as coordination game, 71–72
Roemer, John, 181–182
Rosen, Jeffrey, 154–155
Rule, James, 1, 20, 109

Schelling, Thomas, 59–60
Schiffer, Stephen, 79, 85
Schneier, Bruce, 17, 19, 94, 170–171, 172
Schwartz, Paul, 108, 109
secrecy, privacy and, 68
selective flows of information. *See* information flows
the self
center theory for, 4
exposed public, 7
James on, 3–4
pure ego theory, 4
self-realization and, 3–4
exposed public self, 7
social order and, 7–8
social roles, 7–8
surveillance as threat to, 2
"territories of the self,", 16–17
self-realization
capacity to know and, 12
informational privacy and, 6–8
knowledge and, 13–16
privacy in public and, 12, 16–17
the self and, 3–4
exposed public self, 7
social order and, 7–8
social roles, 7–8
the Stasi and, 126–127
surveillance as influence on, 12
Sen, Amartya, 10–11
shadow conformity, 148–149
group-action goals, 148
Shiller, Robert, 179
Simmel, Georg, 8
SIS. *See* Student Information Systems
Snowden, Edward, 123–124
The Social Construction of Reality (Berger and Luckmann), 15
social justice, fairness and, 187
social norms, 82
social order
the self and, 7–8
self-realization and, 7–8
social roles
common knowledge and, 44, 45–50
capacity to know and, 47–49
conditional thinking, 57
conformity and, 58–59, 62, 64, 65, 67
dominant preferences and, 58, 64, 65, 67
in employment contexts, 68–69
eye contact and, 49–50
game theory and, 47
generators of, 47, 50–53
in health insurance contexts, 69–70
through information flow, 58–59
in investigative journalist contexts, 65–68
ought thinking, 57, 63–64, 65, 67
through reasoning, 48–49
in restaurant contexts, 60–63
in retail sales contexts, 63–64
in university contexts, 64–65
coordination problems and, 44–45, 53–56
definition of, 54–55
development of, 55–56
dominant preferences, 54, 56
group-action goals, 54, 55
proper performance requirements, 55–56

social roles (cont.)
  dominant preferences
    common knowledge and, 58, 64
    coordination problems and, 54, 56
    requirements for, 56
  information exchanges and, 43, 95–97
    relevant probabilities for, knowledge of, 96–97
  privacy in public and, 70
  the self and, 7–8
  self-realization and, 7–8
  surveillance ignored view, 70
Solove, Daniel, 108, 109
SSL algorithm. *See* Strategic Subject List algorithm
Stag Hunt, 91, 92. *See also* Assurance Games
the Stasi, 125–127
  capacity to know, 125
  complicity and, 125
  repressive use of surveillance by, 126
  self-realization curtailed by, 126–127
Strategic Subject List (SSL) algorithm, 27–28
Student Information Systems (SIS), 129–130
subtractiveness, of informational privacy, 99–100, 101–102
  non-conforming uses and, 101–102
Sunstein, Cass, 194
supervised learning, 32
  COMPAS algorithm, 32–33
  training algorithms for, 32
supply, informational privacy and, 100–101
surveillance. *See also* artificial intelligence; pervasive surveillance
  capacity to know and, 12
  capitalism, 23
  as concept, 1–2
  critiques of, 4–6
    in government business contexts, 4–5
    in private business contexts, 5–6
  modern practices, 1
  privacy and, 2
  the self and, as threat to, 2
  self-realization limited by, 12
  trust and, 2
surveillance capitalism, 23
surveillance ignored view, 70

Taylor, Winslow, 130
"territories of the self,", 16–17
tradeoffs, 20, 21
  acceptable, 173–176
    value-optimal norms, 173–176
  artificial intelligence and, 21
  information privacy and, 172
  Notice and Choice and, 103–104, 109, 113–115
    acceptability of tradeoffs, 113–115
    with informed consent, 110–112
Tragedy of the Commons, 99–100
training algorithms, for supervised learning, 32
transparency
  artificial intelligence and, 35–40
    definition and scope of transparency, 36
    for regulatory purposes, 37
  common-knowledge-created, 18
  in Notice and Choice, 115
  r-transparency, explainability with, 41
    explainable and r-transparent, 39–40
    explainable but not r-transparent, 39
    not explainable and not r-transparent, 38–39
    not explainable but r-transparent, 39–40
trust, 18–19
  common knowledge and, 18
  privacy and, 19–20
  risk as element of, 18
  surveillance and, 2
trust dilemma, 91. *See also* Assurance Games
Twitter, 138
The Tyranny of Small Decisions (Kahn), 114

Ullmann-Margalit, Edna, 59–60, 79
United States (US)
  Fair Credit Reporting Act, 154
  Federal Trade Commission, 103, 109
    artificial intelligence surveillance regulation by, 199–201
  Notice and Choice in
    Consumer Protection Privacy Act, 103
    Federal Trade Commission and, 103, 109
university contexts, social roles in, 64–65
US *See* United States

value-optimal norms, for acceptable tradeoffs, 173–176
variables. *See* proxy variables

Waldman, Ari Ezra, 20–21
Washington Post, 151
Weapons of Math Destruction (O'Neil), 183

zero-sum games, 72
Zuboff, Soshana, 23–25, 31, 138
  behavioral surplus, 23

CPSIA information can be obtained
at www.ICGtesting.com
Printed in the USA
LVHW080544131222
735111LV00005B/344

9 781108 486712